BOTANICAL
ESCAPE

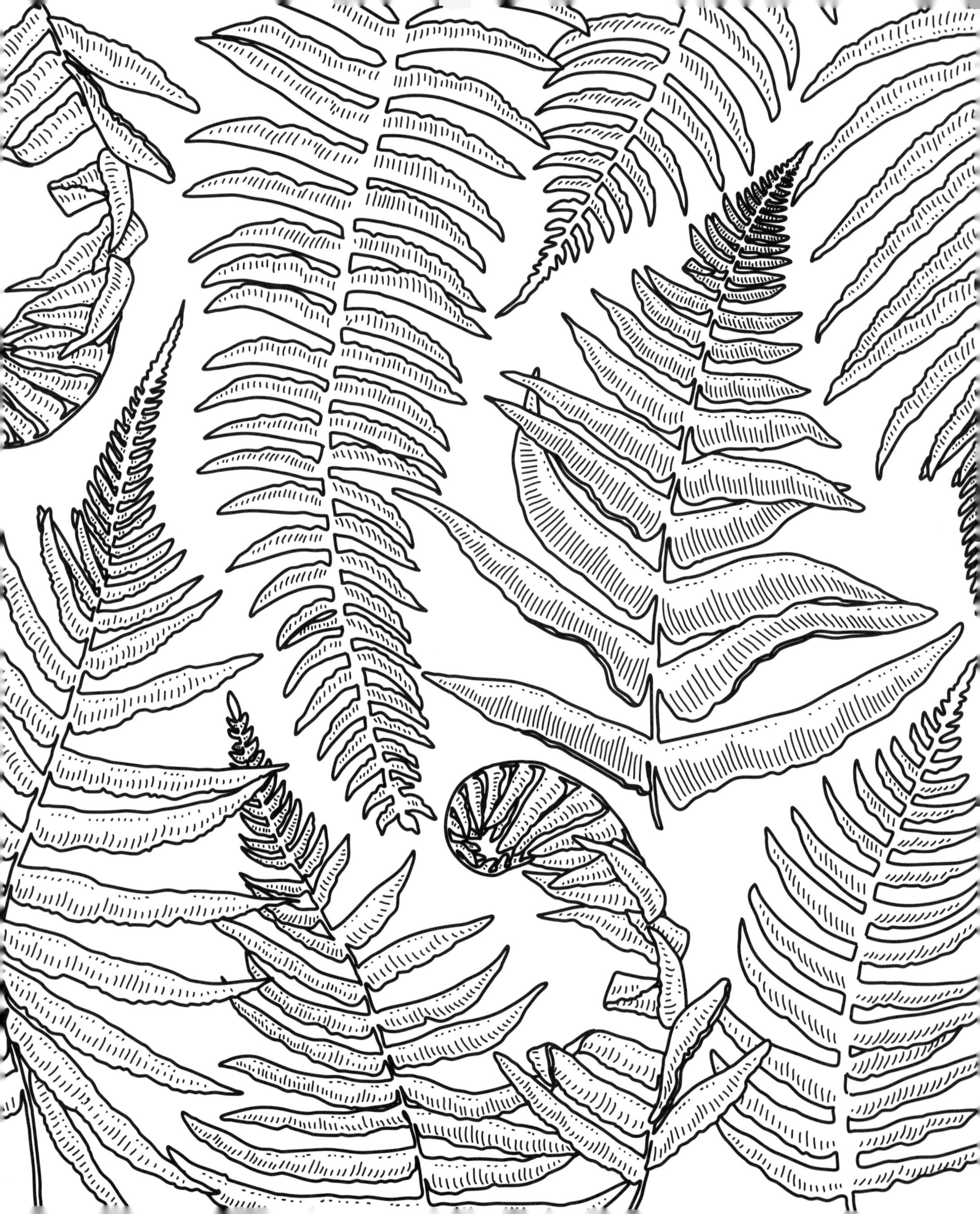

40 Beautiful Tracing Projects to Help You Unwind

BOTANICAL ESCAPE

ANNA OSZVALD

PAGE STREET
PUBLISHING CO.

PAGE STREET
PUBLISHING CO.

First published in 2021 by
Page Street Publishing Co.
27 Congress Street, Suite 105
Salem, MA 01970
www.pagestreetpublishing.com

Distributed by Macmillan, sales in Canada by The Canadian Manda Group.

25 24 23 22 21 1 2 3 4 5

ISBN-13: 978-1-64567-374-3
ISBN-10: 1-64567-374-X

Library of Congress Control Number: 2021931421

Cover and book design by Meg Baskis for Page Street Publishing Co.
Illustrations by Anna Oszvald

Printed and bound in China

trustees

Page Street Publishing protects our planet by donating to nonprofits like The Trustees, which focuses on local land conservation.

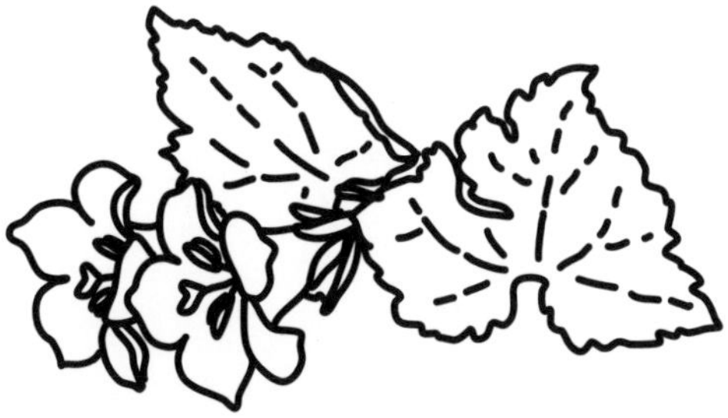

To my lovely cousin, who planted the idea for this book in my head.

And to you, reader. I invite you to switch off and get lost in my botanical universe, while you also learn how to draw modern florals in a fun way.

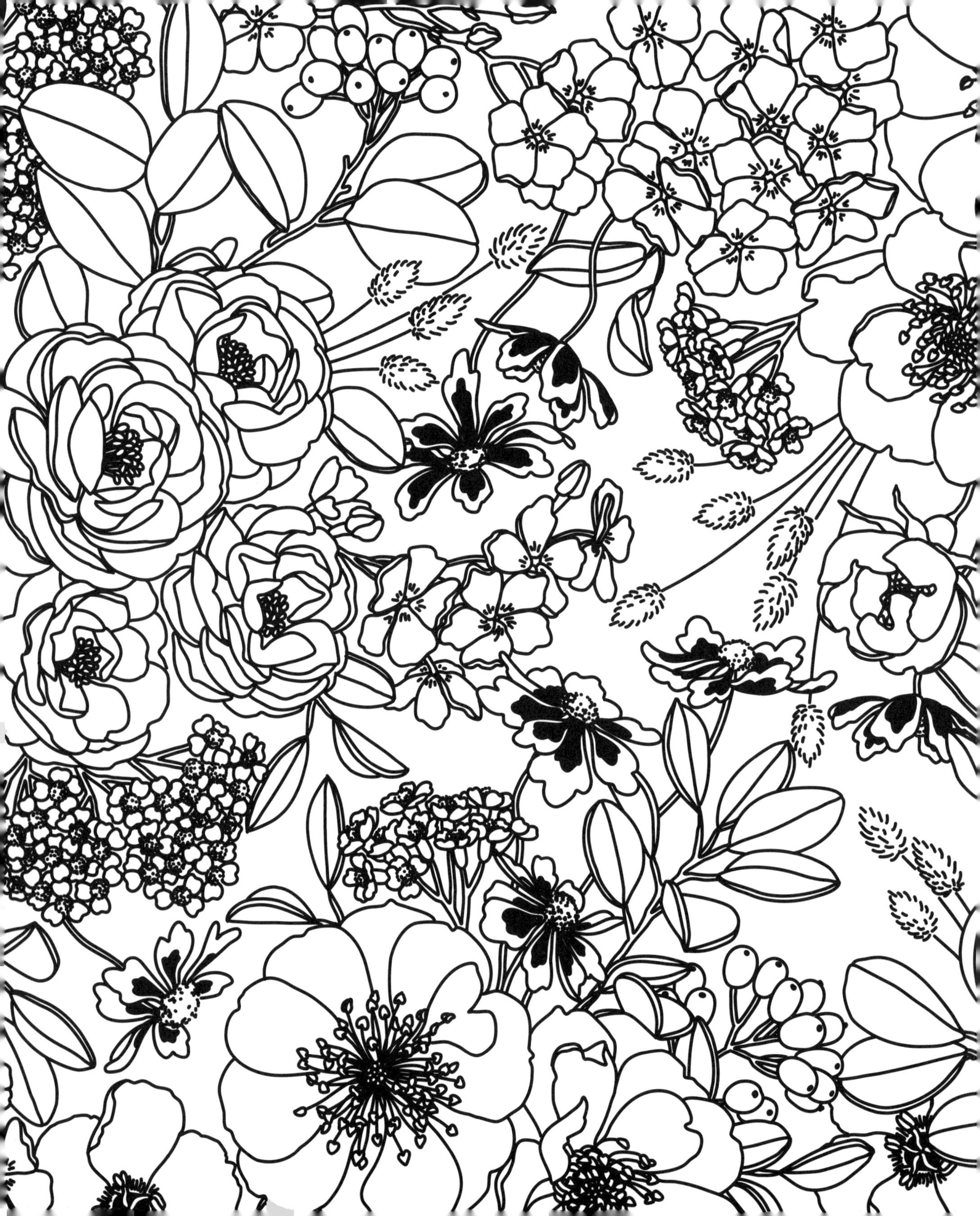

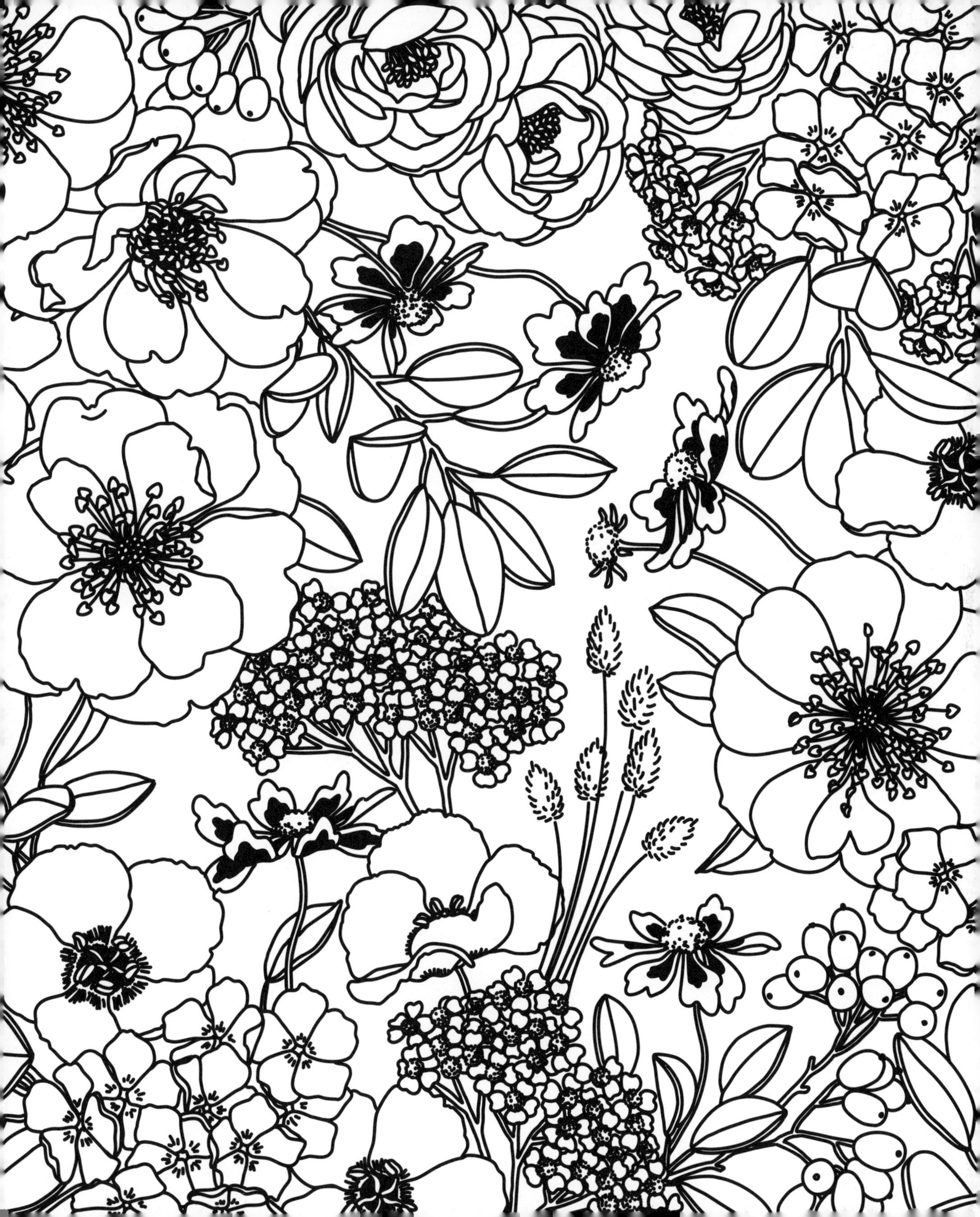

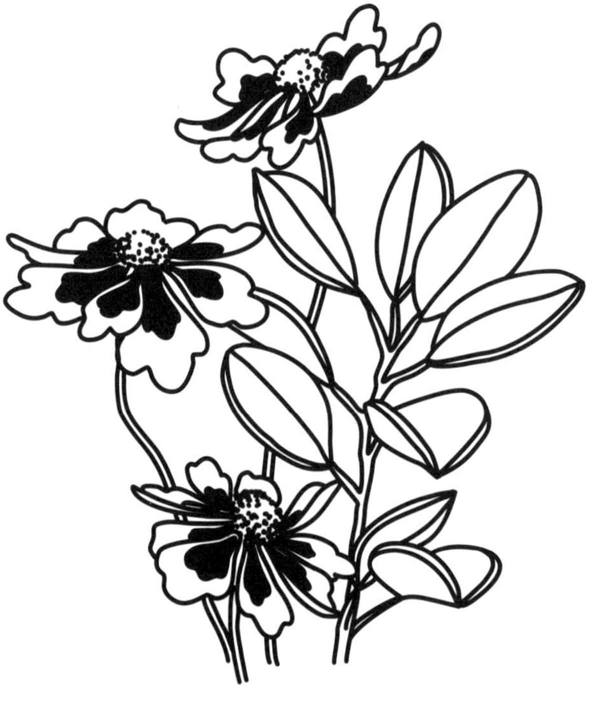

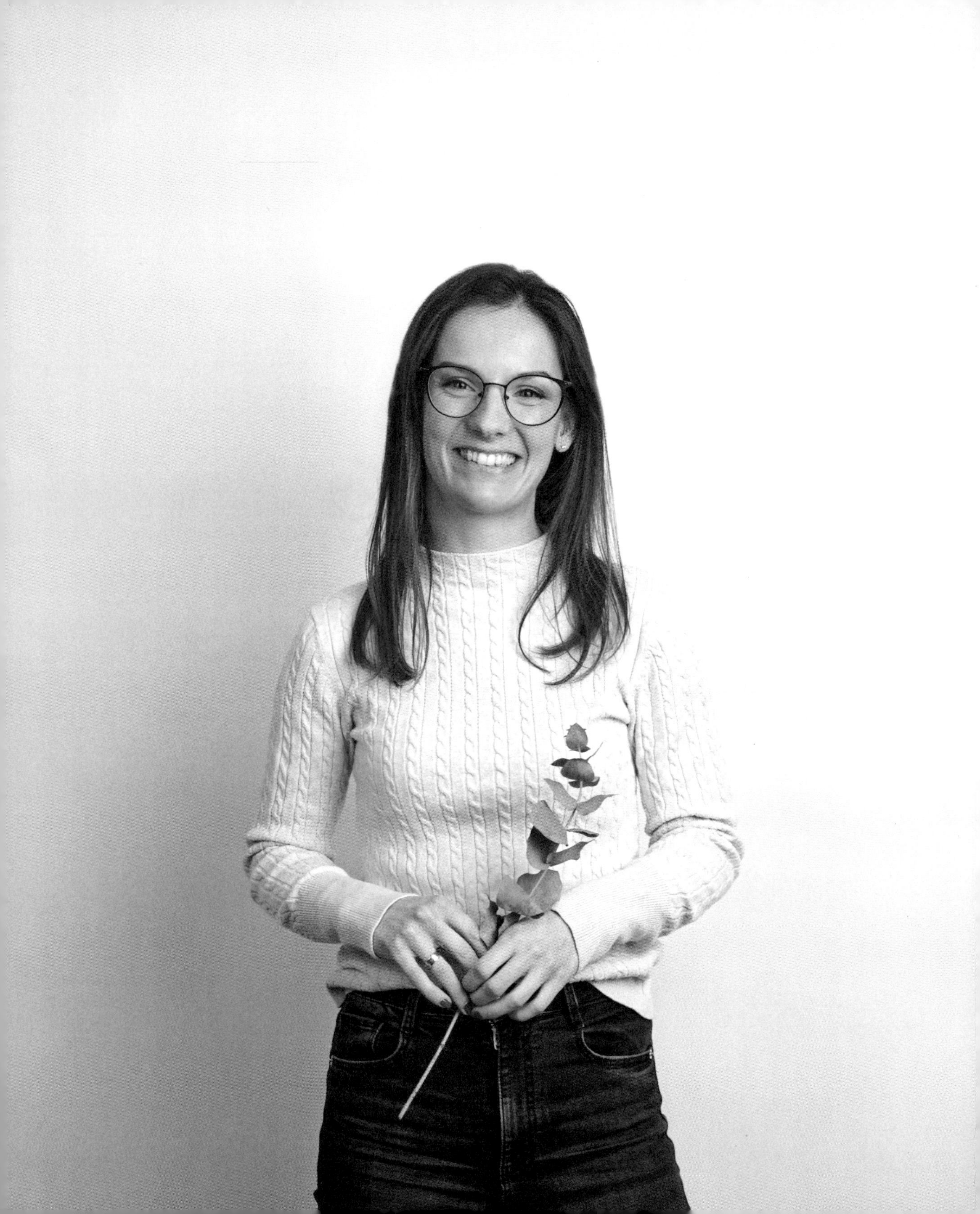

HI! I'M ANNA.

I am an illustrator from Budapest with a serious obsession with lines and botanicals. Oh yes, and details!

I would like to welcome you into my imaginary garden full of beautiful blooms and delicate wildflowers. Step inside and let your mind unwind while filling your aesthetic imagination with all the lush flowers, fresh foliage, playful grasses and lively berries that you will draw in this book.

Anna Oswald

INTRODUCTION

WHAT IS TRACING?

Tracing is basically drawing over a light, pre-drawn image in order to enjoy the movement of your hands while creating something visually satisfying. I could compare tracing to dancing. The only difference is the end result. While you feel joy from controlling your whole body while dancing, you will feel joy from controlling the motion of your hand while tracing.

Tracing can help put you in a relaxed mental state while teaching you how to draw these beautiful flowers. Tracing is also a method of storing new shapes in your muscle memory. Remember when you learned to write? There were exercises where you had to draw over the pre-drawn letters. This book uses that same teaching method with modern botanical illustrations. As you draw these flowers following my guidelines, you will be able to recall the shapes in a future drawing session and add that special wow factor to your own sketches.

WHAT IS INSIDE?

There are 40 projects in the book, starting with flowers, then going through some leaves and berries and finally ending with gorgeous floral arrangements. All of the chapters start with easy illustrations. As you go, they become more challenging to trace as shading comes into play, adding an extra layer of detail. Shading allows us to capture the depth and vast variety of three-dimensional shapes within the flowers.

I love details. I believe that the simplest drawing can turn into a professional illustration by adding one perfectly caught detail. This is what I would love to show you in this book. Come on, let's go through some basics!

HOW TO USE THIS BOOK

There are 40 individual tracing projects in this book, printed in light gray—similar to a pencil sketch—waiting for you to bring them to life. Aren't you excited to see these illustrations in their full glory? Each project comes with a tutorial page, where you can read my tips on how to draw the elements of each illustration and where you can see a hint of the beauty of the finished flowers. The tutorial page leads you through the steps of drawing the flowers with process images, like the following:

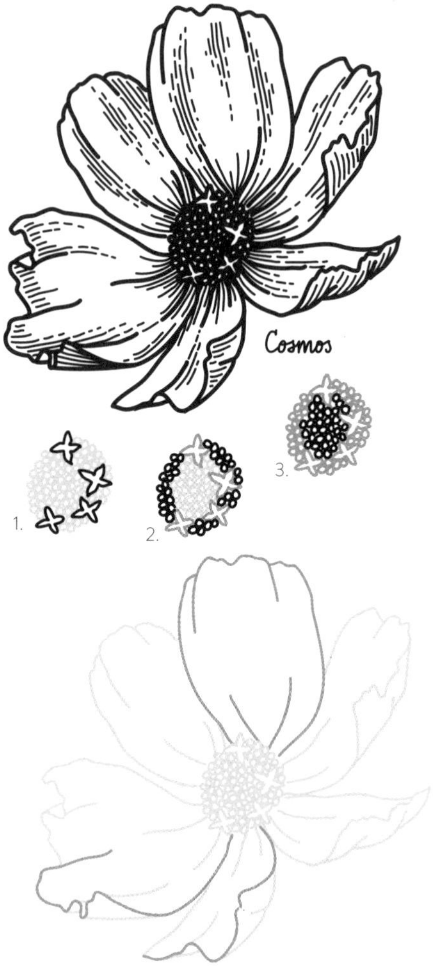

You will find a reference image of the flower on the page in full black. This is the finished look of the flower. This image serves as a map, to show you how the lines look and what to aim for.

The numbered step-by-step images show you the order of laying down the lines in the densest area of the illustrations. Let's see what they mean in this case.

1. Trace the four starlike shapes (shown in black).

2. Start adding little circles close to each other (shown in black).

3. Fill in the inner area with little circles (shown in black).

After the steps you will find an image in all gray. This image is for you to practice. The dark gray lines highlight the starting points for you. In some of the more complex, shaded projects, you will be called to create your own version of shading on this gray image for added practice.

As you may have noticed, I use shades of gray and black to help you visualize the lines drawn in each step. Here is an example.

- Light gray: not outlined yet
- Dark gray: outlined previously
- Black: draw them in the current step

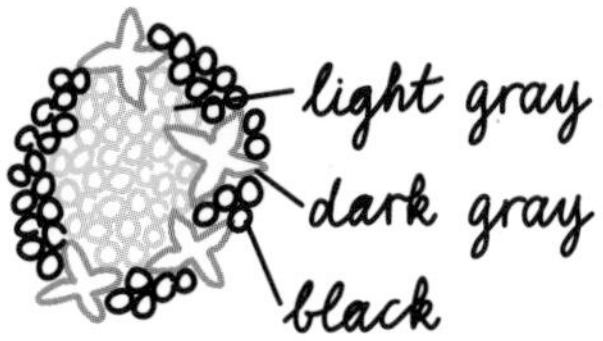

As you work through these steps, remember to take a deep breath. The goal is to help you get comfortable with tracing and to have fun!

One more tip: You don't have to stop at tracing over the gray outlines. Grab colored pencils or a light wash of watercolor and add color to your drawing. Or if you would like to practice even more, you can draw over the full black images with a metallic gel pen. It will look fabulous!

BASICS

In this section, I will walk you through the basics of achieving success in these projects. You'll learn which tools you will need to draw and trace the flowers. I will also share my secrets, tips and tricks for shading, sketching and drawing in general. And you will also read about my beloved shading style, which comes into play at the end of every chapter. This will be fun, I promise. Let's jump into it.

STYLE

My drawing style has a very simple, fundamental component: The lines themselves all have a consistent width. This gives my work a clean and modern look. You can re-create this look easily by using even pressure on your pen tip throughout your whole stroke.

TOOLS

You don't need any fancy tools to draw the outlines. Just grab your favorite pen and go ahead. You can use a fineliner pen, a ballpoint pen or a gel pen; the only thing that matters is that you choose a darker color like a simple black fineliner or one that has full coverage, such as a gold or silver gel pen. And finally, make sure to enjoy how the pen runs on this wonderfully smooth paper.

My favorite pen for drawing line art is the Faber-Castell Ecco Pigment fineliner in 0.6 and 0.2. It has beautiful deep black ink, and the tip dances on the paper so smoothly. I usually use my 0.6 (thicker) one for the outlines and the 0.2 (thinner) for the shading.

The one thing you'll want to remember is to always use a thicker pen to trace the outlines. And when you are finished, switch to a thinner pen to trace the shading lines and get lost in the jungle of dashed lines.

STROKE DIRECTION

I am sure you have already realized that there is a direction for you where it feels more comfortable to draw a line. Don't be afraid to use this to your advantage. Feel free to rotate the book while you're working. Of course, if you like challenges you can also keep the page straight! This will act as a wonderfully effective practice method for building up your drawing skills. As a hint, here are my comfy directions. Feel free to trace over them to discover yours.

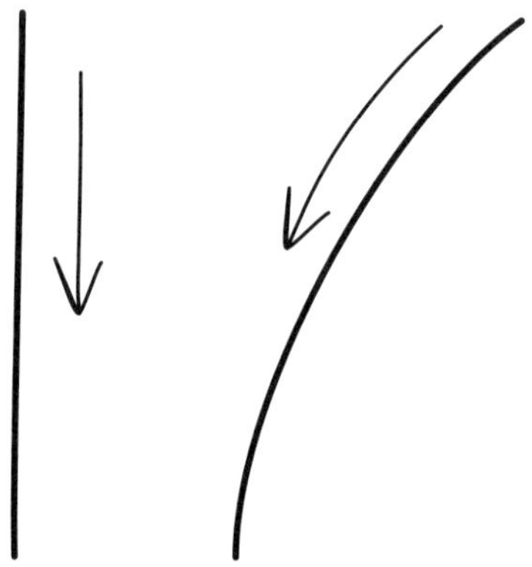

For right-handed people, it is easier to draw a curve in a similar fashion to an uppercase C. Once you fix your wrist on the paper, the hand acts as a compass. For left-handed drawers, the curve would follow a shape similar to an uppercase D. Follow your instincts while tracing; you will feel it right away!

FLOWER ANATOMY

I will refer to the different parts of flowers throughout the book to explain the order of drawing the outlines. To make sure we all speak the same floral language, here is a guide:

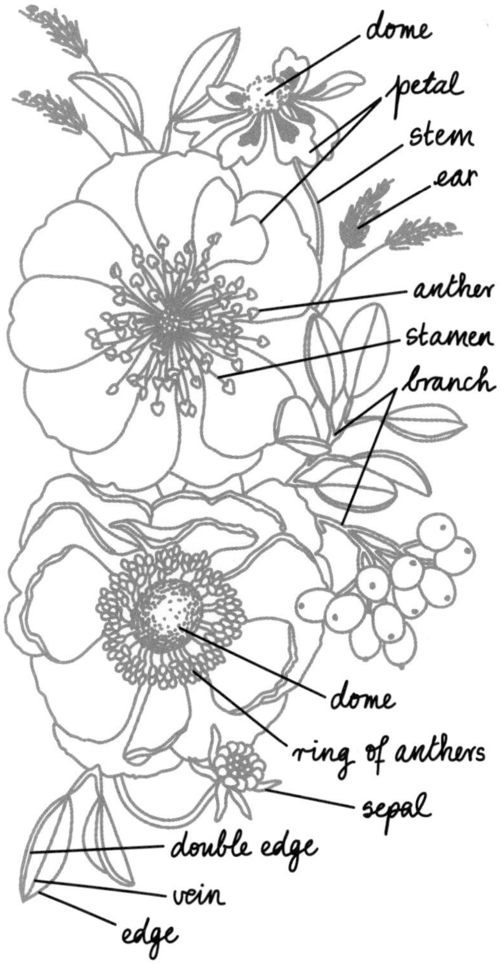

THE LINE

I learned an amazing trick from my primary school art teacher, which I'm sharing with you now. If you would like to draw a long smooth line, which you'll need to do while working on the projects, place your pen on point A and start to draw the line toward your body slowly. Let your eyes run a bit quicker than your pen, so focus your eyes closer to the end point and not on the tip of the pen. Your line will automatically run in the correct direction and you will be able to reach the end point more precisely. It may sound silly, but it truly works. Give it a try!

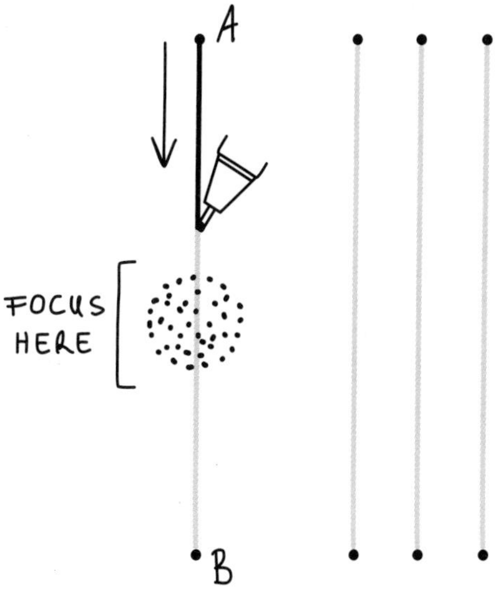

SHADING BASICS

I love to capture all the details in nature, and I am excited to take on the challenge of capturing them with only ink lines. Here I will teach you how you can do the same.

But wait . . . nature is so diverse, full of curves and edges, which form unbelievably complicated three-dimensional shapes. Light and shadow play on these shapes to create a beautiful melody full of gradients. How could we draw them with simple lines and a single pen? This must be absurd.

The basic idea of shading, in this case, is to create gradients using only parallel or almost parallel lines. The lightness/darkness of an image is defined by the density of these lines. Here are examples on lighter and darker surfaces. These are identical lines, differing only in the density, and the result is clearly distinctive.

Whether you are creating a light or dark area with your lines, as long as you draw the lines equidistant from each other you will create a homogeneous surface. Okay, that is how we draw homogeneous surfaces, but flowers rarely have them. They are usually full of curves, folds, valleys and hills, which require gradients. Let me show you how to create them.

I use carefully designed dashed lines to illustrate a gradient. From dark to light, draw the horizontal lines shorter and shorter and leave a bit bigger space between the dashes toward the light area. To add an extra shade to our palette and achieve a really dark effect, I also add a second layer by drawing diagonal lines on top of the existing ones.

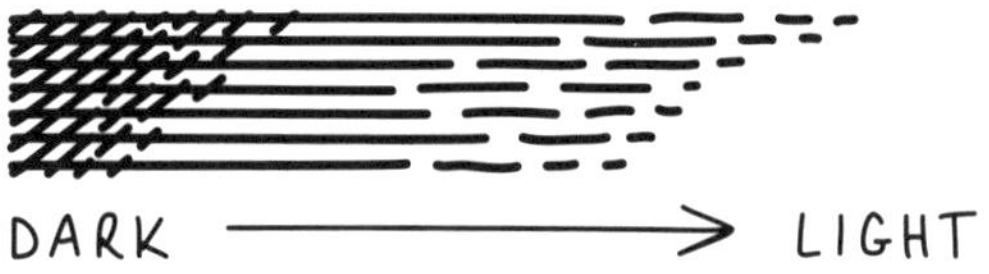

As you can see, the gradient can be broken up into four shades. The darkest is at the left, where I added the second layer of diagonal lines, then the simple parallel lines are already a little lighter, then the dashed area is lighter again, and the end is the plain white of the paper.

Once again, these dashed lines are carefully designed. Too tidy looks unnatural. I always say that spaces should not be neighbors because they hate each other.

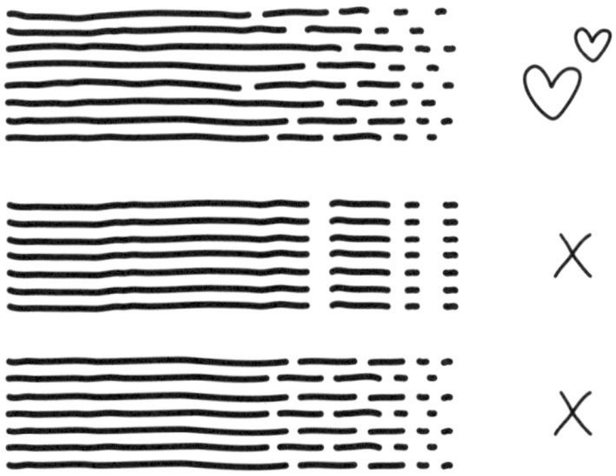

Okay, one more important component. Let's see how this method works with different shapes.

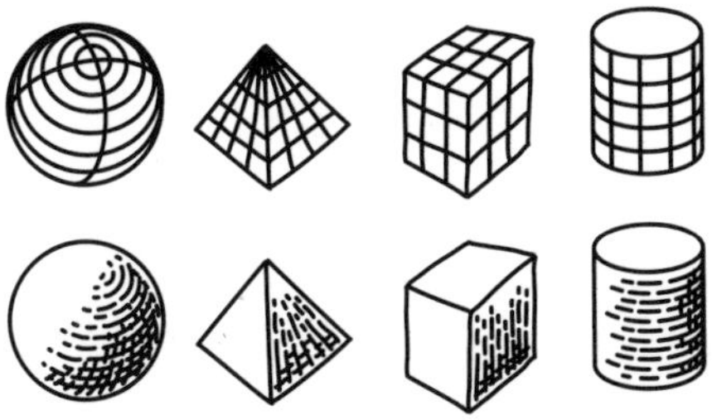

On the top shapes you can see the wire frame representation of the three-dimensional objects. The lines follow the surfaces very precisely; they can even portray a shape without shading. On the lower row of shapes, the shading lines follow the same directions for a clean look. We are lucky because it is easy to define the direction of the shading lines of each petal with the veins there to act as a guide. Throughout the projects, you will see how I follow the direction of the veins to create realistic and beautiful shading.

Here is a guide for shading petals. Look how the lines follow the shape and provide way more detail than the simple outlines.

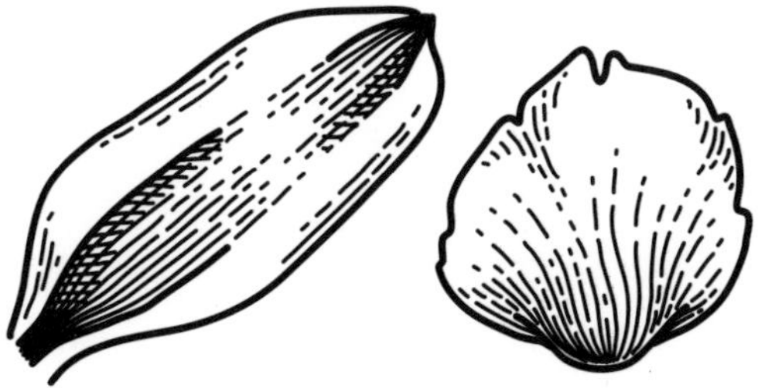

There is another shading method I use to illustrate the center of flowers. I refer to it as "stippling" or "dot work" throughout the book. The basic idea is that you create gradients by varying the density of ink on a particular area, similar to the previous shading method. The only difference is that the surface is covered with dots or very short strokes, not long parallel lines. To make an area dark, add more dots, and to make it light, add only a few. I like to move my hand in a spiral motion while I am stippling. Here's an example:

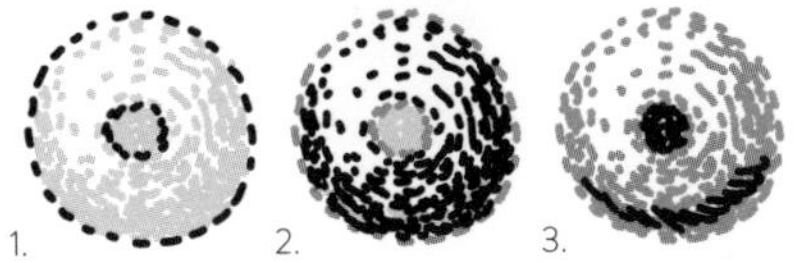

MY BEST ADVICE FOR GETTING STARTED

Here are my best tips for getting the best, most beautiful results.

1. First think, then ink!

You always want to stop for a second before you start tracing. Clear your thoughts and imagine how your hand will draw the next curve. This will help minimize mistakes and make your illustrations look flawless.

2. Warm up by scribbling—always!

Both your pen and your hand need a few warm-up strokes before you start on the project. Let your pen reach its best ink flow while it is offstage. Then, when you are both ready, step into the limelight and go for it.

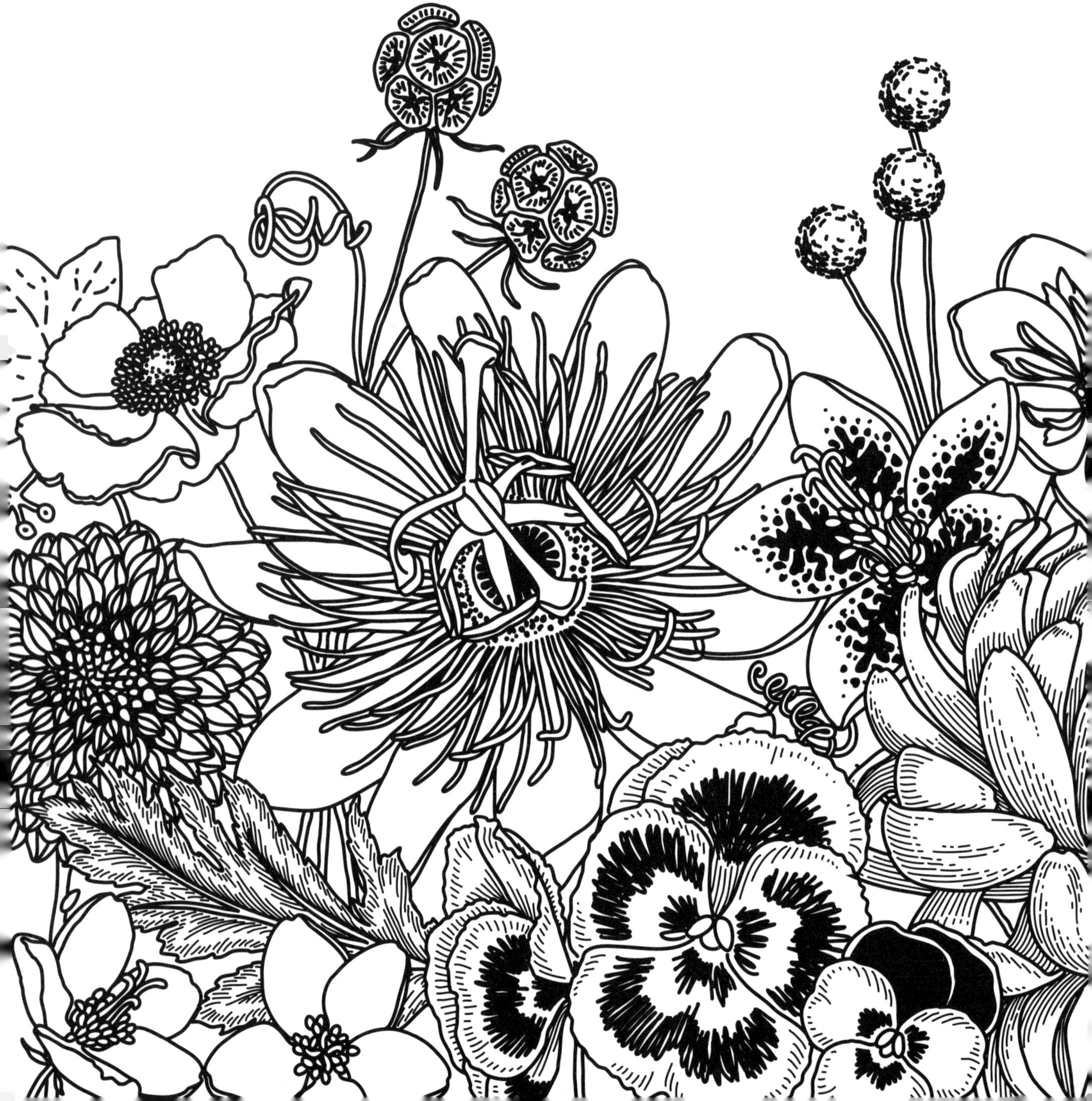

FLOWERS

And we are finally here. This chapter is the entry into my imaginary garden. Here you will find flowers, from simple to detailed and complex. Feel free to jump around. The projects can be worked individually in no particular order, but you will see that they get more complex as you go.

Don't forget my motto: First think, then ink!

Take a deep breath, clear your thoughts and you are good to go! Have fun and enjoy the motion of your hands.

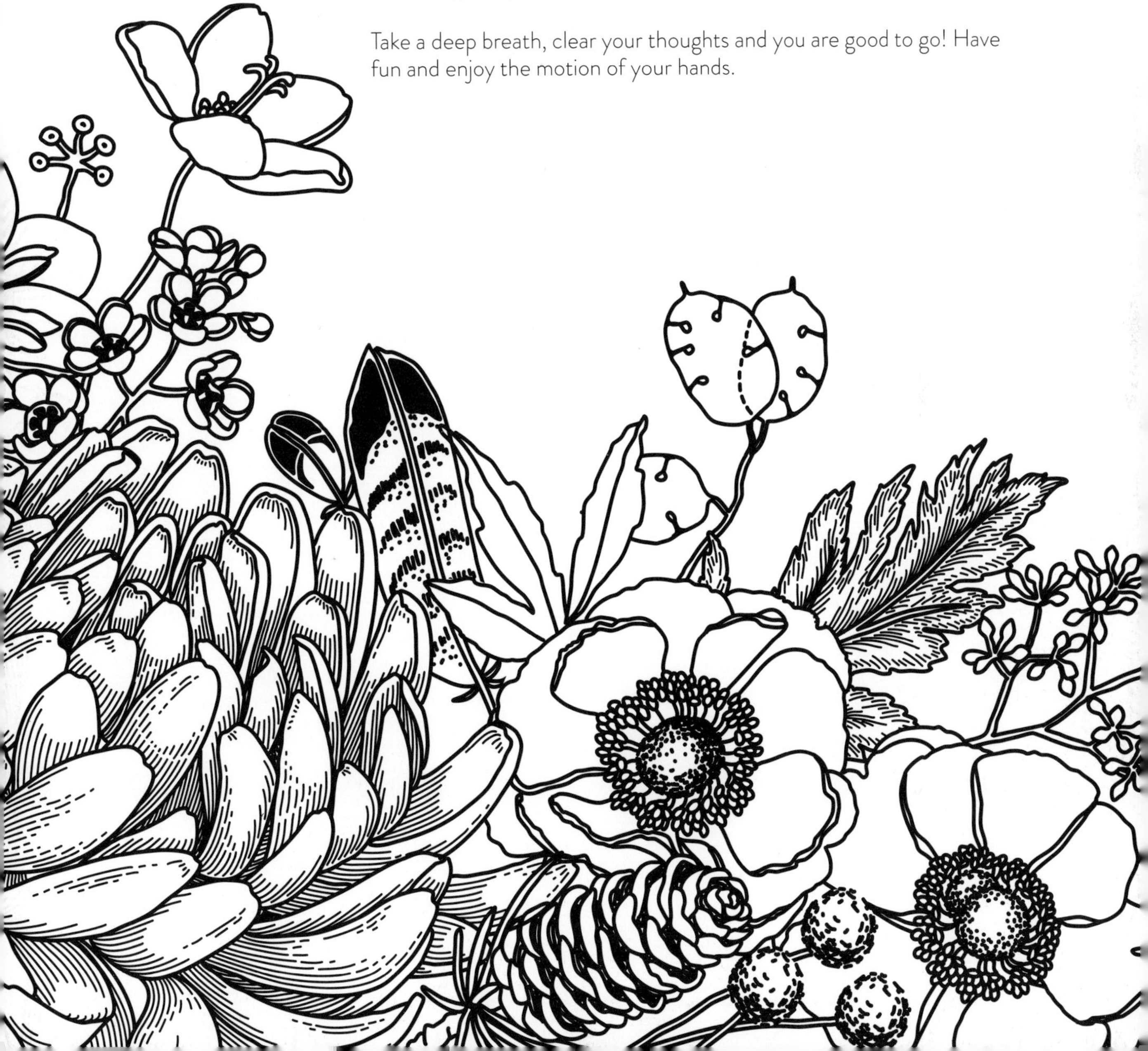

HELLEBORE

Hellebore's simple row of egg-shaped petals are so pure. Can you picture this whimsical wreath worn by a beautiful bride or a fairy? I was not sure if I should leave this illustration so simple, but it just took my heart as it is.

I used to make flower crowns for myself from daisies when I was a little girl playing in the garden. Now as an adult this might look a little silly, but sometimes I can't resist making one while I am having fun in the park.

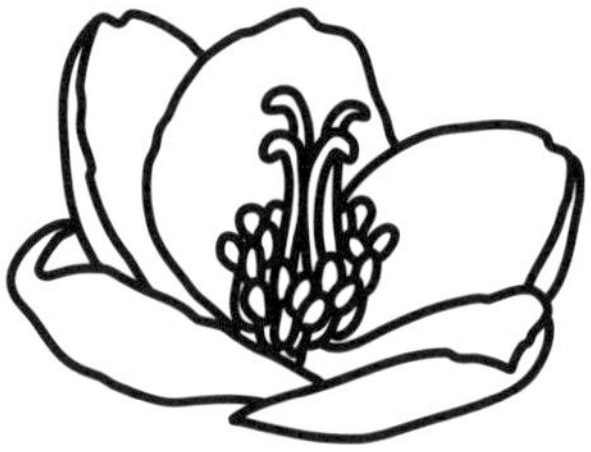

For the hellebore at an angle, start by drawing the petals that are covering the center of the flower. Continue with the central part. First trace the anthers that are fully visible in the front and move backward. Hellebore has three or four spikes in the center that look like candy canes. Here you also want to go from front to back.

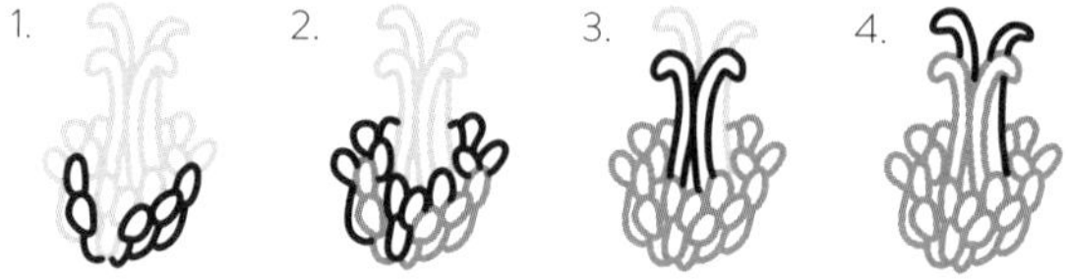

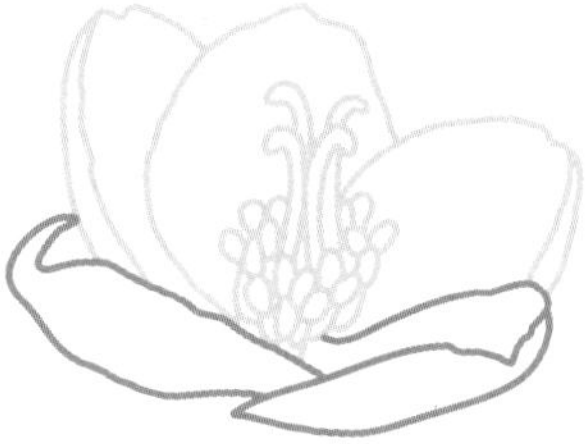

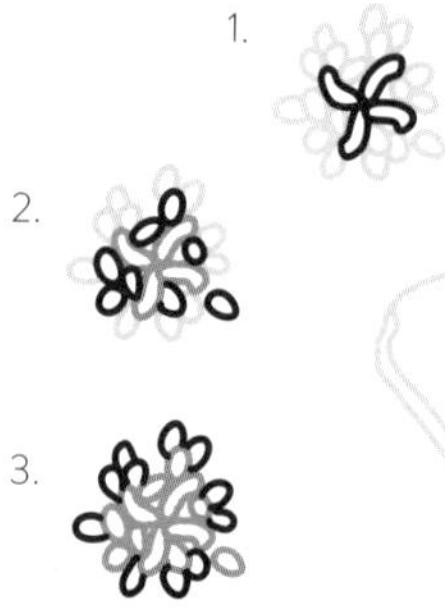

Following the top view illustration, start by working on the flower's center. First outline the four spikes in the middle, then add in the small ovals for the anthers. Make sure you draw them big enough to have a tiny white space in the middle of each one.

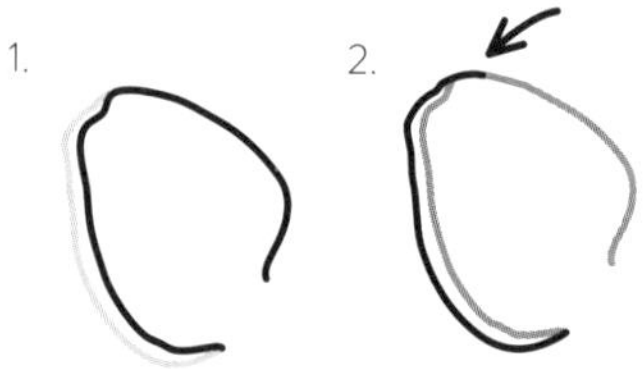

Finish up the drawing with the petals. Pay attention as you draw the double edges to draw them nice and parallel. After drawing the first layer, start your next stroke on the already existing line in order to have the smoothest joint.

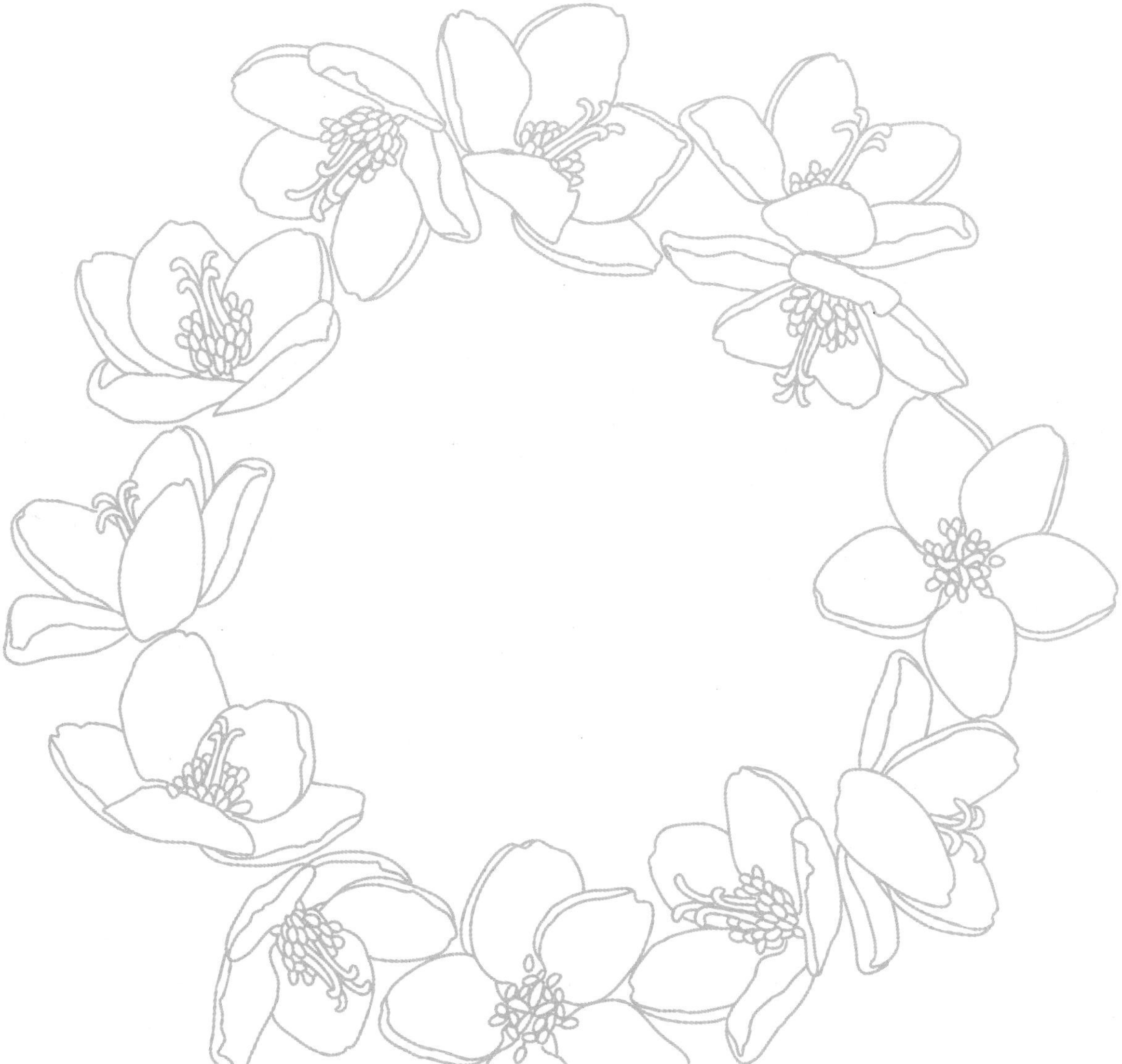

POPPY

I'm sure there are more people who love poppies than those who don't. Needless to say, I am a big fan. I always wanted to draw a poppy field, and now I found a great purpose for bringing you ultimate joy with one. I kept it simple, wanting to capture the incredible delicacy of this flower. I love all of its states, from bud to full flower to wilted, as well as the playful curves of the stem—they instantly bring a smile to my face. In addition, this is an incredibly effective way to improve drawing long parallel lines! Get ready and jump into the challenge.

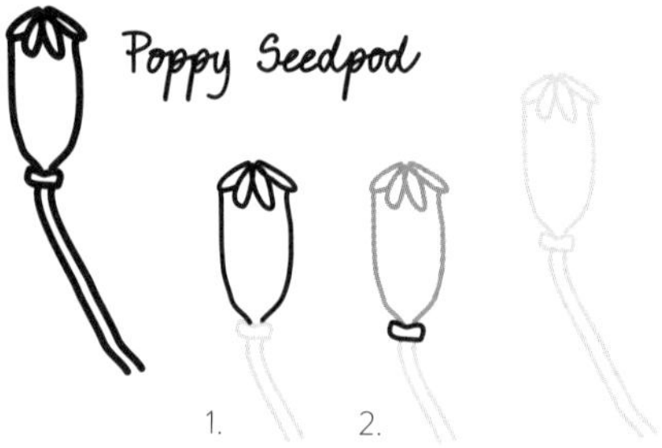

The seedpod remains after the flower has lost all of its petals and anthers. Start with the four ovals at the top. Then draw the two sides and connect the stem and the seedpod with a tiny oval.

The wilted poppy seedpod has some anthers hanging from its bottom. Draw some stems to connect the anthers.

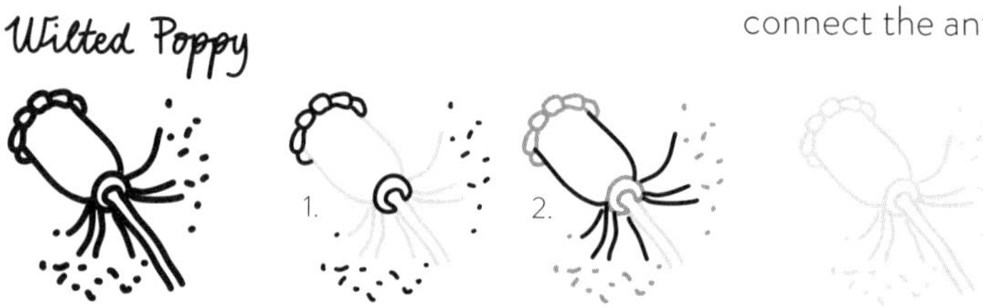

For the center of the poppy flower, start with the starlike shape and outline of the seedpod. Then stipple some anthers around it. Finish off by adding in the dark spots around the base.

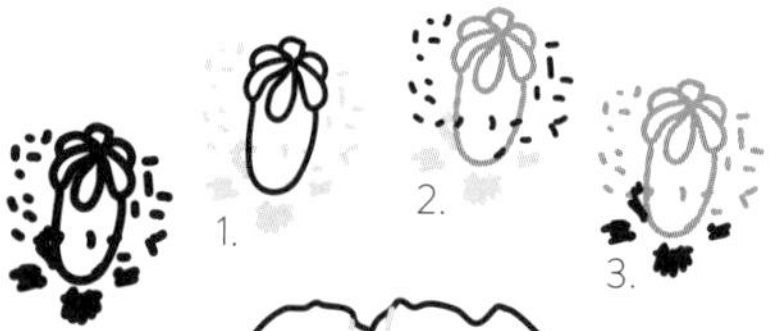

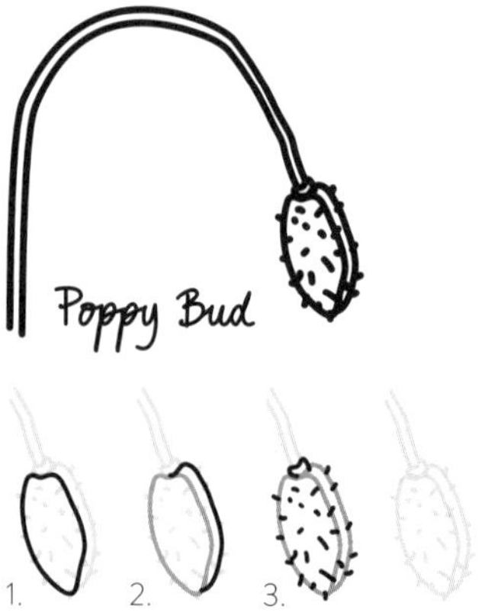

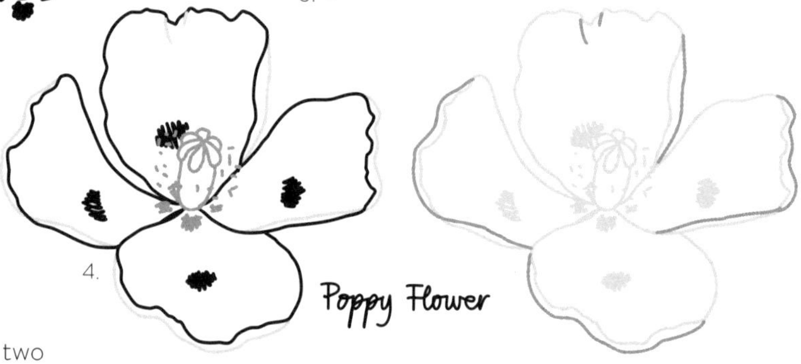

The bud is a hairy little thing. It has two sides; draw the closer one first. A little ring connects the bud with the stem, appearing like a kidney shape. Add random short strokes to illustrate the hair.

Draw the petals as shaky as possible to imitate the natural folds of this flower. The dark spots make the petals even more spectacular. Use a continuous squiggly stroke to capture their density.

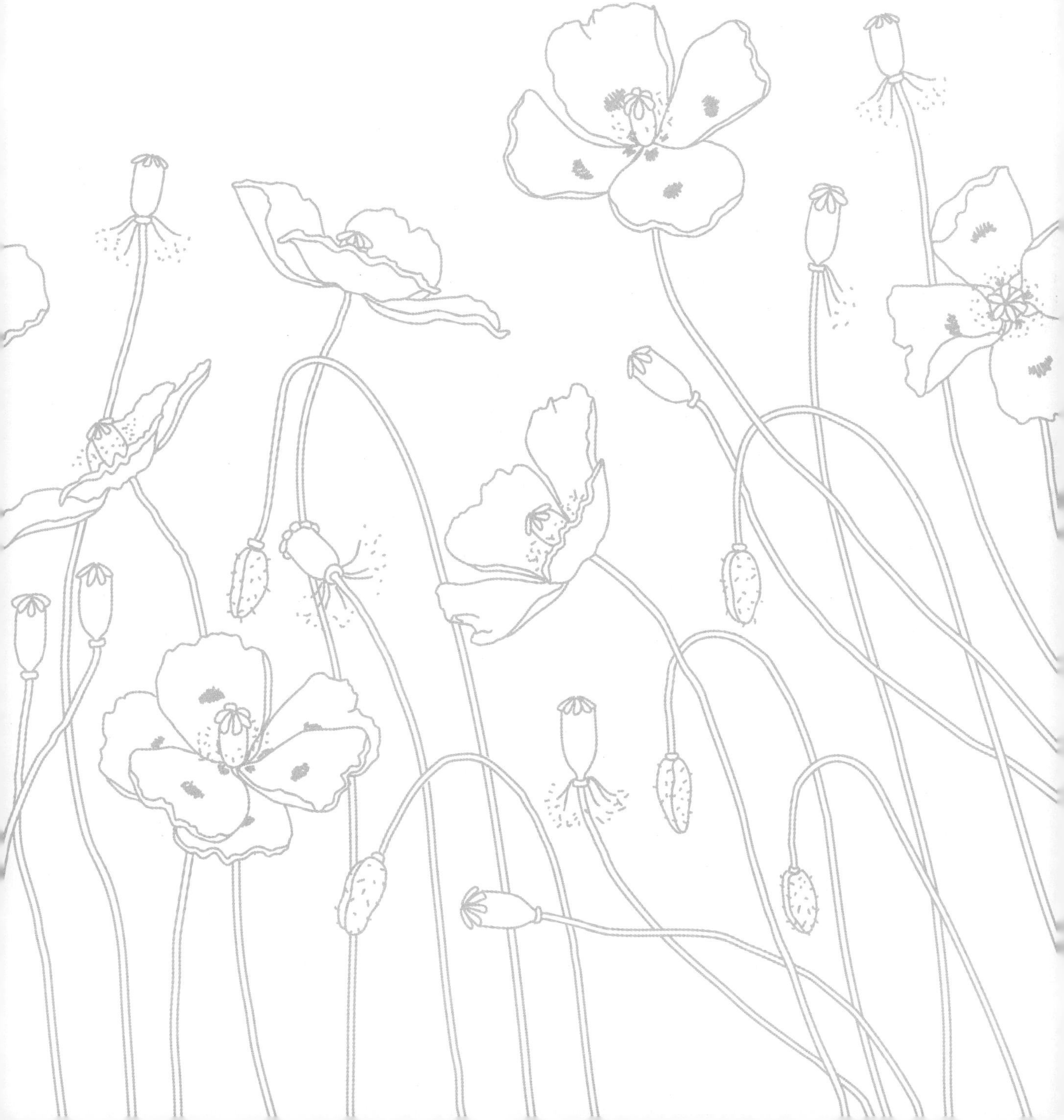

PEONY

Peonies are like superstars—they steal the show from any other flower. They simply cannot be ignored. The luxurious petal ocean is soft as silk and full of details that captivate the eye. The center creates the perfect contrast to the dense bunch of anthers. I feel like I could get lost forever in the thousands of layers. Let's take a deep dive and switch off our minds for a few minutes.

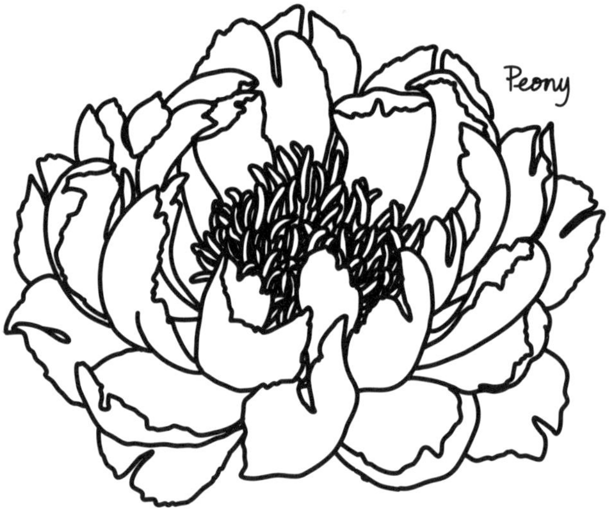

I like to start with the petals that hug the center. Sometimes they also shield some of the anthers, so these lines create the boundary of the central messiness. From there, create the center of anthers then finish off the petals working outward from the middle.

The anthers are like short sausages and usually have a slight bend, but can have a variety of shapes. Here are some examples.

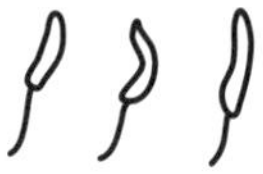

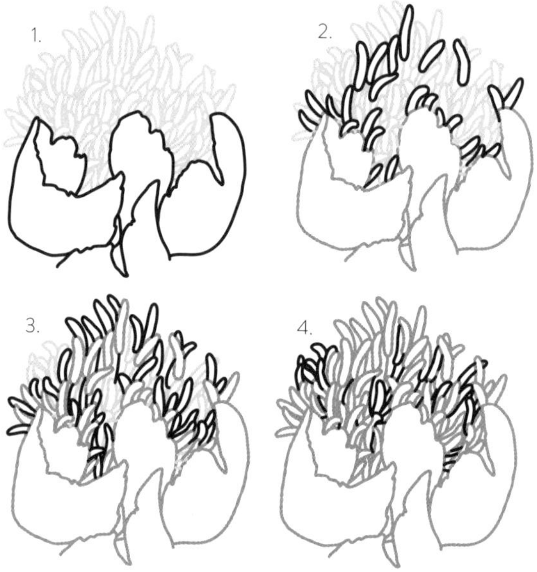

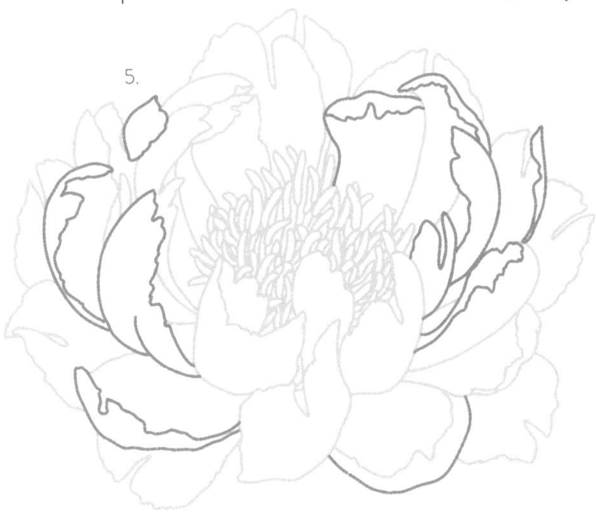

The anthers stand in several layers. Start by tracing the anthers that are fully visible, then begin filling out the ones in the background.

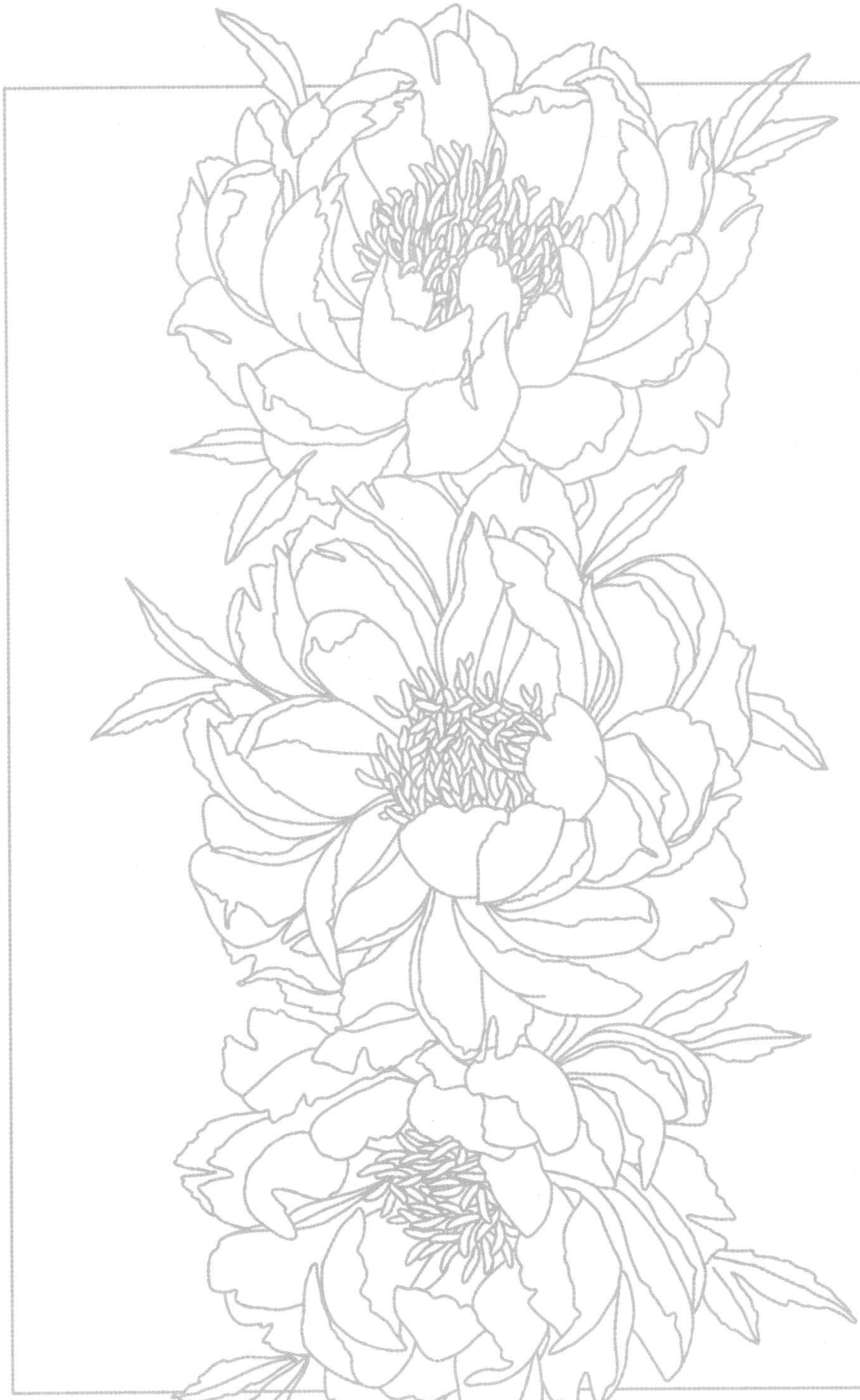

ANEMONE

I love the contrast of the black velvet center and the ultralight silk petals of anemones. This flower is a perfect example of how I like to match flowers in an arrangement. Contrast makes the magic. This is why I use anemones in my illustrations again and again. I also want to show you the pure beauty of this flower on its own.

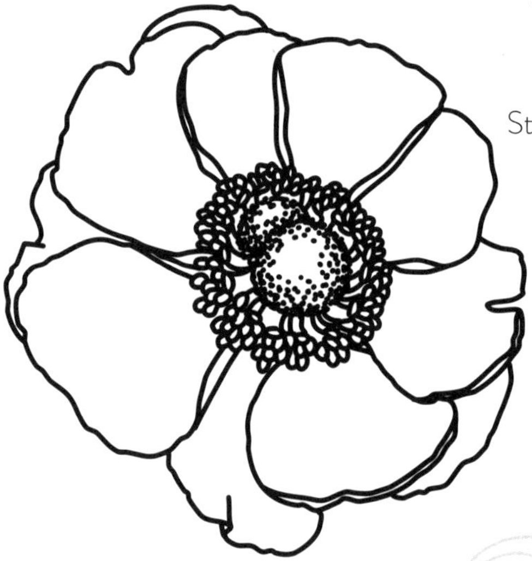

The central dome is built up from dots. Move in a spiral motion around the dome. Stipple more dots at the edge and decrease them toward the center. This creates the highlight, which will make the illustration look more three-dimensional.

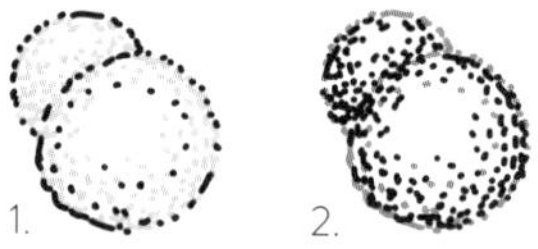

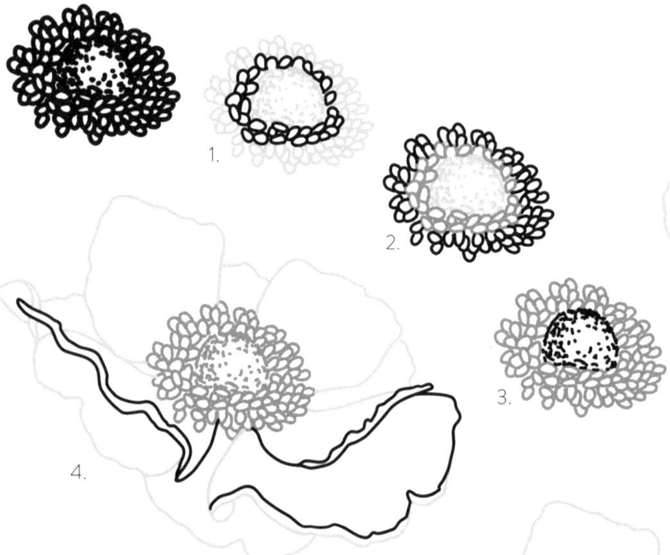

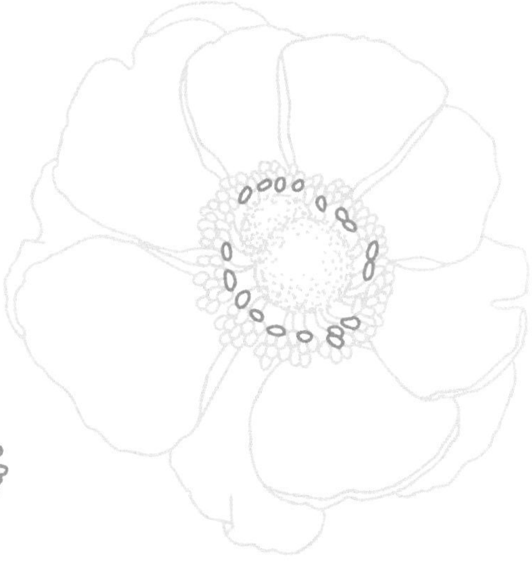

The edge of the petals are detailed by hills and valleys. The double edge adds body to the lightweight, airy petals. Pay careful attention to draw the edges narrow and parallel.

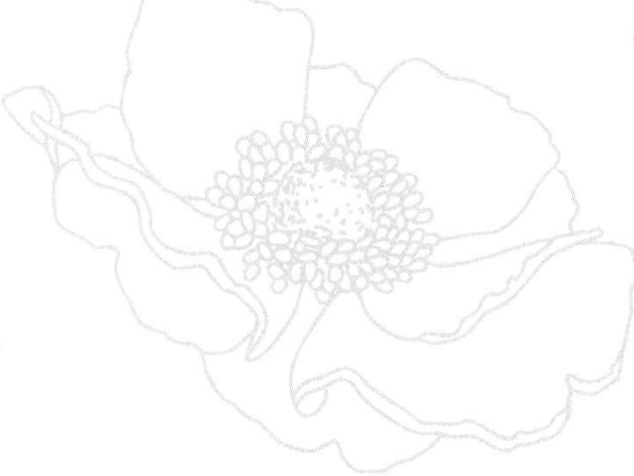

When creating the anthers, I like to start with the dense center part. They are laid down in several layers. Start by outlining the fully visible ones. They look like small ovals, and there are many tucked behind, which appear as semiovals.

DAHLIA

Dahlias are native to Mexico and Central America, and they are known for their amazing diversity. Even with all the different floral shapes in this illustration, it doesn't showcase the full variety of dahlias! The color range is also amazingly wide, from a café latte to almost black-burgundy. After drawing the outlines, it is definitely worth it to add color to this illustration. What are you feeling? A deep moody palette or some sun-kissed nudes?

For this more fanned-out dahlia, start by drawing the center as tiny circles. First draw the outer ones, then the ones in the middle. Keep them big enough so they have a little white spot inside of them. Draw some spikes around them.

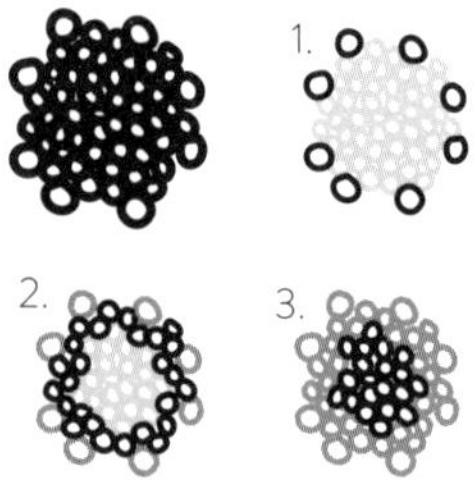

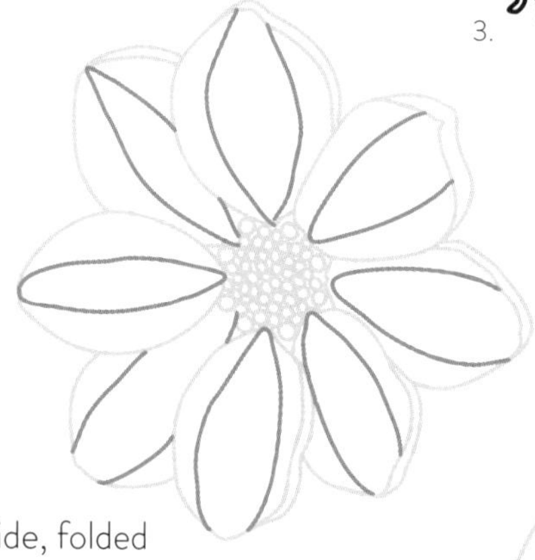

For this smaller dahlia with wide, folded petals, start at the center with the larger circles and fill in the space with smaller circles. The petals have two visible folds, which complete the look of this flower.

Here are some examples of the petals, showing how amazingly diverse they are. Practice drawing smooth lines with even pressure.

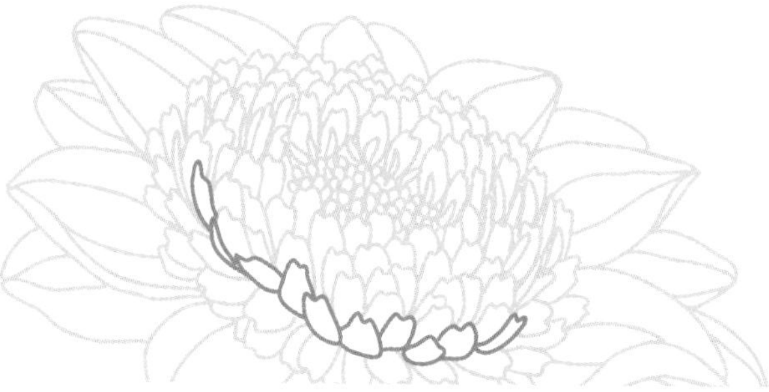

This dahlia is like a pom-pom full of petals. Start by drawing the darker ones that curl up and add them all in layer by layer.

PASSIONFLOWER

I think we can agree that tropical flowers are unbelievably rich in fascinating detail. And passionflower is a perfect example! How can nature create such complex structures when a simple tulip would do the trick?

One summer I had a passionflower plant on my balcony. I couldn't stop studying its blooms and buds, and it always took me on a tropical getaway, if only in my imagination. Take a deep breath and jump into the ocean of lines and shapes.

1.

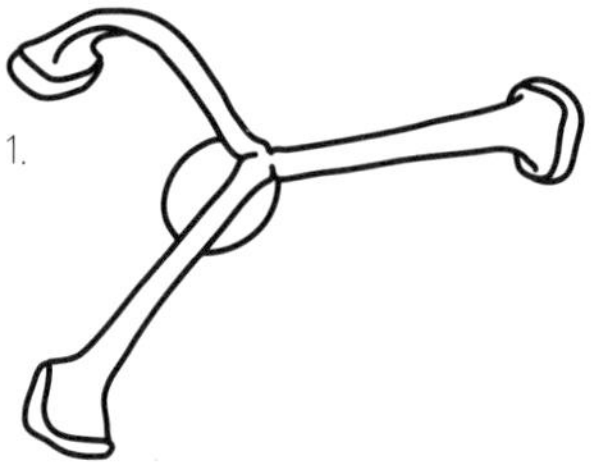

Start with the first layer of the propeller-like center. Then create the second one with anthers at its ends. Be careful to draw the sides parallel. Next, add the tiny dots and zigzag strokes to complete the central structure.

2.

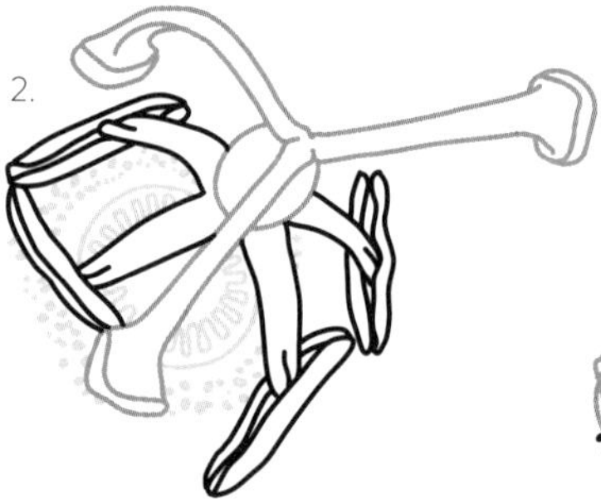

3.

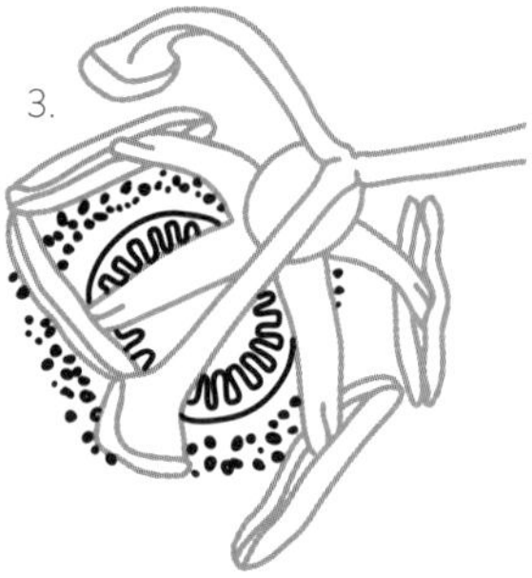

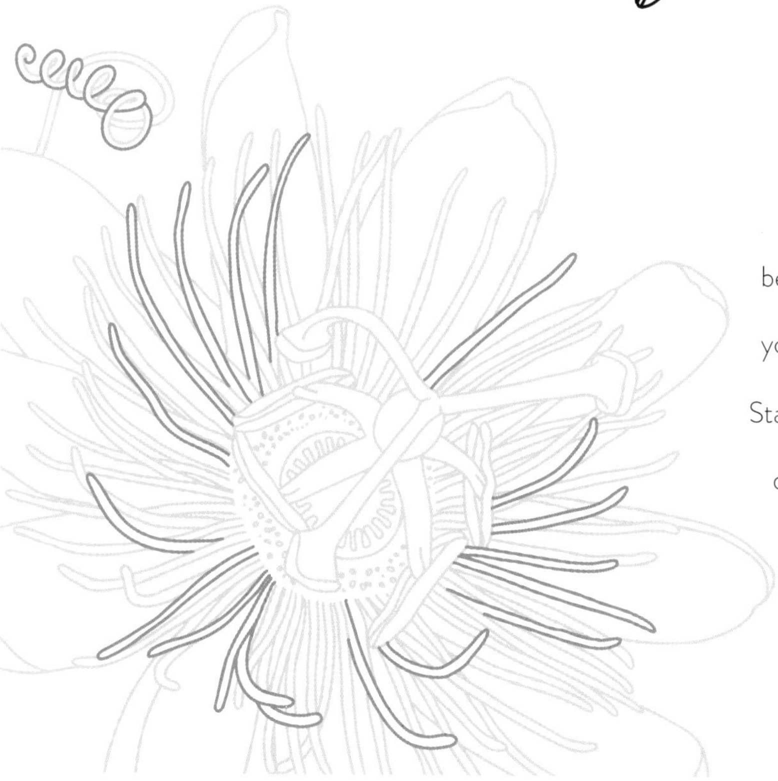

The crown is a row of threadlike filaments, which may look complicated to draw. Using your best stroke direction (see page 14) makes it a lot easier. Remember, you can rotate the book as you go.

Start with the fully visible filaments, indicated in dark gray. They will define where to start and end the upcoming outlines.

To achieve the most stunning result, draw the filaments similar in width.

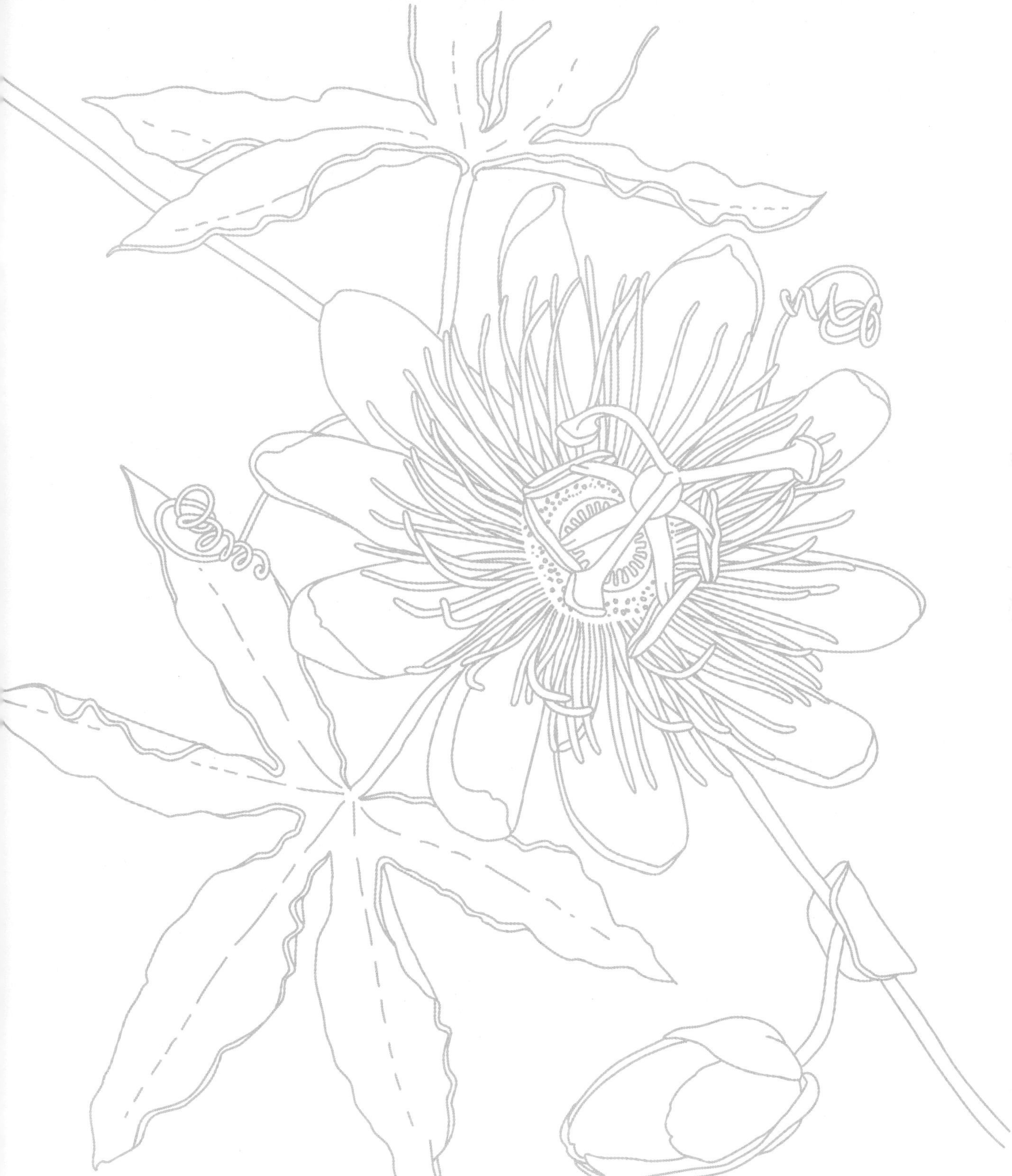

ZINNIA

My grandmother's garden was full of zinnias. Oh my gosh, what a riot of color! Zinnia has vibrant pinks, oranges and yellows, but my favorite part is capturing the details of the center. It has a ring of tiny flower-like anthers that really steals my heart. Then there are the cute, heart-shaped petals leaning in several layers around the center. I left one zinnia all filled in for you to enjoy looking at as you bring your own to life. Let's jump into this flowing stream of kindness and joy.

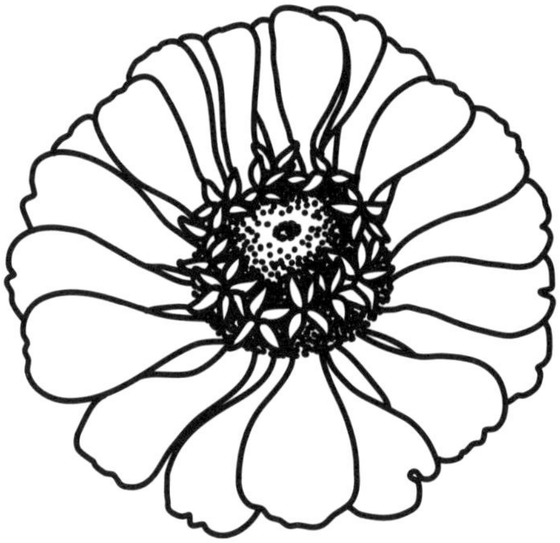

Start to draw the ring of anthers, as shown in both step 1 images. Pay attention to the layers because they might overlap. Leave a small white area in the center of the anthers so they can pop from the darker dome.

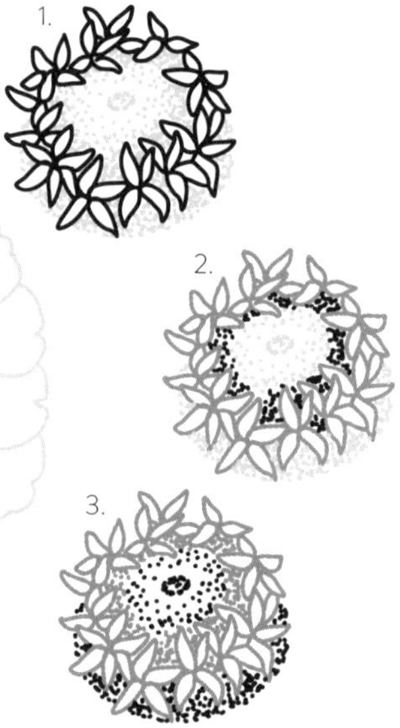

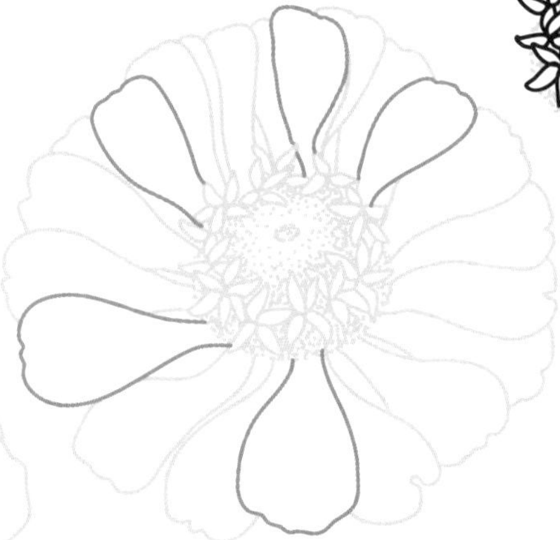

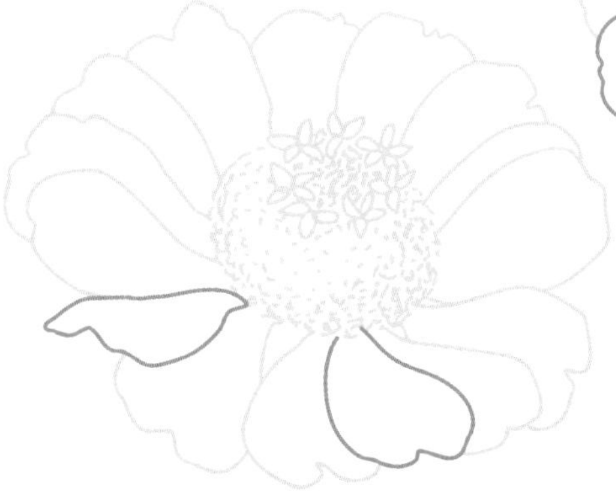

After outlining the anthers, start working around them by stippling in dots, as shown in both step 2 images. Add as many dots as the paper can hold to create a really deep shadow.

Stippling plays a key role in this illustration. Varying the density of dots will create shadows and highlights. The petals are an easy heart shape. Trace over them in one continuous motion and start with the ones that are fully visible, working backward from there.

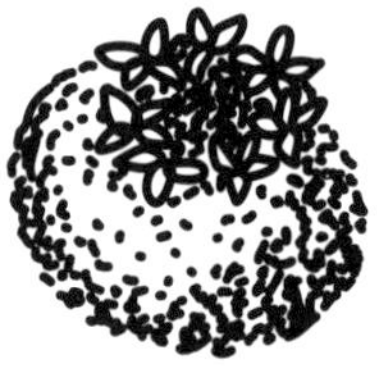

The dome requires more variation, as you can see in both step 3 images. The perimeter and one side are darker, but make sure you leave a highlight area. This gives depth to the illustration.

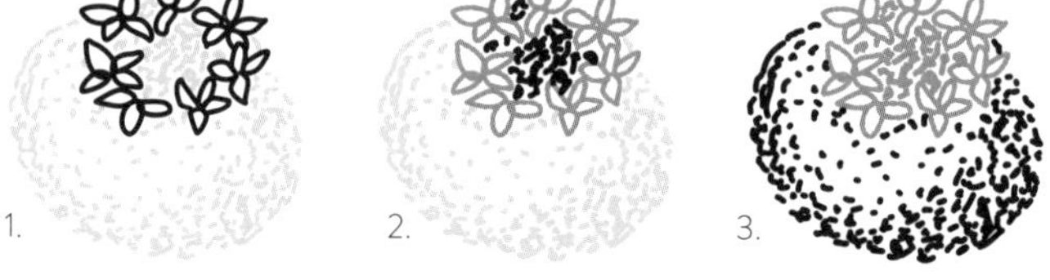

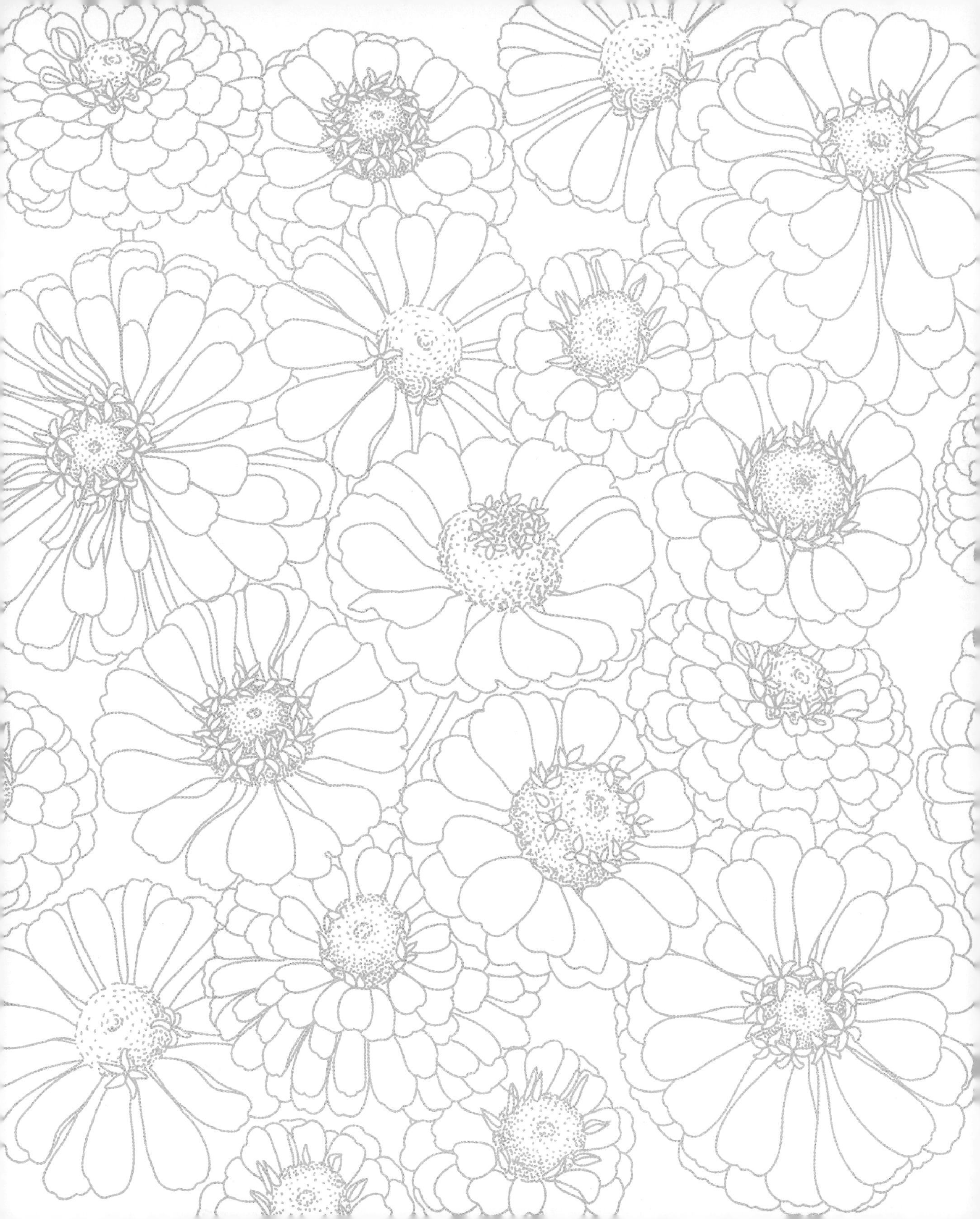

PANSY

I am totally blown away by the diversity of this flower. I absolutely adore the color variations and combinations, and they are one of my favorite flowers for a beautiful spring or autumn arrangement. I was also super surprised when I found them growing wild on an evening walk. The wild ones are tiny, like the smallest ones in the illustration. Tracing the different sizes of these flowers all follows the same logic. Instead, we will be focusing more on the shading.

Here you'll practice adding your own shading lines for the first time! Remember that you can practice by tracing and then try adding in your own in the blank illustrations.

1.

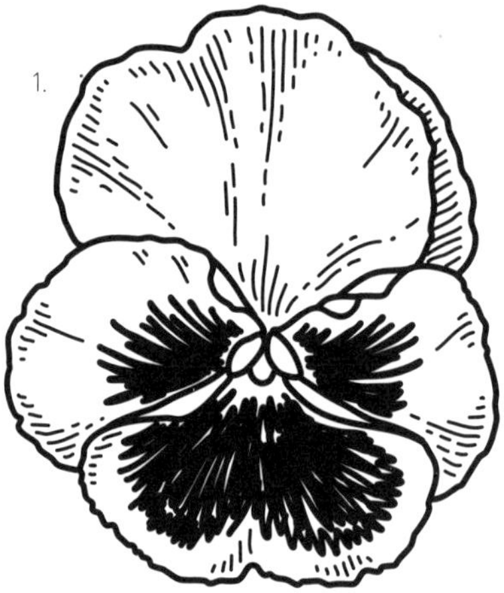

Start drawing the outlines of the flowers with a thick pen. Begin with the two ovals and semicircle in the center. Move on to the lowest petal, then add the two on the side. To finish, add the two upper petals.

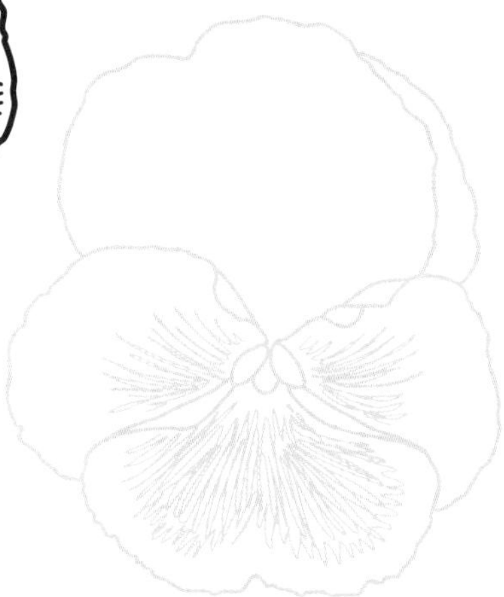

2.

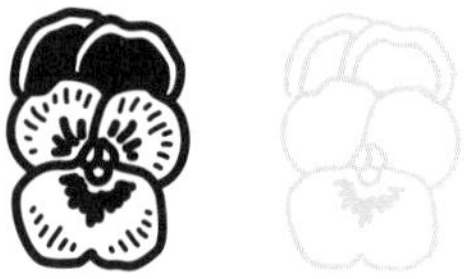

Grab a thin pen, and add in the shading lines. Be careful to make the spacing even and add a slight curve to the lines. Start the shading lines at the edge of the petals, but leave a tiny gap. This little detail makes such a difference!

3.

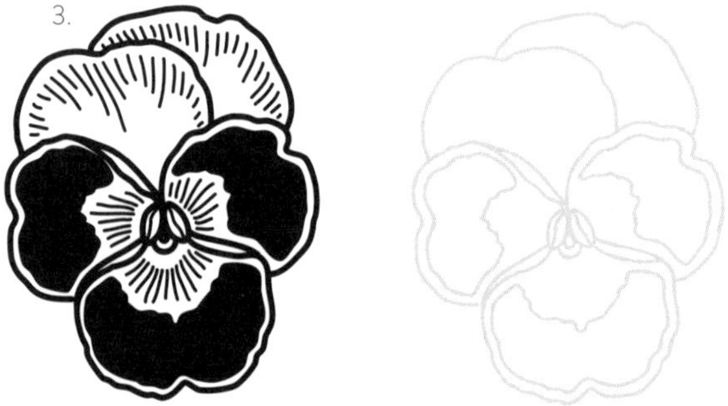

To create the dark patterns, switch back to a thick pen. I use two methods. You can either draw the outline of the dark area and fill it in completely (as in examples 2 and 3), or if the strokes are visible, fill in the dark area with a long zigzag stroke (as in examples 1 and 4). It gives the flower an interesting texture.

4.

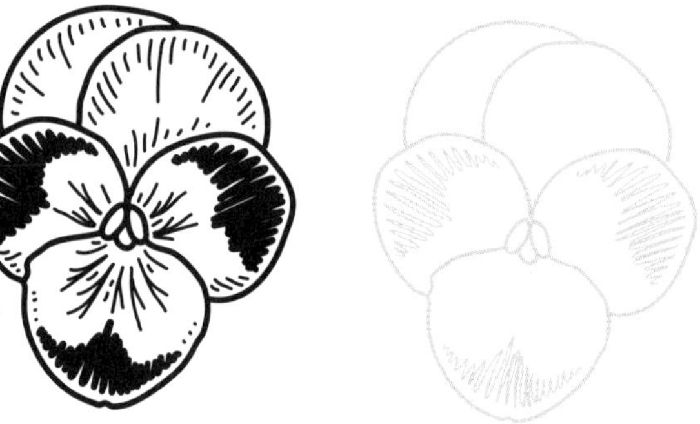

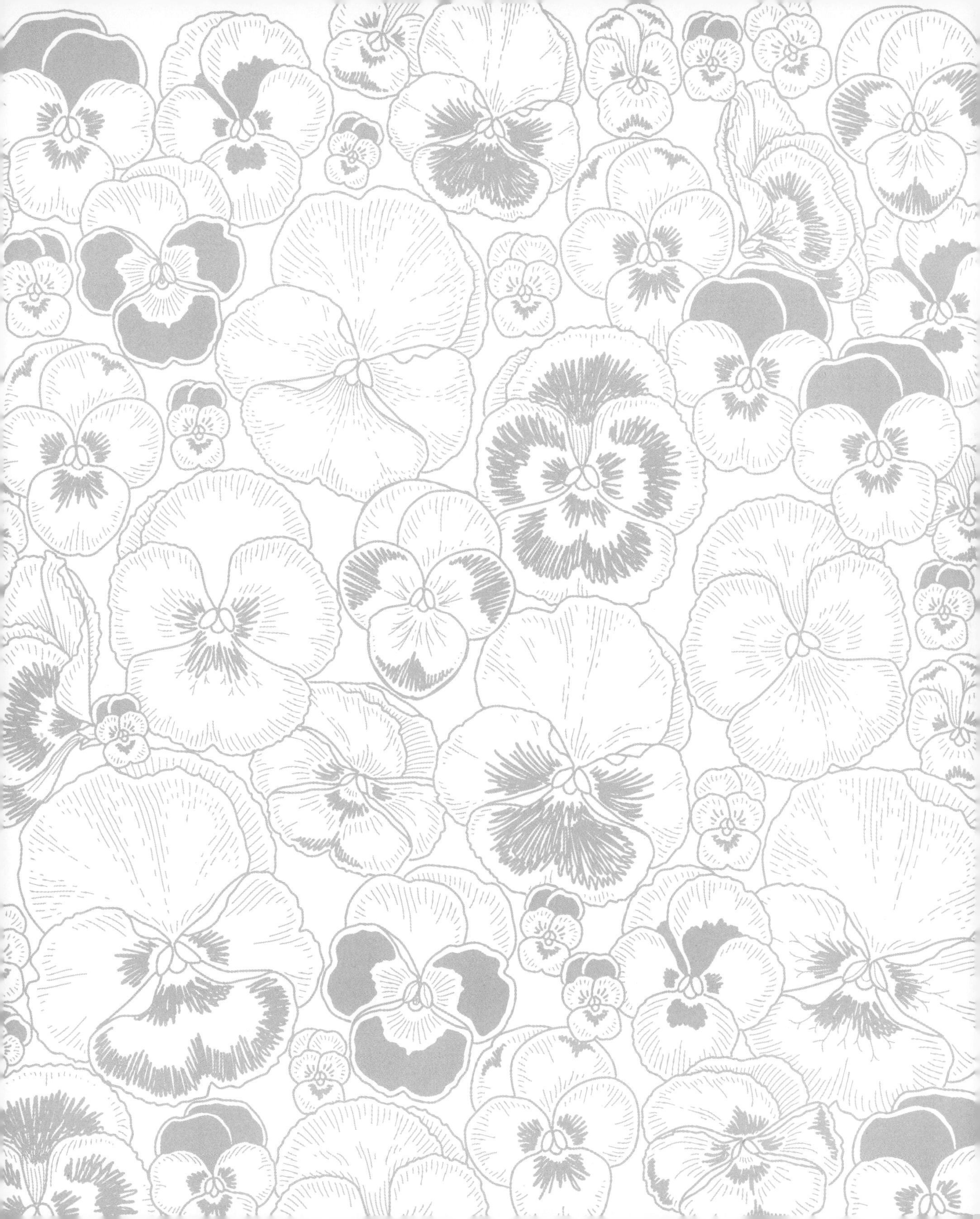

HYDRANGEA

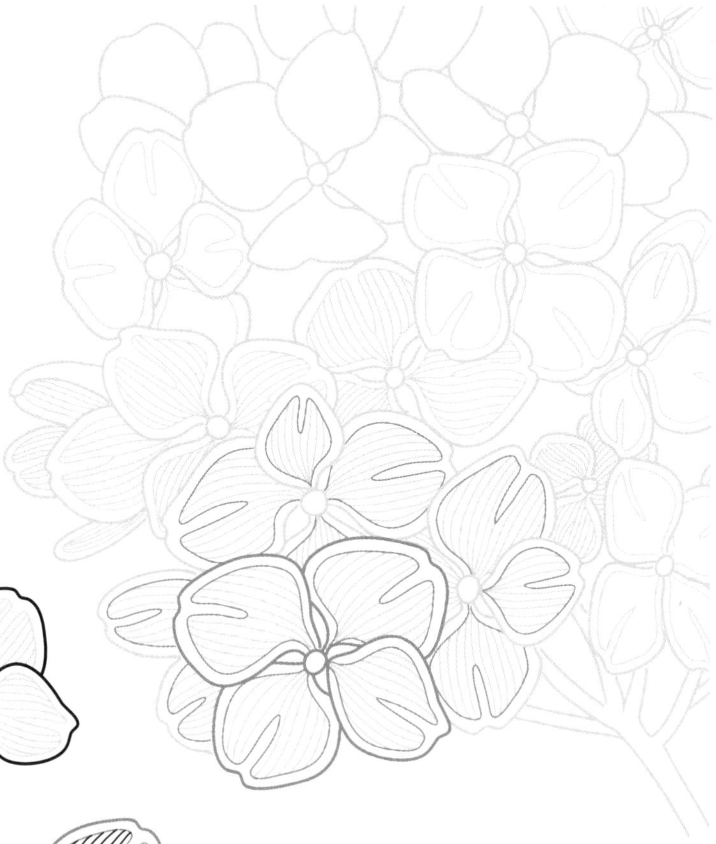

This illustration is based on a hydrangea plant my mother gave me a few years ago. She has a wonderful bush in her garden. The only tweak I made to this version is the pattern of the petals. This kind of linework helps improve fine motor skills. Drawing these parallel lines requires close attention, but it is easy because the lines are not too long. Let's grab a pen and get lost in the flowing lines.

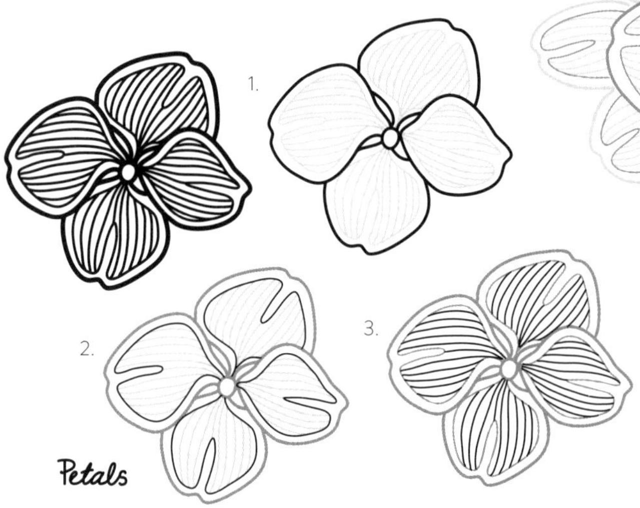

The leaves are pretty advanced this time. Look at all the details of the outline. Try to draw both sides without lifting your hand. The veins—drawn with a thin pen—are defined by the tiny shading lines. Be sure to leave a gap between the two rows—this makes the veins pop.

Draw the outlines of the petals with a thicker pen and then use a thinner pen to create the interior pattern. Start with the center of the flower and draw the fully visible petals (step 1), then draw the partially covered ones. With your thin pen, draw the outline of the pattern first (step 2), then fill in the whole area with parallel lines (step 3).

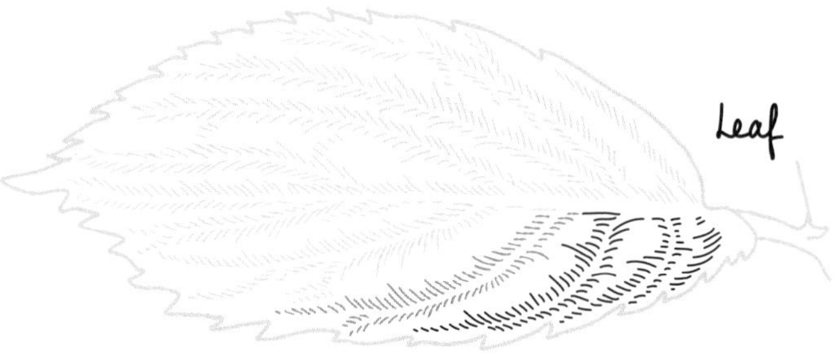

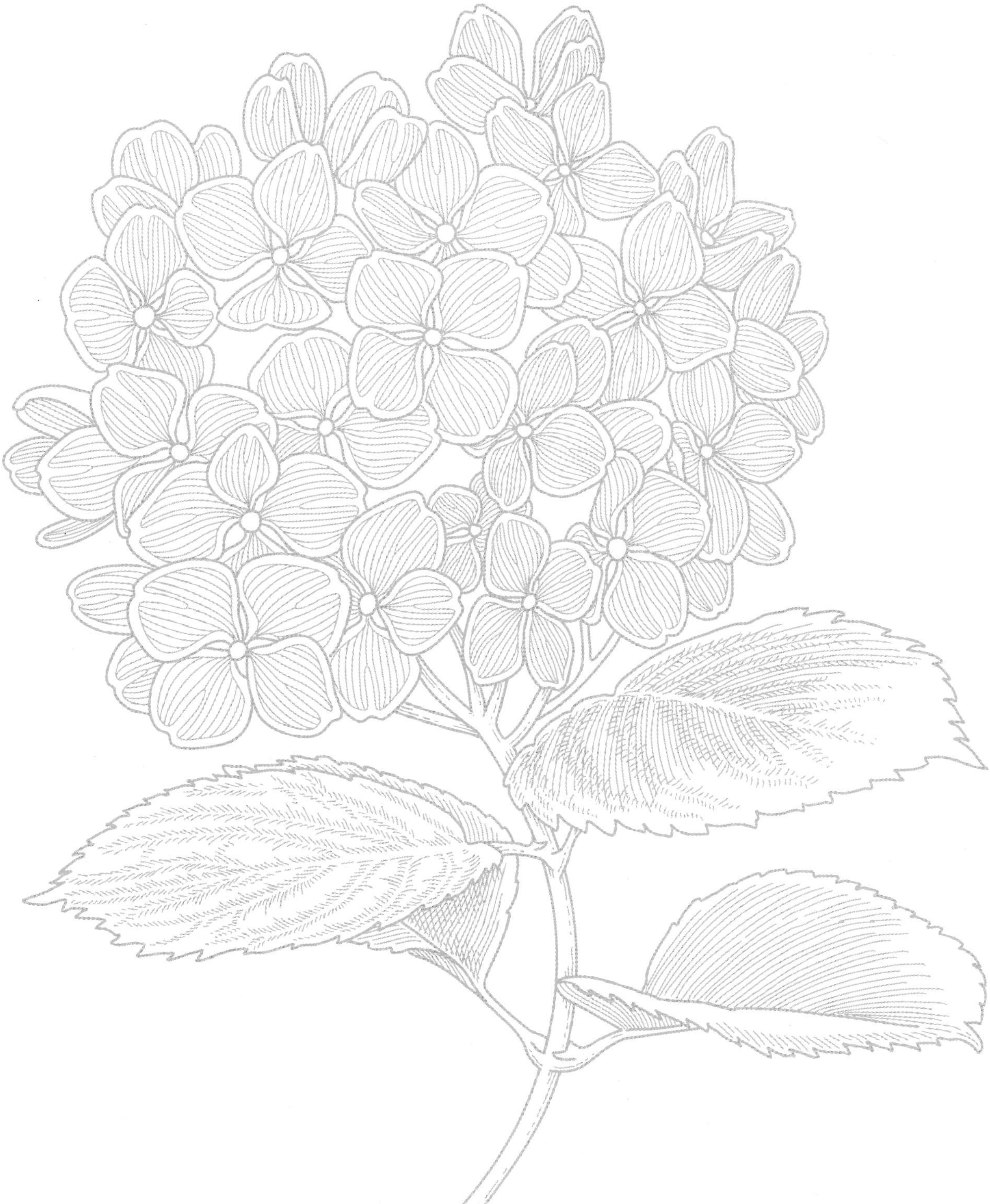

SUNFLOWER

This beautiful, highly detailed illustration gives you the opportunity to dive deep and practice your line art. Let's take a look at the way I built it up. When you are ready, create your own shading for this flower in the Shading Templates on page 107.

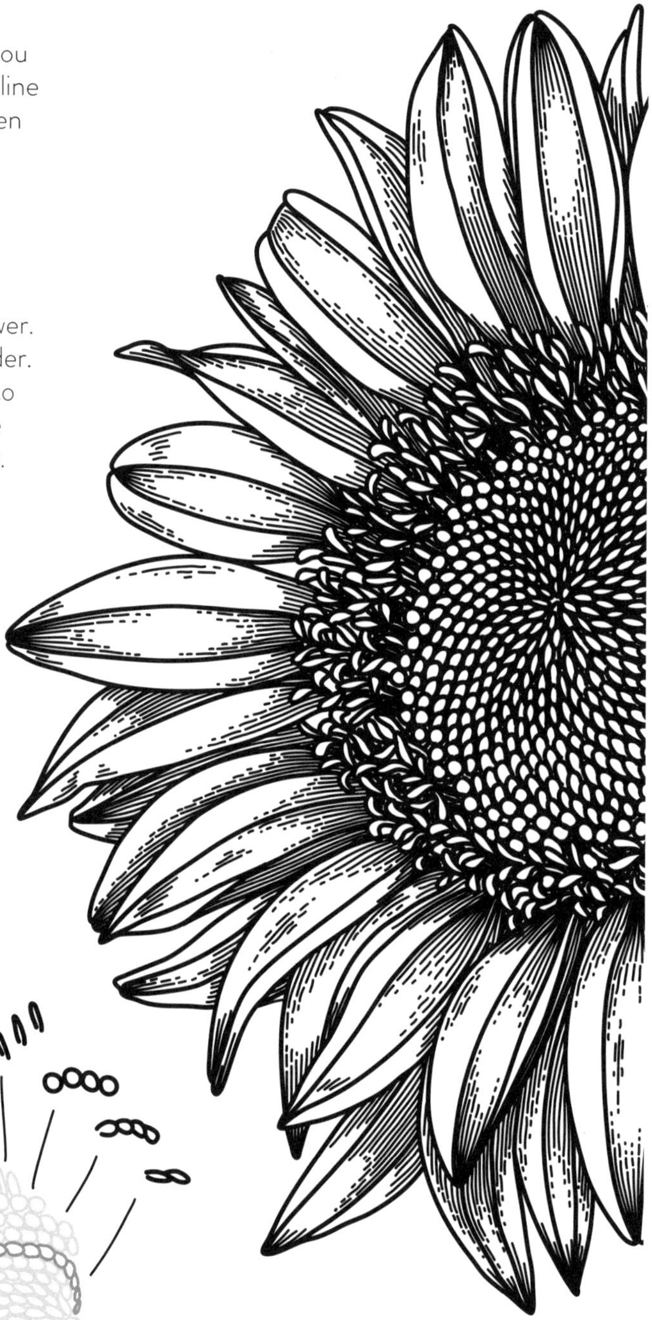

I suggest starting with the center of the sunflower. The seeds are clustered in a surprisingly tidy order. Start with the round seeds at the edge and try to follow the spiral layout. As you get closer to the middle, draw the seeds more pointy and narrow.

There is a ring of anthers around the seeds. This is a rather messy area full of playfully bent teardrop shapes. Fill the white areas around the anthers with ink to add depth to the illustration.

Start drawing the petals with the outlines first. Create beautiful gradients with carefully designed dashed lines (see page 16).

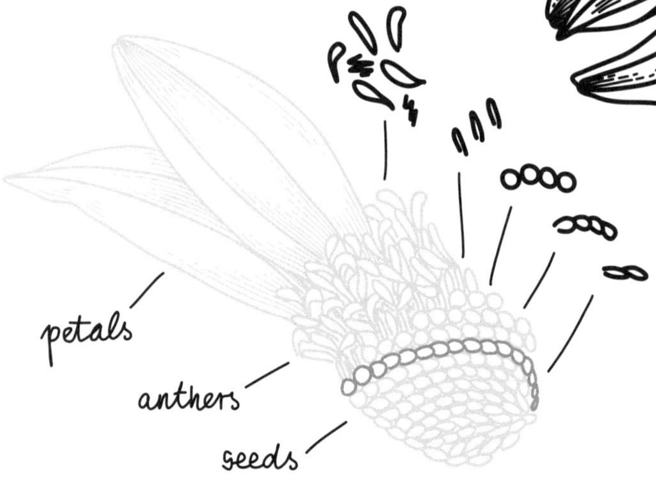

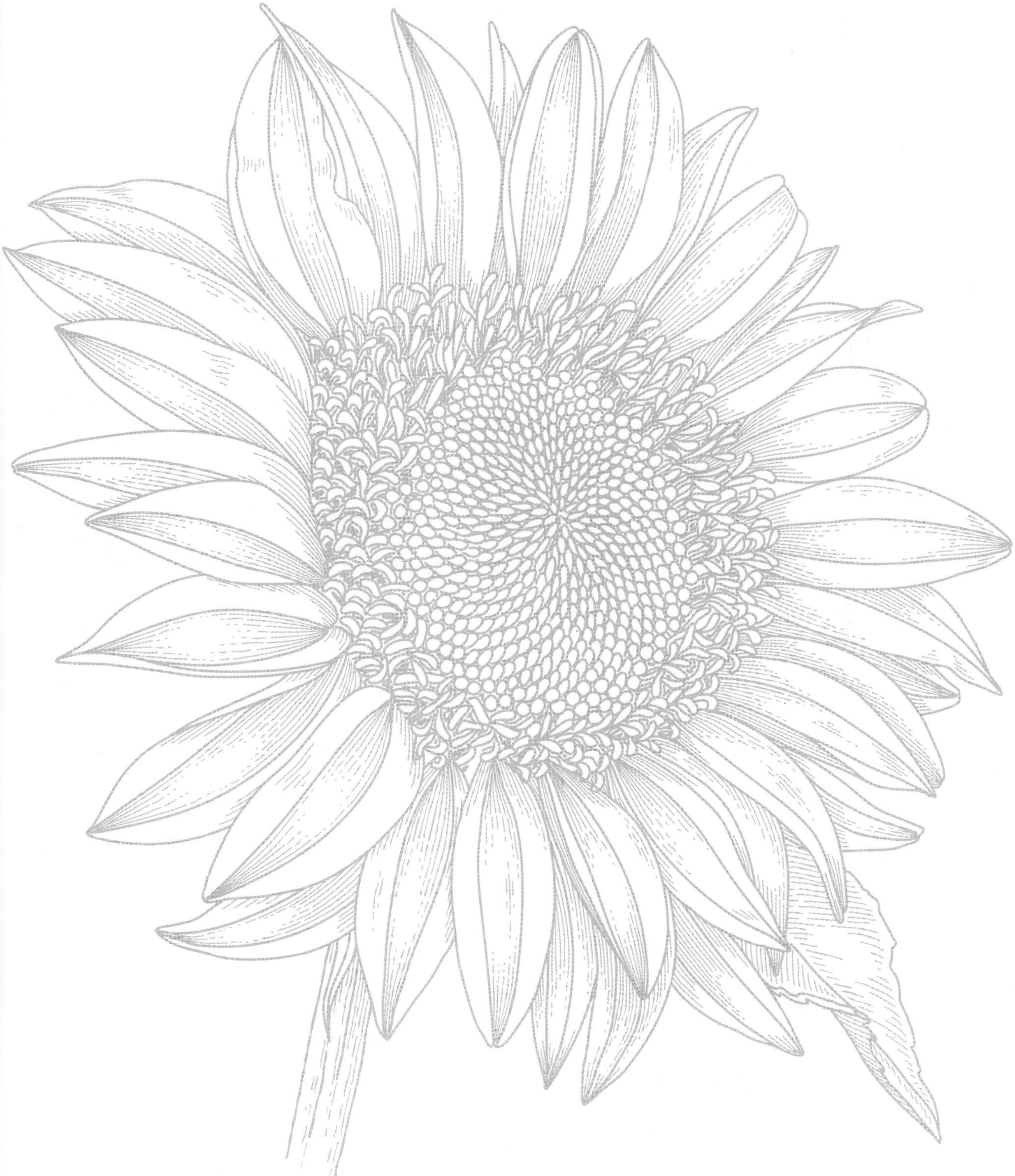

RANUNCULUS

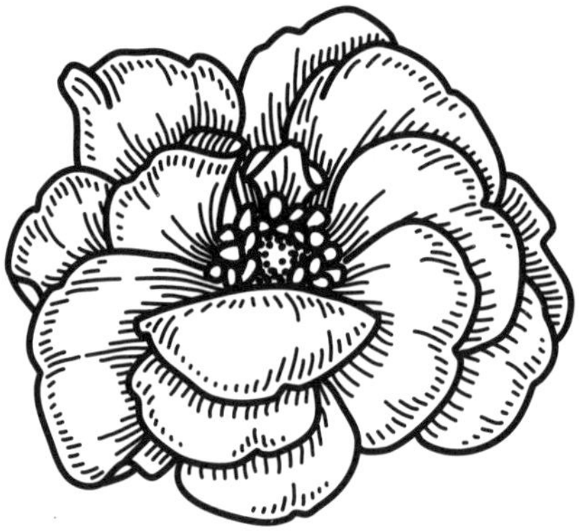

This flower, with its delicate and ultralight petals, is one of my personal favorites. There are so many variations of this flower, and they vary in density from a dozen up to a hundred petals. Let your mind relax and get lost in the layers of beautiful petals as you trace. Work with a thicker pen at the outlines, and use a thinner pen for the shading lines.

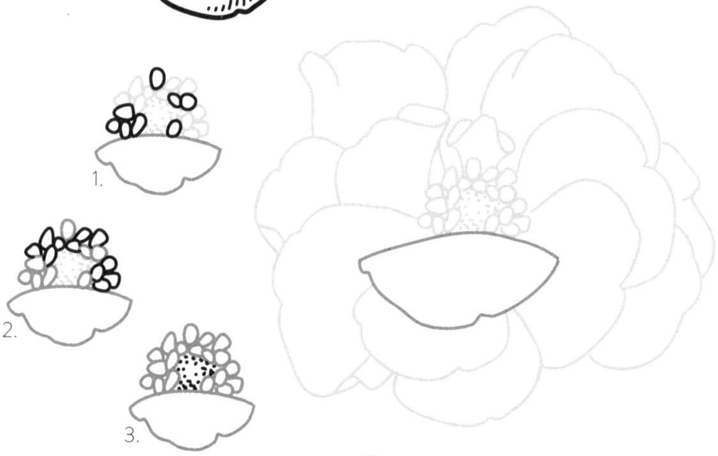

I like to start working on the central area of the flower by outlining the ring of anthers first. Add some extra detail to the ring of anthers by drawing some full circles first, and then tuck some others behind them (see steps 1 and 2). Next, move on to the little dome in the center (step 3), creating depth with loose dot work.

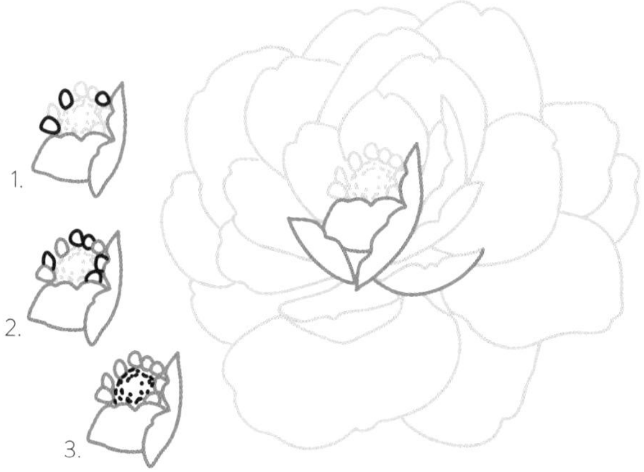

To create the petals, start outlining the ones that are fully visible, then outline the ones around them. Move from the inside toward the outside. Switch to a thinner pen and add in the shading lines, paying close attention to the direction and slight bend of each line.

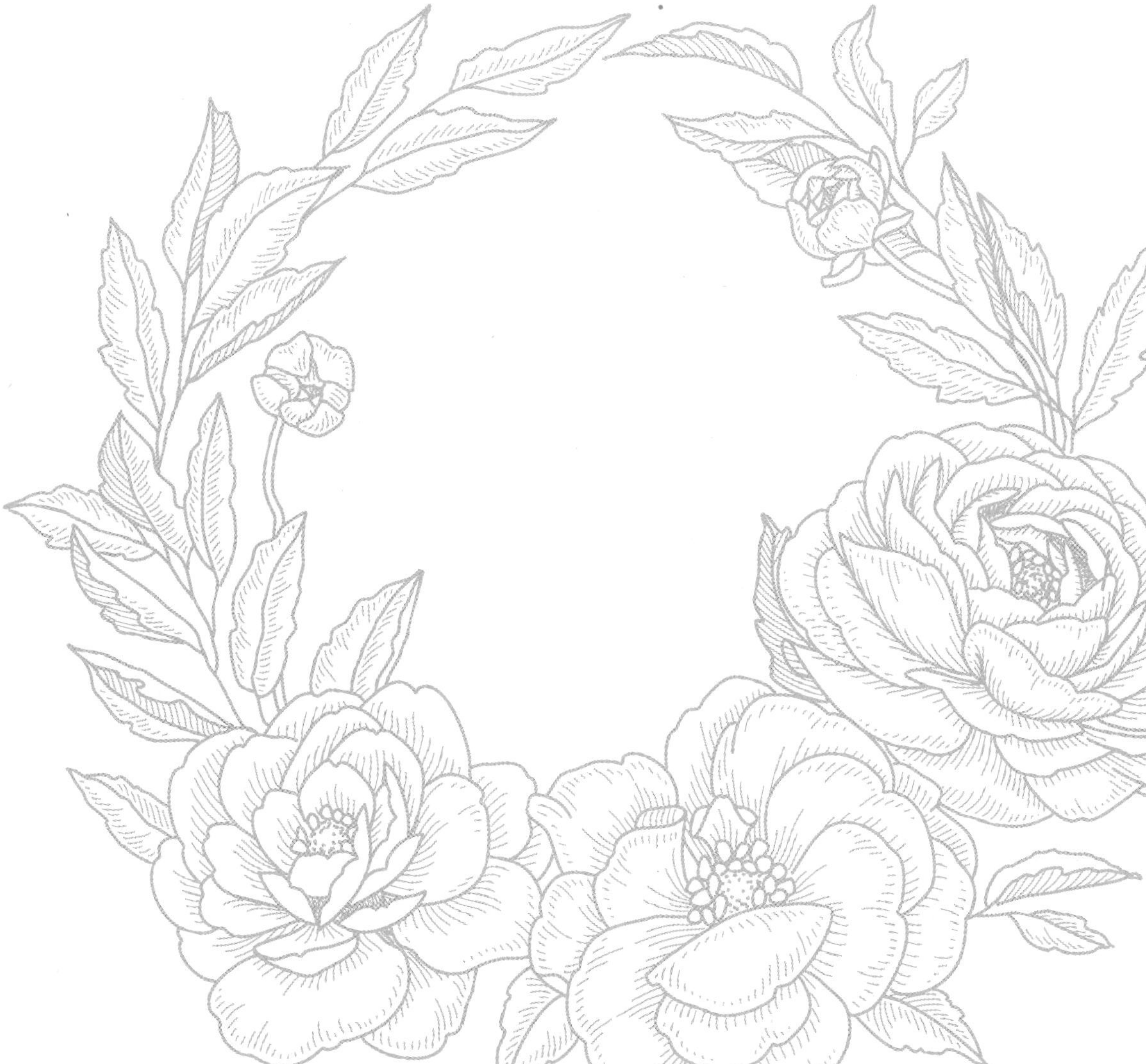

COSMOS

I discovered cosmos when I started drawing flowers as an adult. As a cut flower you buy for your home, it hadn't been on my map somehow. But I have to say once I started drawing, I welcomed this flower into my heart immediately and it became one of my favorites to capture. The center is so playful and detailed, and the beautiful folds of its petals are begging for pen and paper. Since then, I have also discovered a plant a few corners away from my home, blooming from summer until the first frosts. My family and I always stop by and breathe in some of its happy vibes. I left one cosmos in black for you to do the same while practicing.

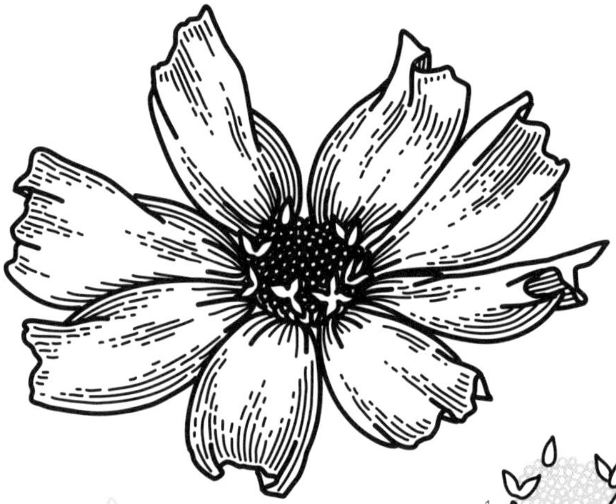

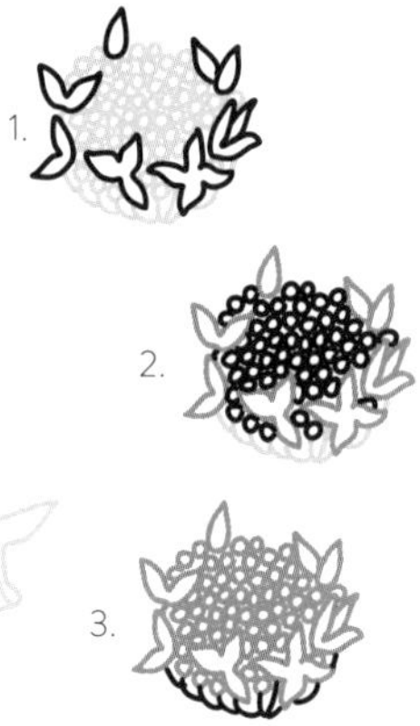

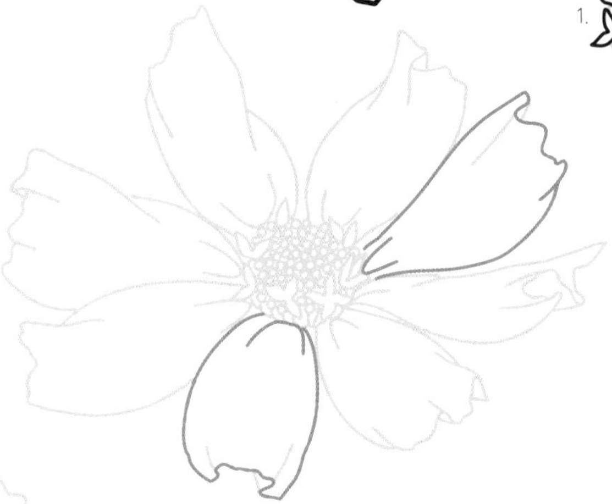

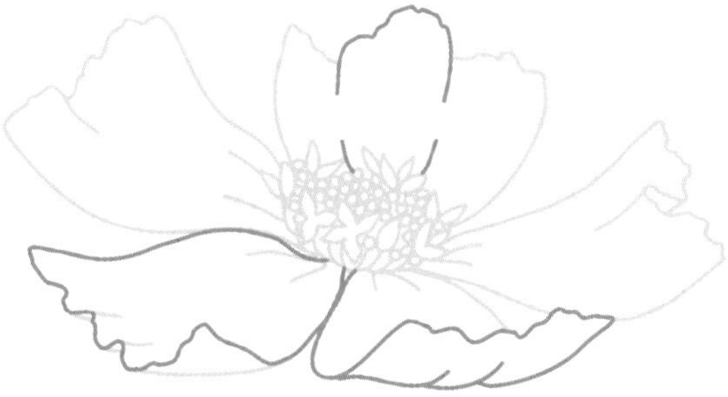

The center has some spectacular star-shaped pieces. Draw those first, as in step 1. Be sure to leave the inside of these shapes white to make them stand out.

Next, draw a bunch of circles to illustrate the anthers, shown in step 2. Finally, add some stamens below the anthers, as in step 3.

Begin by drawing all the outlines of the petals with a thick pen, then use a thin pen for shading. Create your own version of shading on the gray images.

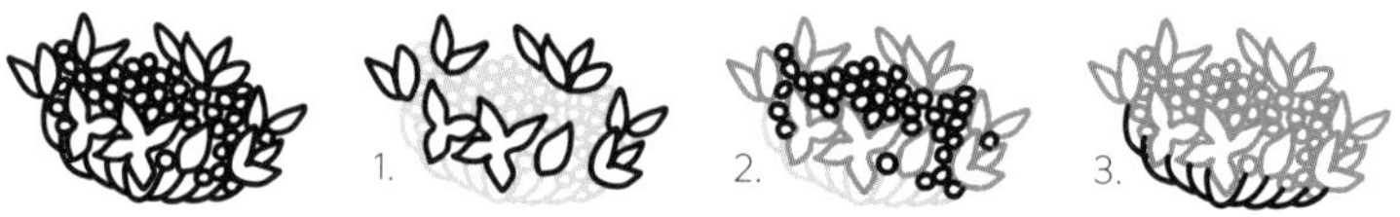

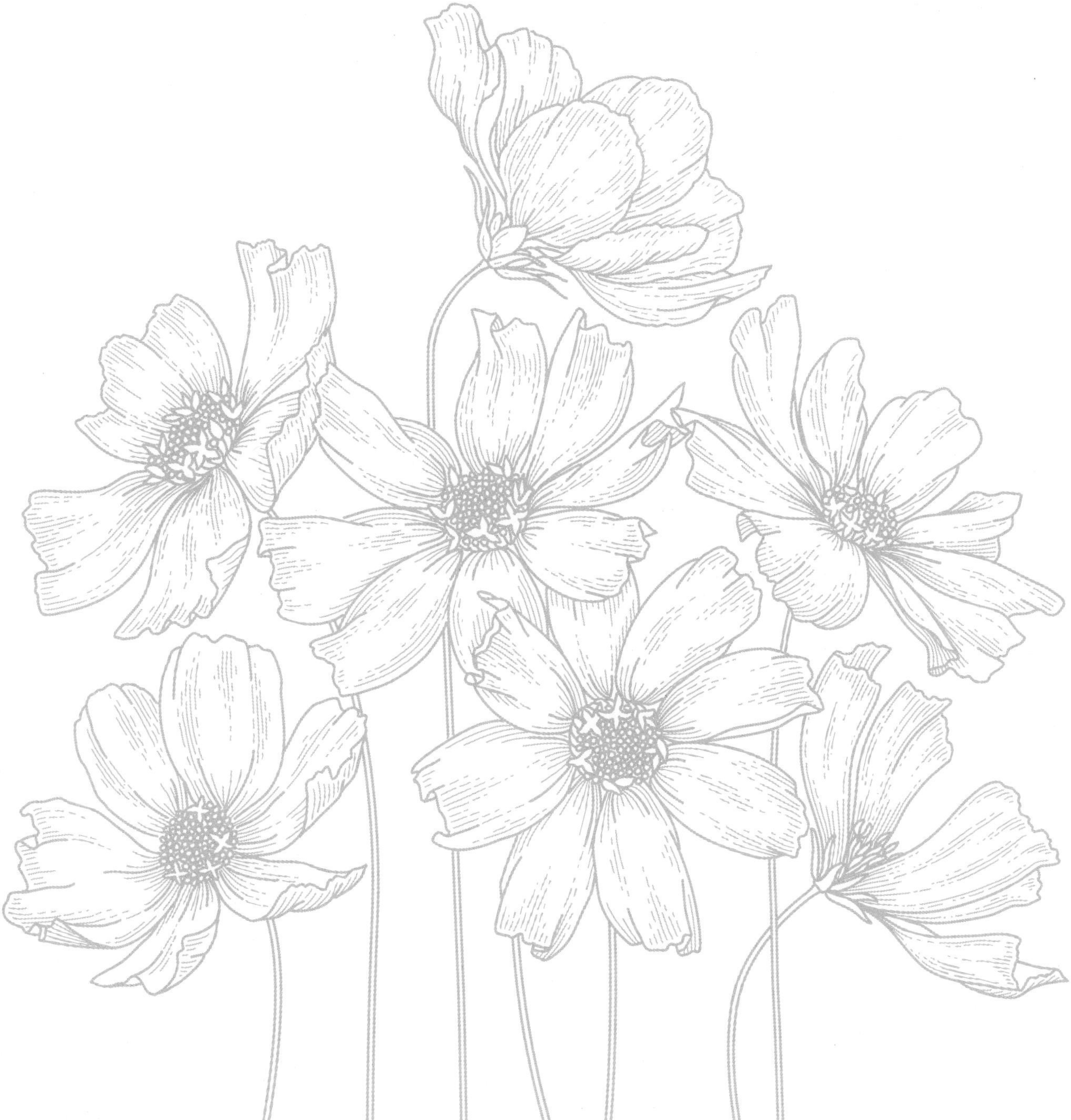

CONEFLOWER

My love for the coneflower is quite new. I started to adore them from the first moment I drew them. I enjoyed drawing the central structure so much that I wanted to draw one again and again. You will get addicted too. After the second illustration I still didn't have enough, but I couldn't find any good reference photos online. So I decided to grow them on my balcony, where they seem to live the happy life of A-list models.

1.

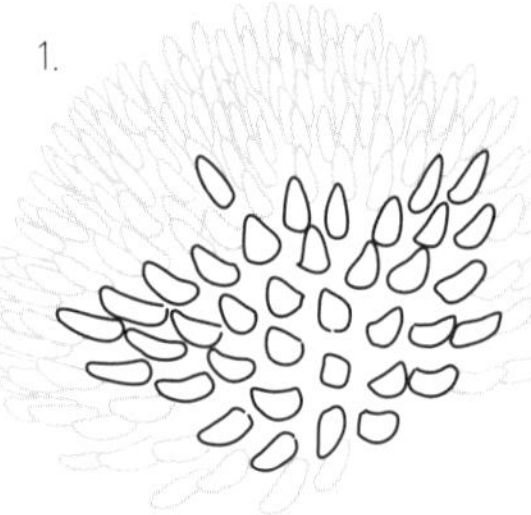

2.

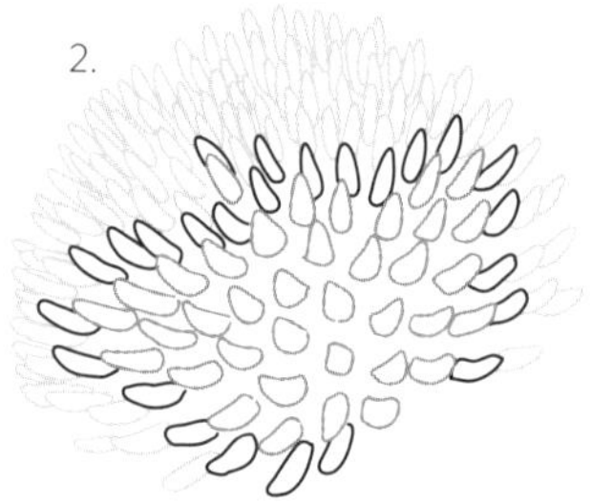

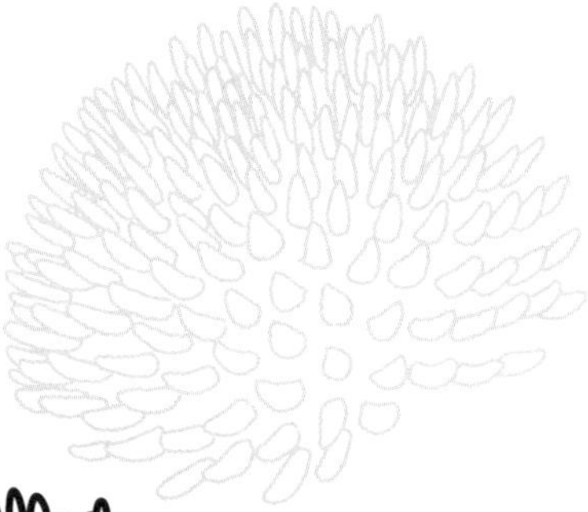

Start by drawing the outlines of the spikes in the middle (step 1), and move outward layer by layer (step 2). Once you've completed them all, fill in the areas between the spikes with black ink using a thicker pen.

Outline the petals with your thicker pen as well. Then switch to a thin pen and draw the first layer of shading lines within them. Keep your line widths uniform, applying even pressure on your pen tip throughout the whole stroke. Pay attention to the gaps between the lines. They will define the tone of the gradient.

There is a second layer of shading here to create extra depth in the darker areas, as shown in step 4. Keep these lines parallel, drawing at an acute angle to the first layer.

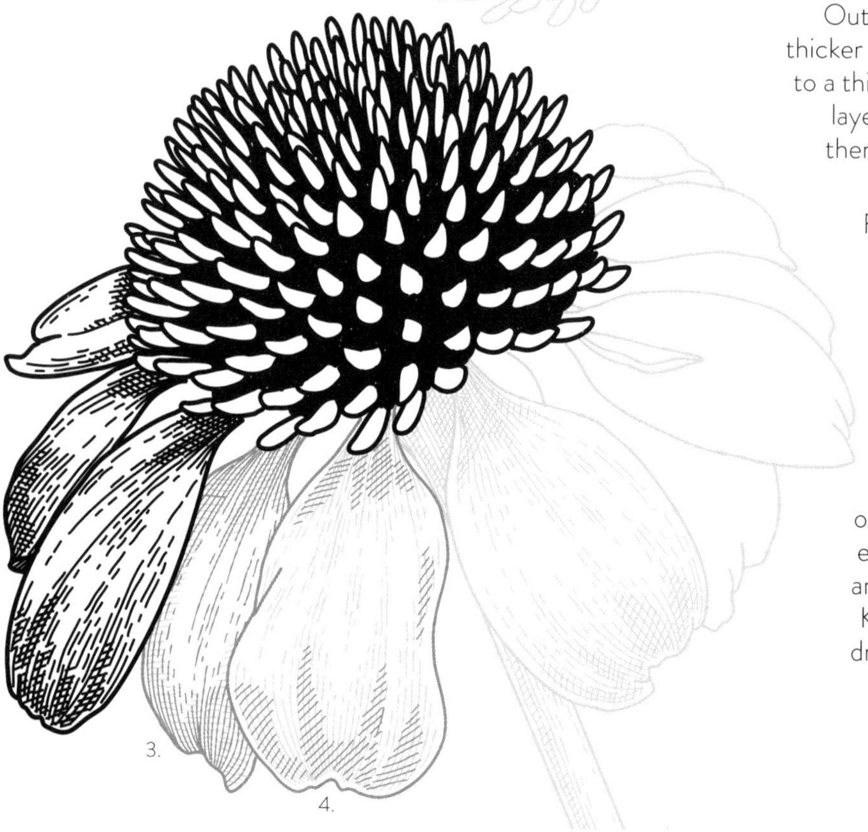

3.

4.

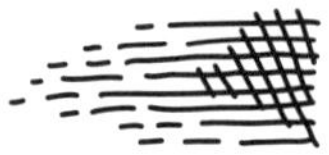

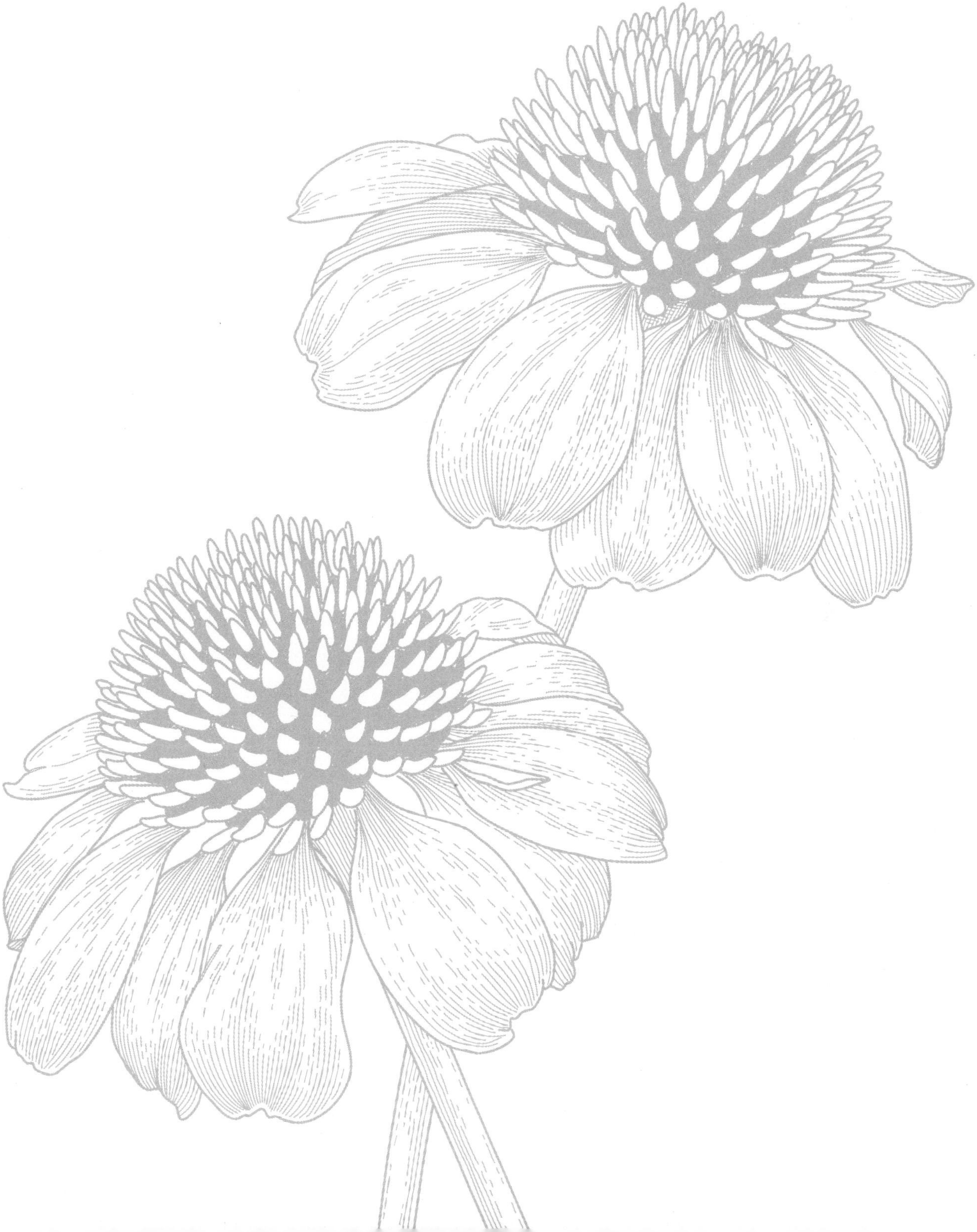

CHRYSANTHEMUM

I rarely buy chrysanthemums for my home. But to draw them, and especially to shade them, is a dream. The long narrow petals are perfect for shading with parallel lines, making it easy to create even gradients on them. The tons of layers on top of each other give you the opportunity to create stunning contrast with deep, dark shadow areas. You can see a hint in full black at the beginning of the chapter on page 19. Create your own shading on the empty petals, or practice adding it in to the full flower with the Shading Template on page 111.

I recommend building up the illustration starting with the outlines of the petals. To challenge yourself, draw one side of a petal with one smooth stroke, then draw the other. Meet at the tip of each petal where it has a little valley as a detail.

After outlining the illustration, grab a thinner pen and start working on the shading. Keep your lines evenly spaced and the gradients well designed, as described on page 16. Remember, keep the gaps of the dashed lines separate.

Shading the leaves requires an important trick. The lines should look like one stroke interrupted by a gap, like the ones I marked with dark gray. This makes the surface of the leaf beautifully coherent.

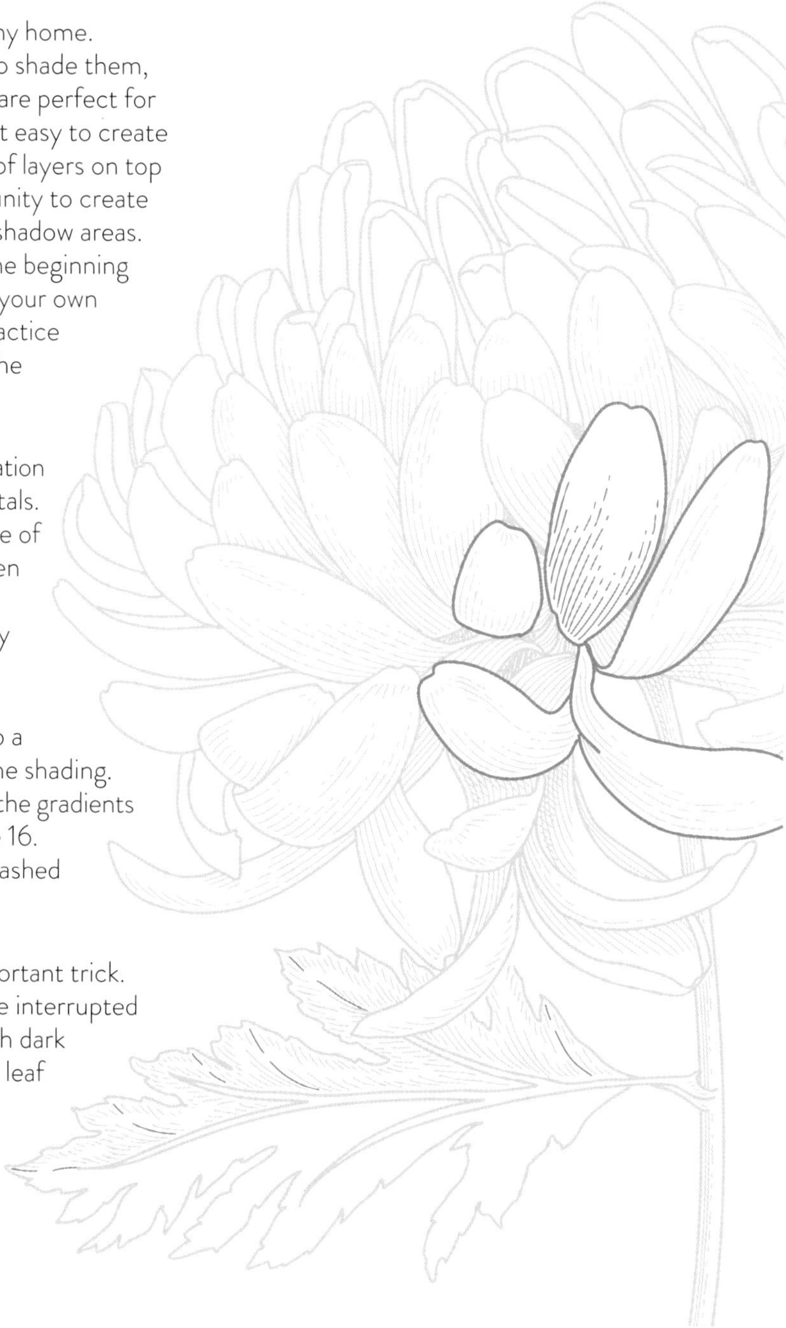

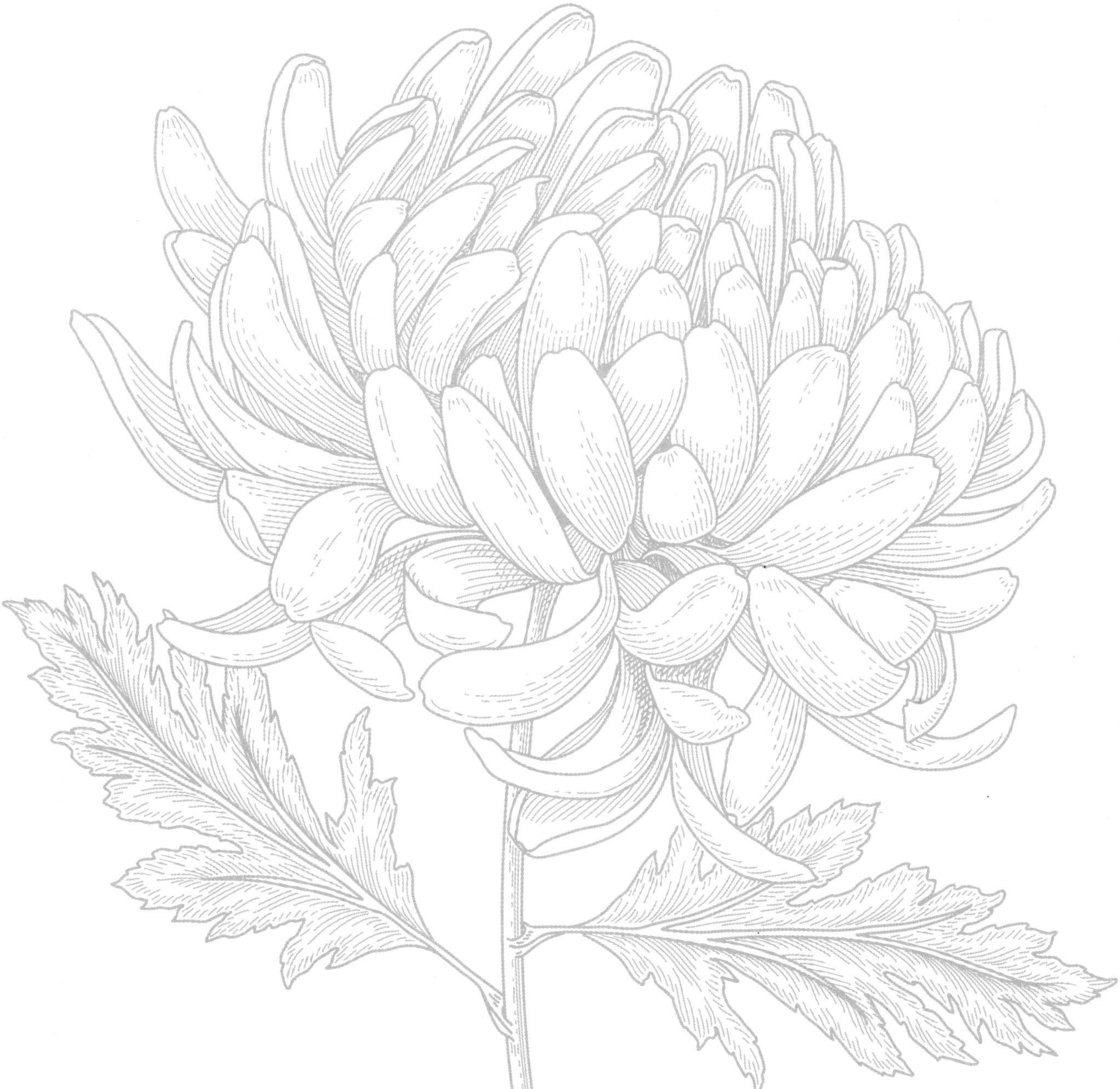

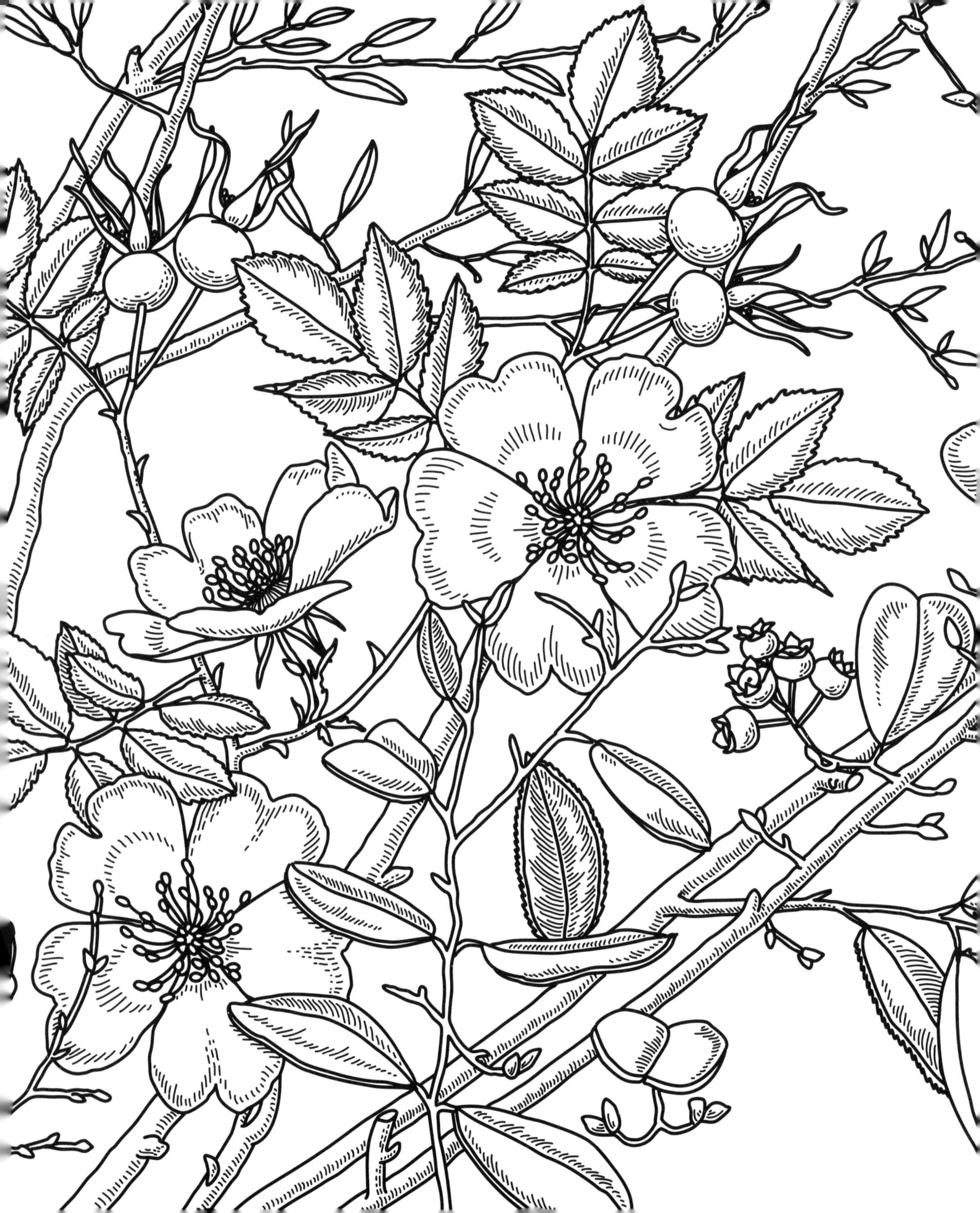

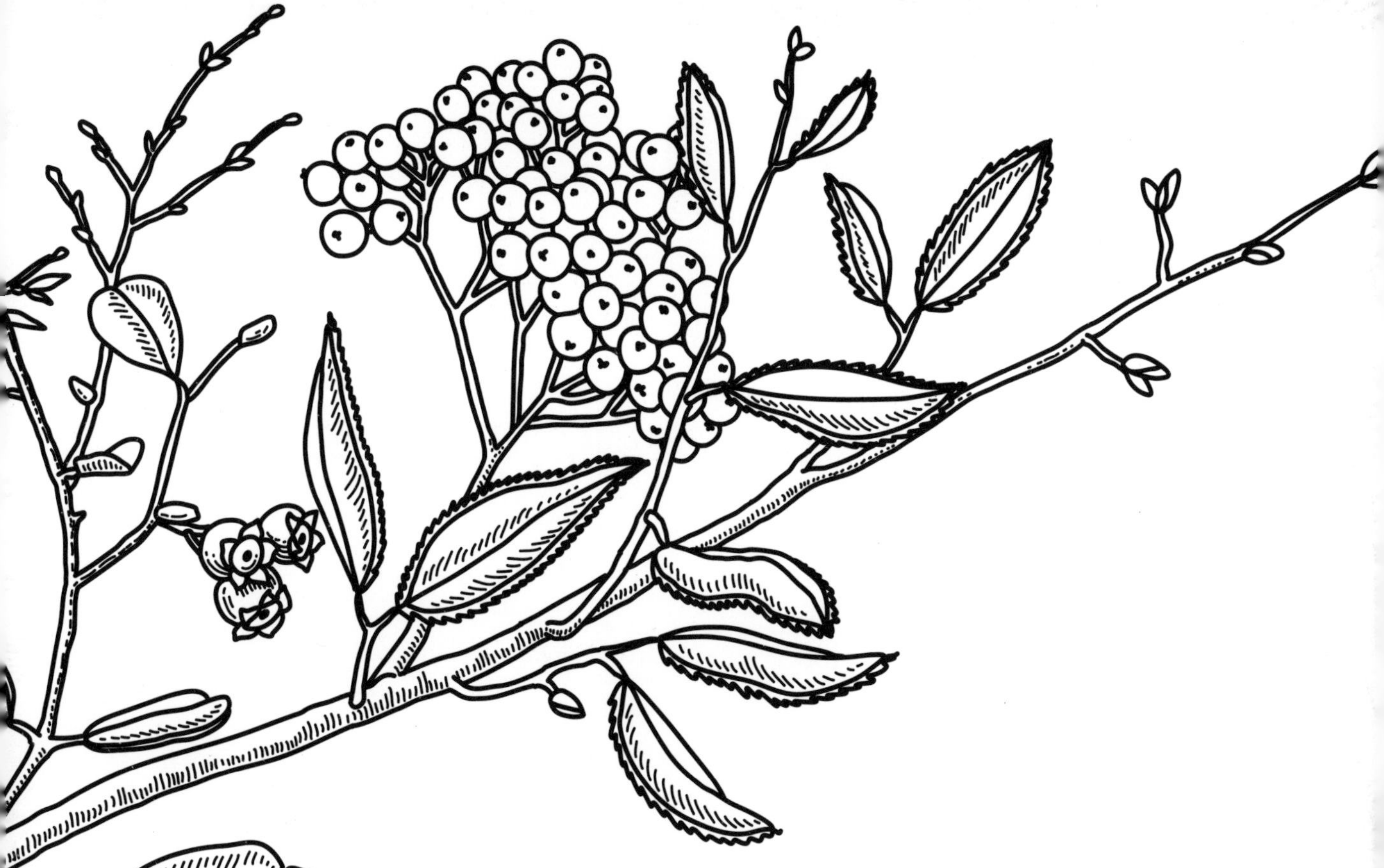

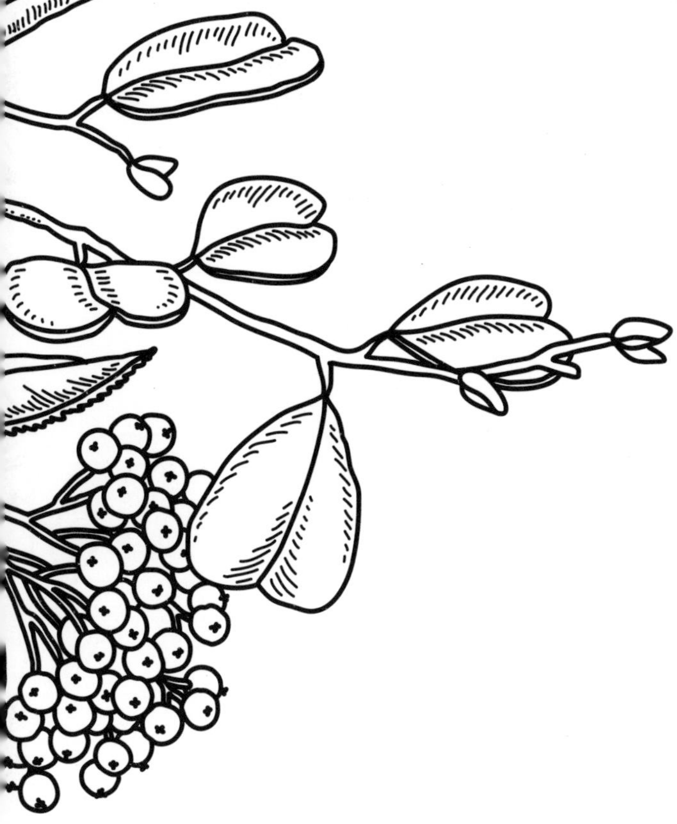

LEAVES AND BERRIES

Leaves and berries make such an impact in a floral arrangement. This chapter features some of my favorite greenery and some lovely berries, which will elevate the look of any floral artwork. They are great eye-catchers, and I love how they add different textures to a composition.

Are you ready for some fun embellishments?

BERRIES

I am the luckiest wife on earth because my husband is my biggest fan and critic at the same time. He immediately points out the strengths as well as the weaknesses of an illustration. My illustrations with berries are usually ranked very high. He sees something extra, and special, in the compositions with berries. And honestly, I love to incorporate them a lot because they add texture and interest to any floral arrangement. It is so satisfying to draw all the little elements of these complex structures—the perfect escape!

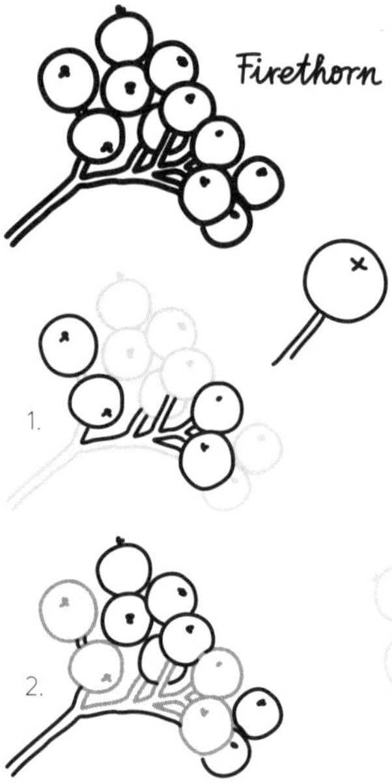

The key to drawing realistic berries is layering. For the firethorn, first find the berries that are on the top of the bunch and show up as full circles. The lower layers appear as semi- or incomplete circles, or even less. The little branches give meaning to the whole structure. Keep your lines parallel and as close together as possible.

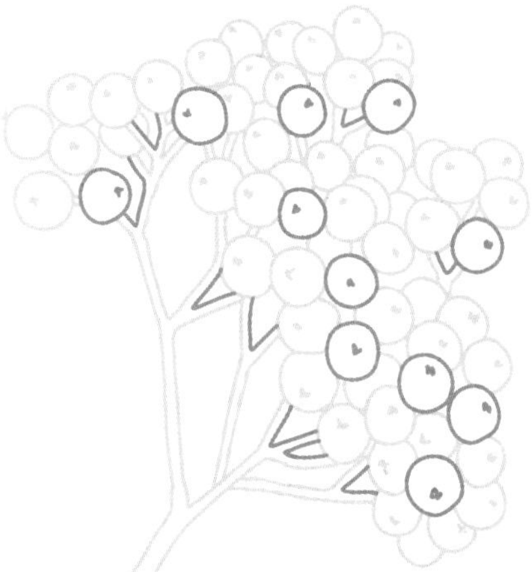

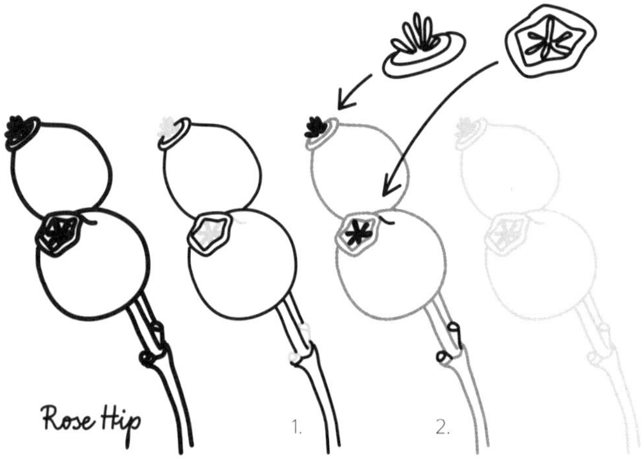

Blackcurrants are the shiny little stars of a composition, and they are so easy to draw. Outline the body of the currant and the small oval inside. Add three little spikes to the bottom, defining the direction of the currant. Finally, color it in but make sure to leave the inner oval white for the highlight.

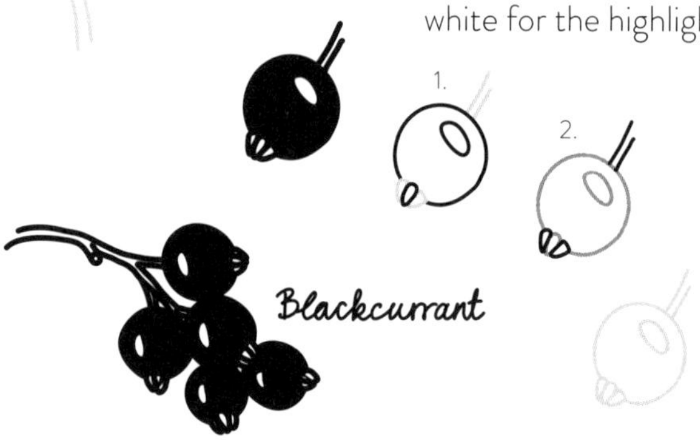

For the rose hip, start by drawing the central details with a ring, then fill it with a star-like shape. For the side view, the star appears as a tiny pom-pom. To build the branches, take note of how they are broken up into several segments. Start with the bottom one, then trace the one above it, highlighting any small details as you go.

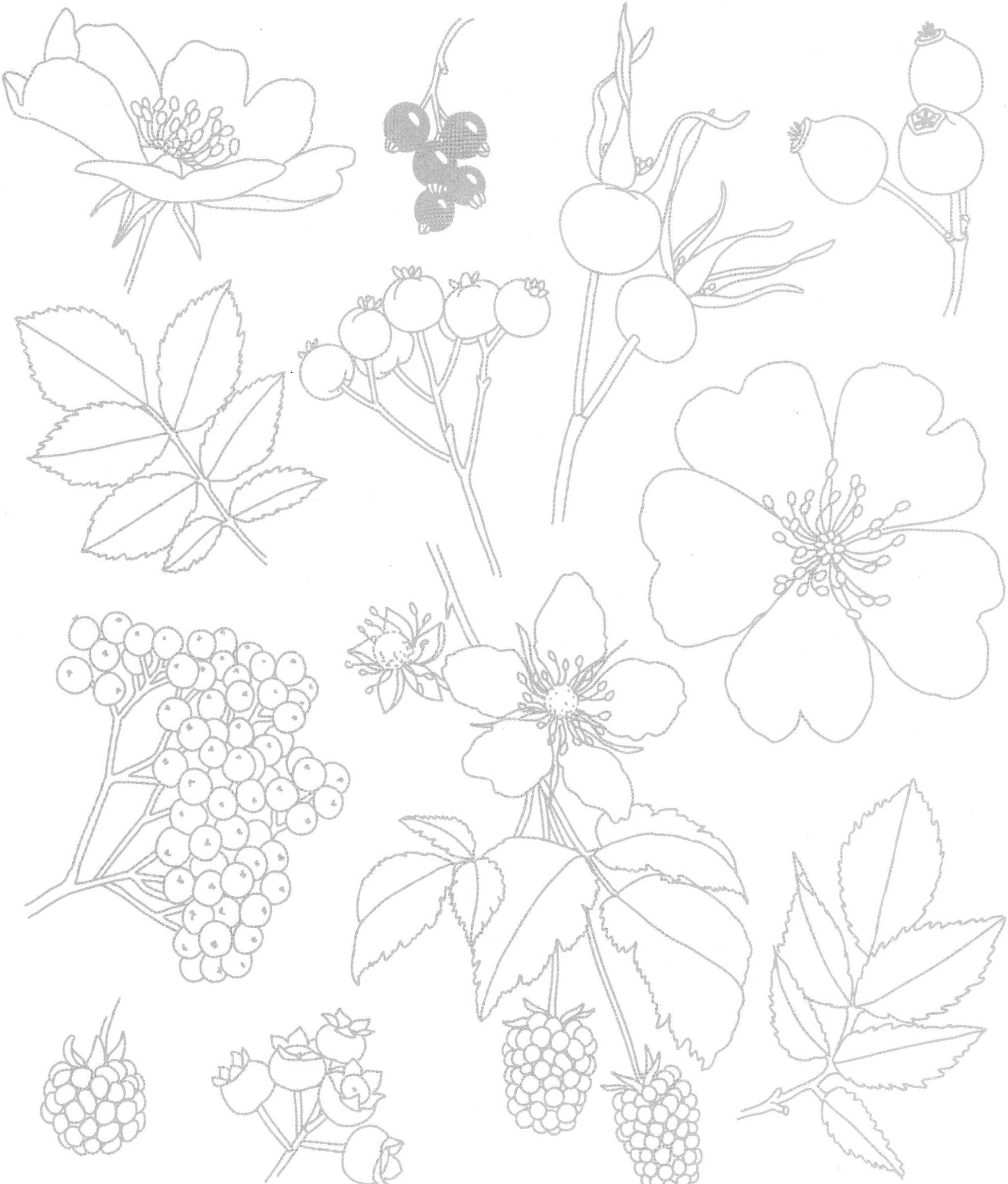

BRANCHES

My son asked me the other day which is my favorite flower. I stood there and thought about all the beautiful flowers I draw every day. And if I put my hands on my heart, I swear I love flowers, but I adore foliage too. The grayish green palette of eucalyptus or an olive branch are the most beautiful things on earth to me.

I present you with this wonderful wreath full of breathtakingly decorative and easy-to-draw leaves and branches to show you my favorites.

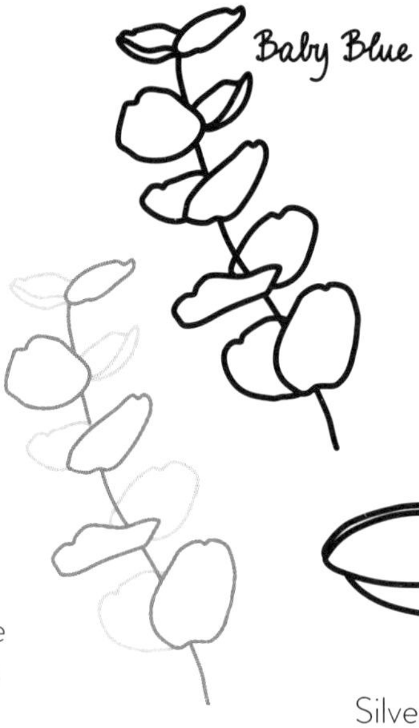

Baby blue eucalyptus's round, heart-shaped leaves sit on a thin branch. Draw the full leaves and the branch first. Then add in the background leaves.

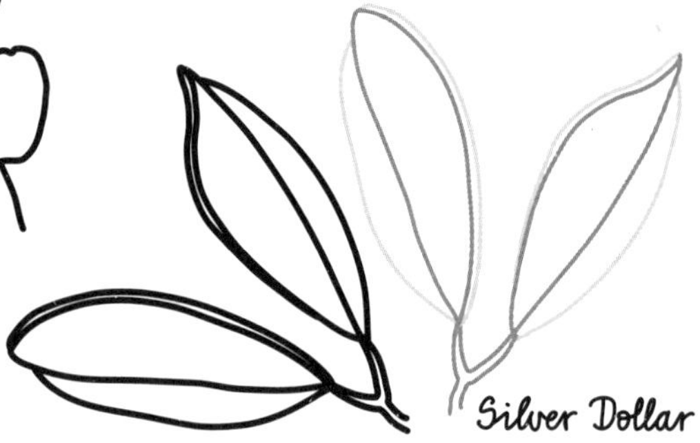

Silver dollar eucalyptus leaves have smooth edges, making them the easiest leaves to draw. The only thing that needs attention is the sides. I illustrate the edge in parallel lines, giving dimension to the leaf.

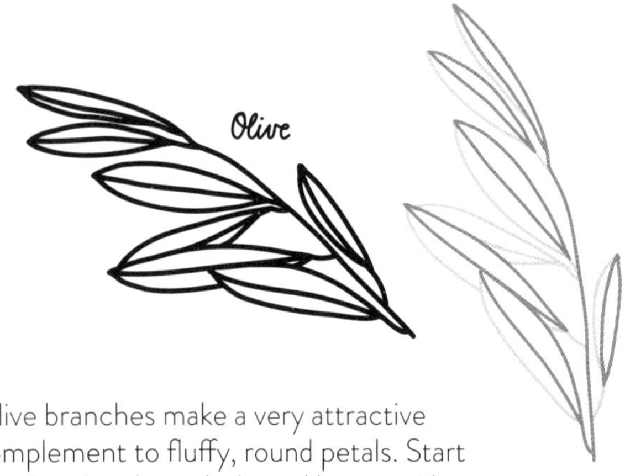

Olive branches make a very attractive complement to fluffy, round petals. Start drawing the almond-shaped leaves with their centerline and draw both sides with a slightly bent line.

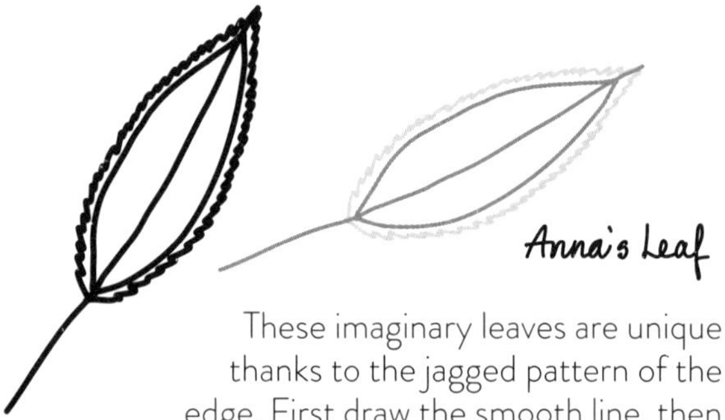

These imaginary leaves are unique thanks to the jagged pattern of the edge. First draw the smooth line, then go parallel with the zigzag. You will improve fine motor control with this challenge.

Build up the pine branch from a central branch, and add a row of slightly bent needles spaced out evenly. Then add some needles that are crossing over the others.

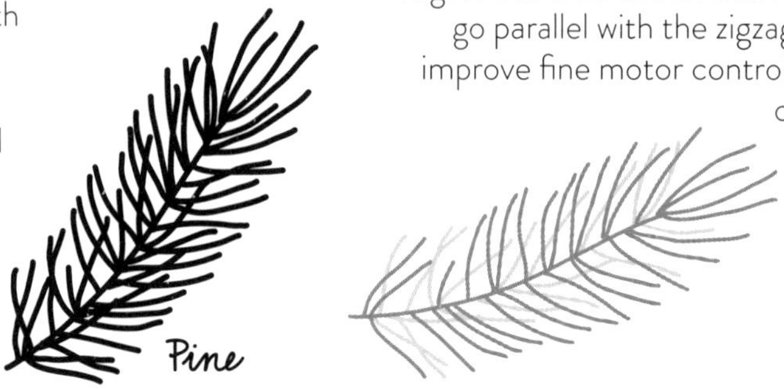

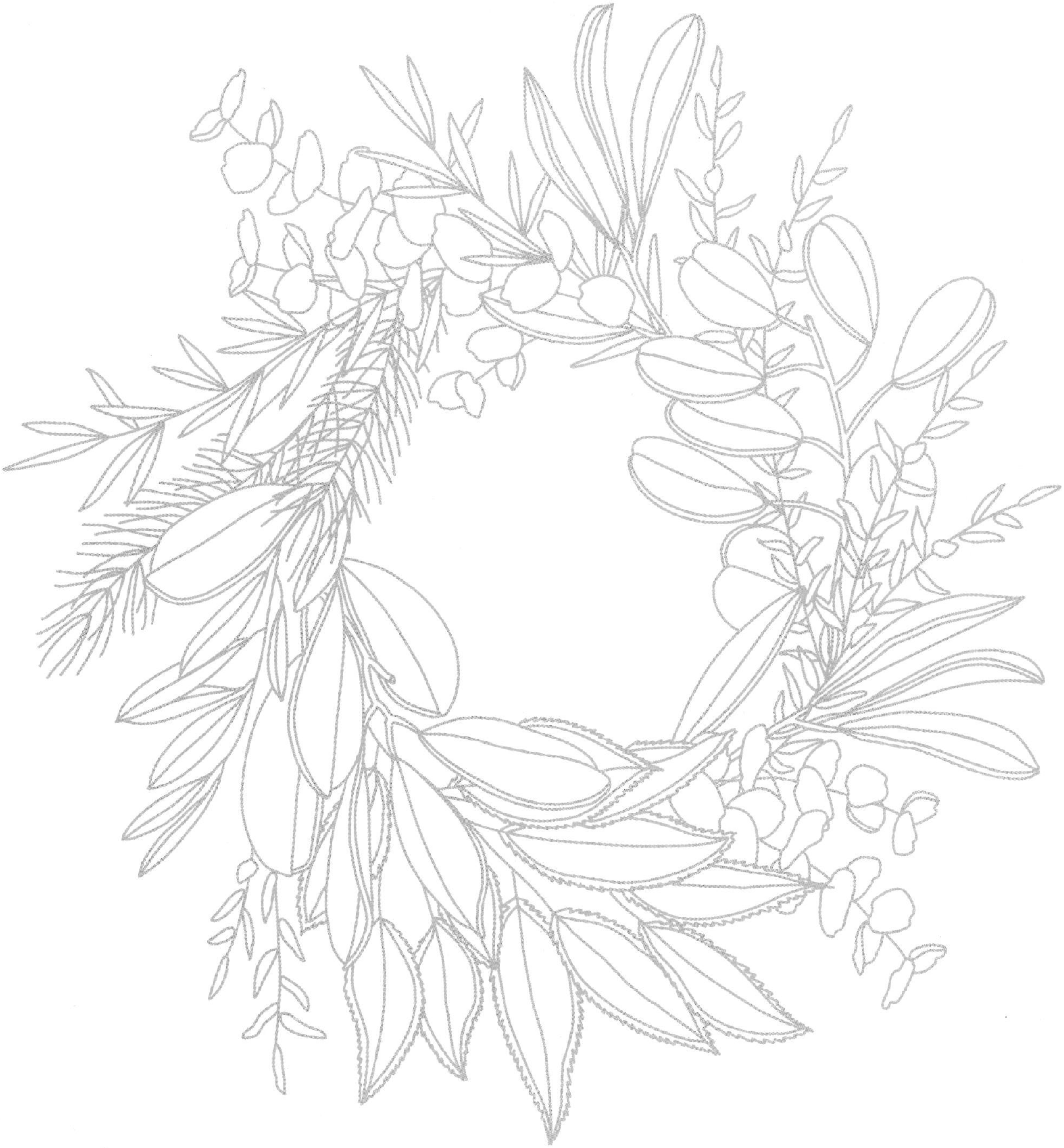

TREASURES OF THE MEDITERRANEAN

This collection of treasures reminds me of the summer holidays I spent in Mediterranean countries. Close your eyes and imagine the beautiful seacoasts and the scent of lemon, lavender and pine.

You can add an extra glow to the page with a deep terracotta or navy background.

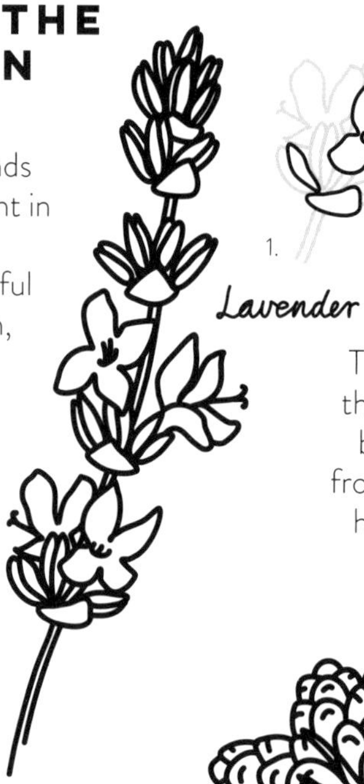

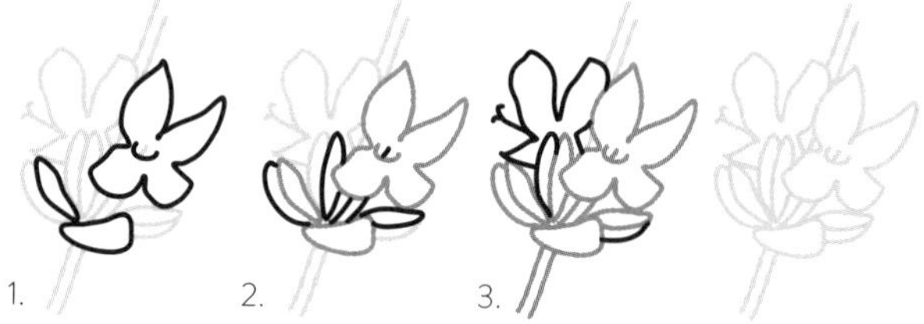

This lavender is so simple, but layering elevates the look. Draw the triangular leaf under the little bunches first. The rest of the buds are built up from an oval and a tucked half-oval. The flowers have a pretty simple shape, with a little central detail to create a more realistic look.

Drawing a star anise is a very good way to practice controlling your lines. Try to complete the round center without rotating the paper. Start with the first banana shape and complete the circle. As a finishing touch, add the seeds by drawing in the crescent moon shapes.

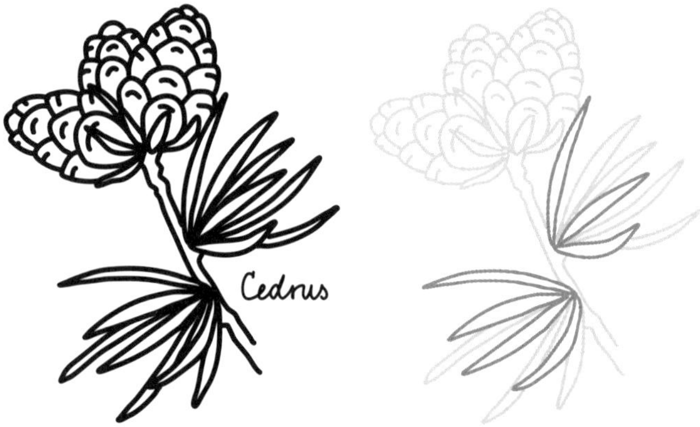

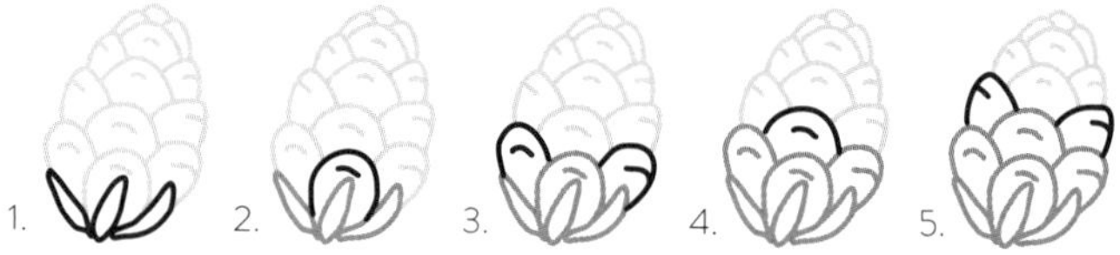

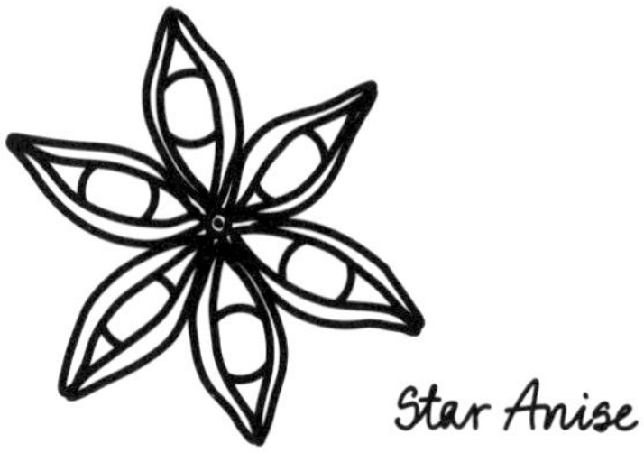

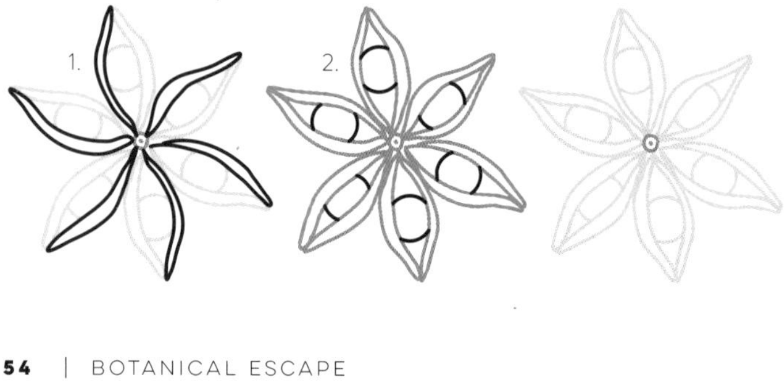

Cedrus has groups of needles on its branch. Find the needles that are closest to you, and draw them first. Then outline the ones further away. Drawing the pine cones is like climbing on a ladder. Move from the bottom to the top.

EUCALYPTUS

I showed you some different types of eucalyptus leaves already, but now for the flowers. They don't need to be part of a bouquet; they shine brightest if we can take a closer look. This fuzzy little thing is a real challenge to draw at first sight, but hopefully after tracing it, guided by my lines, it will feel joyful and exciting. The outline of the leaves is really simple. They don't have a particularly conspicuous texture, so simple parallel lines for shading fits. They are the background to let the flowers be the queen of the illustration.

Remember, draw the outlines with a thick pen and the shading lines with a thinner pen.

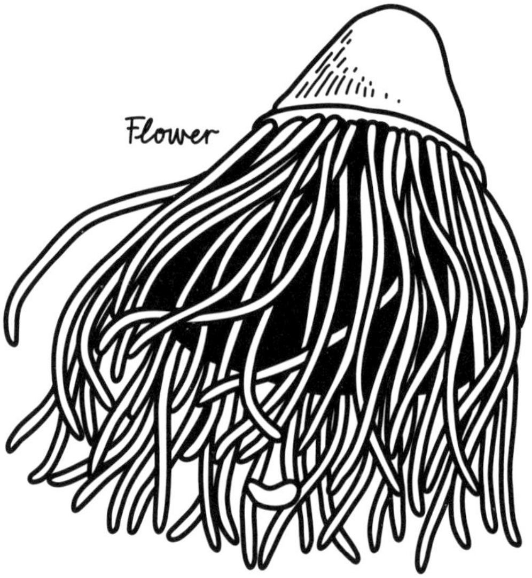

Draw the outlines of the filaments first, paying attention to the layers. They cross each other so playfully. Some parts are hidden by others. Then fill in the areas between the filaments with black to illustrate the depth of the center.

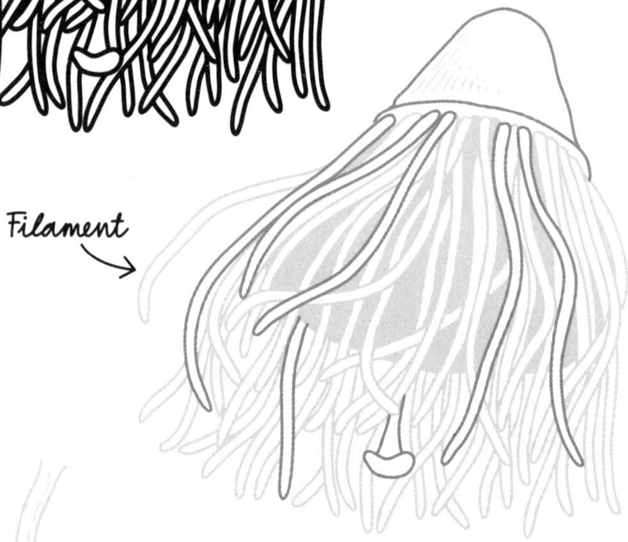

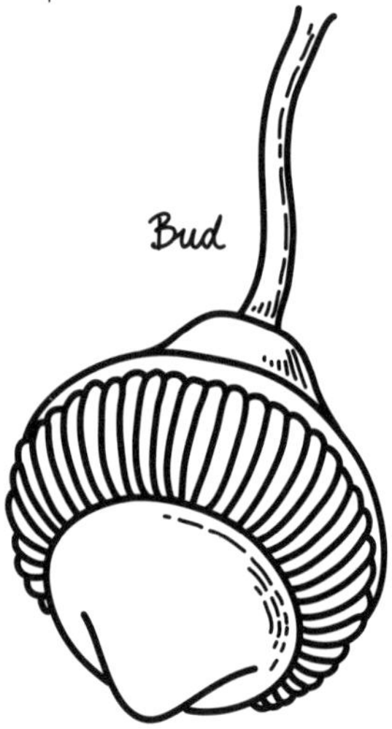

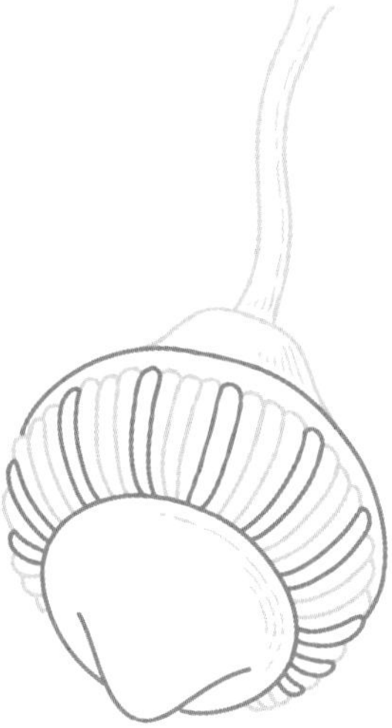

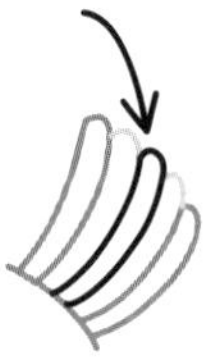

The buds are also full of filaments, but they are still beautifully organized by the little cap on the top. Draw the cap first, then add the filaments spaced evenly around. These filaments are tubular, and to illustrate that, end them in a semicircle at the top.

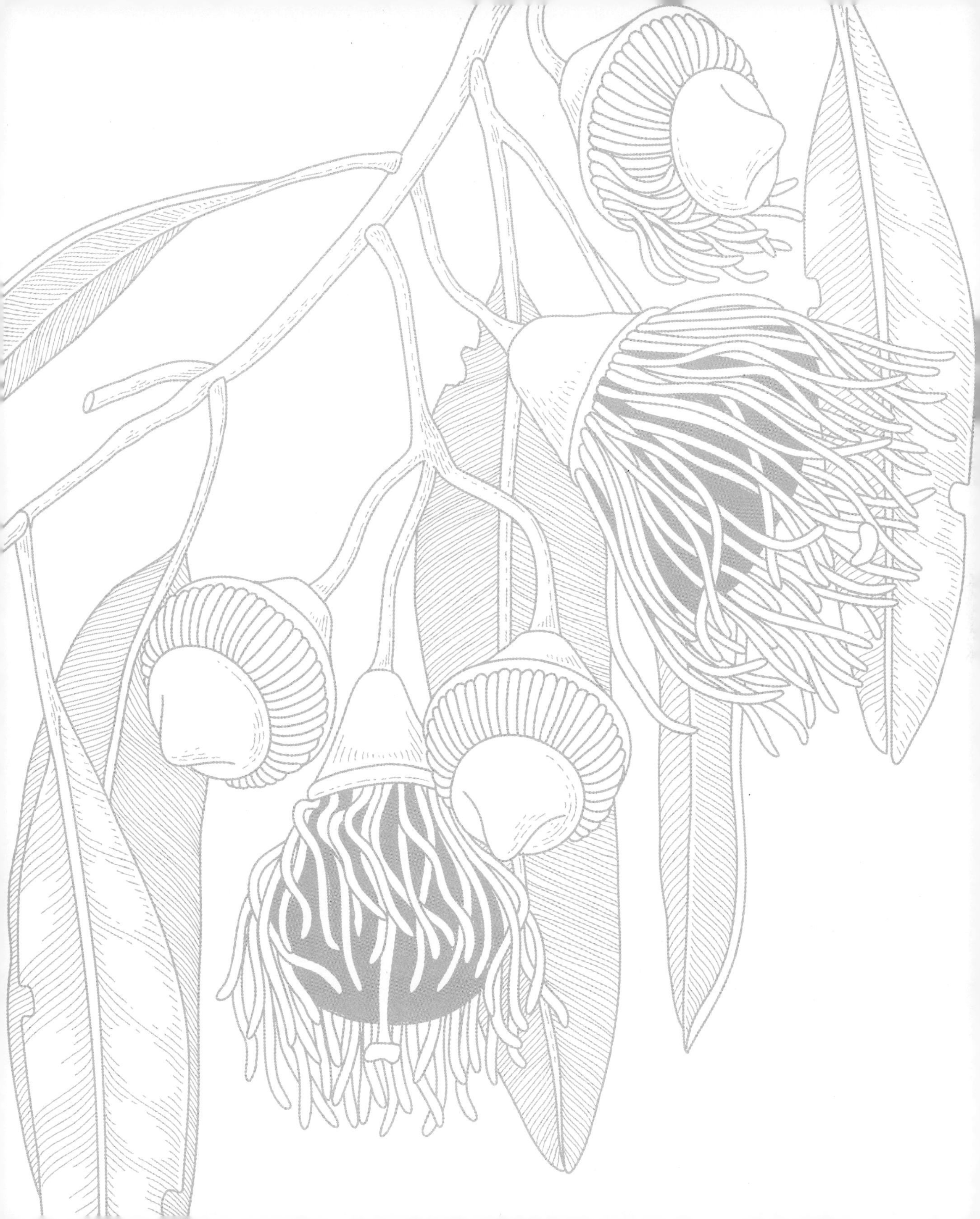

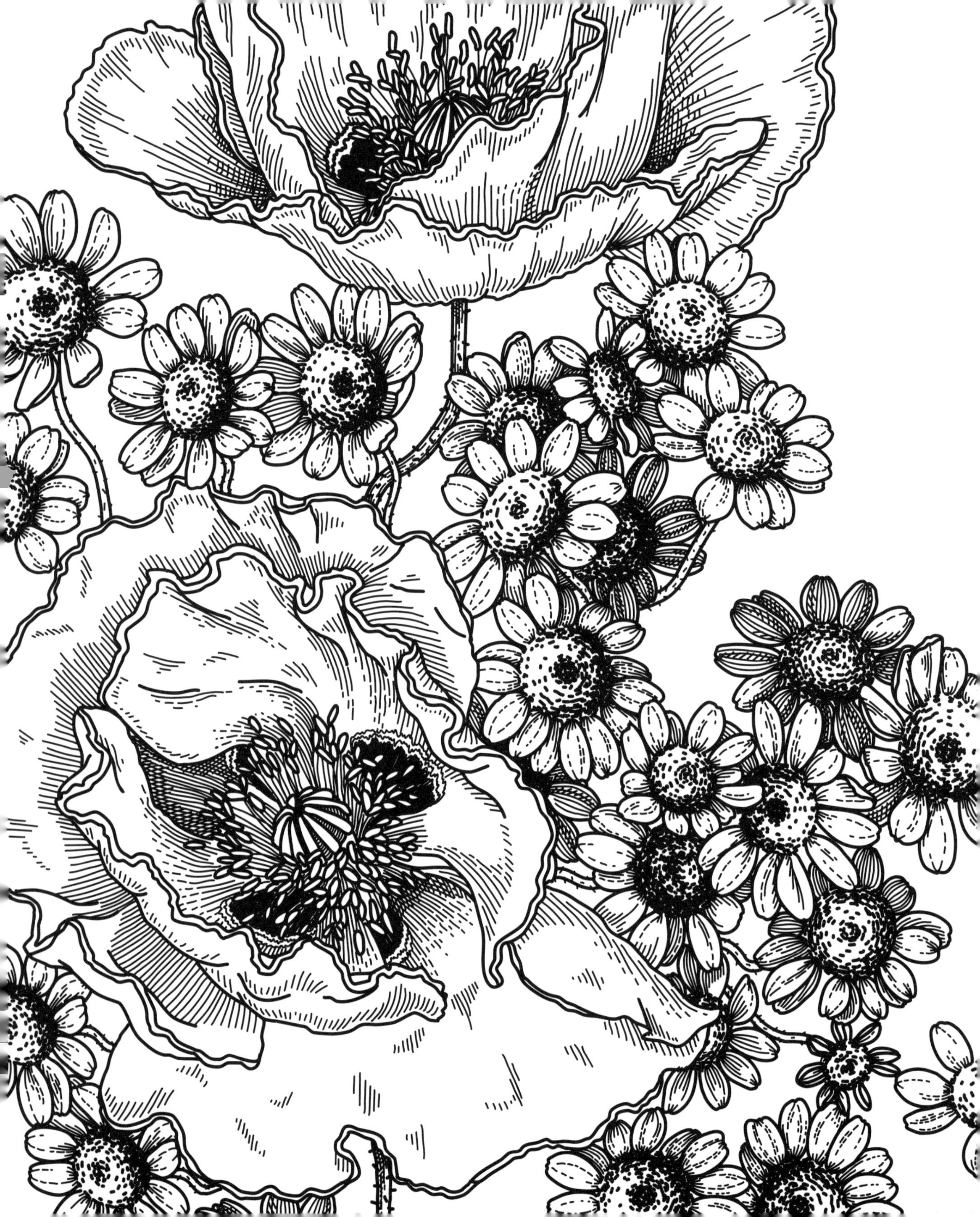

STUNNING ARRANGEMENTS

The key to these illustrations is contrast. I love to match round, fluffy petals with edgy leaves and dark berries. And luckily, thanks to the amazing diversity of nature, the possibilities are endless. I enjoyed creating this chapter so much! Picking the best matching flowers for a composition is like the icing on a cake.

You will find hints for drawing some elements in these arrangements in the Flowers chapter (page 19); see the reference at the bottom of the tutorial pages.

I hope you enjoy tracing these projects just as much as I enjoyed designing them!

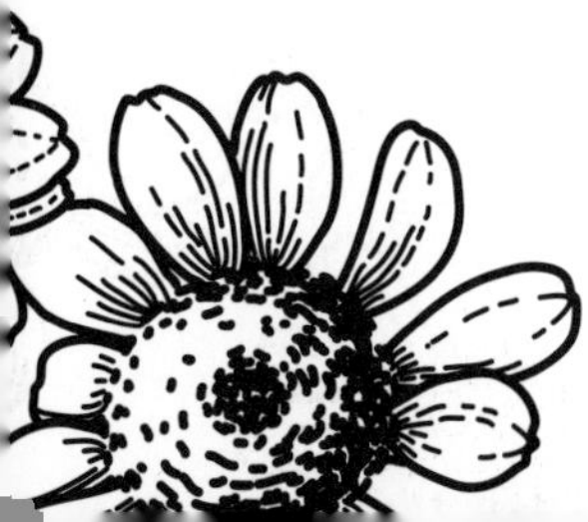

BOHO BOUQUET

Grasses are wonderful filler, and they add a unique boho vibe to almost any bouquet. They look beautiful in a bunch, but also look gorgeous on their own in a vase. I love to pick them during a walk. They last so long, and are so easy to find—they grow literally everywhere.

Grasses are easier to draw than you might think. Here, less detail is more. Leaving gaps creates the illusion of a lightweight, airy feel.

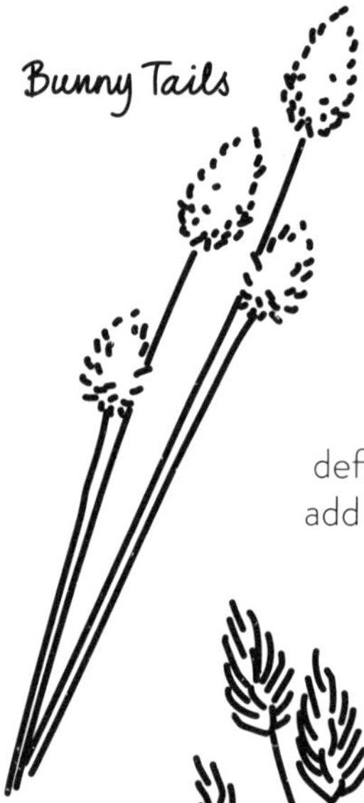

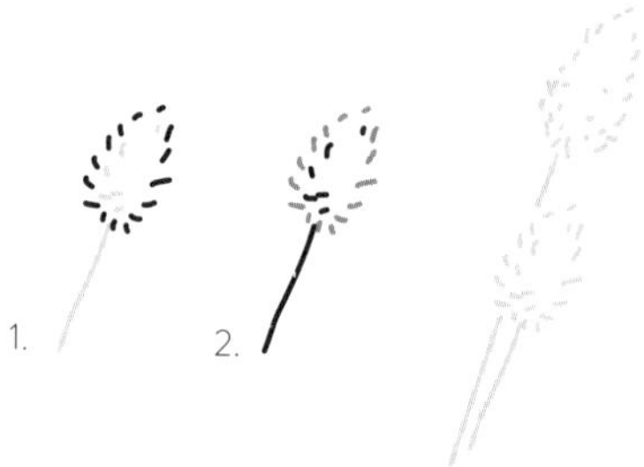

First draw the outer strokes, which define the shape of the flowerhead. Then add the few inner strokes. Keep your lines a bit random for a more organic look.

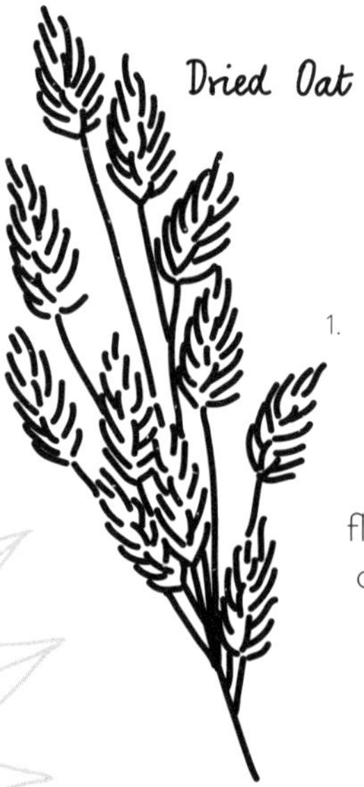

For the dried oat, draw one edge of the flowerhead closed and the other more open. Leave a gap in the center for the final random strokes.

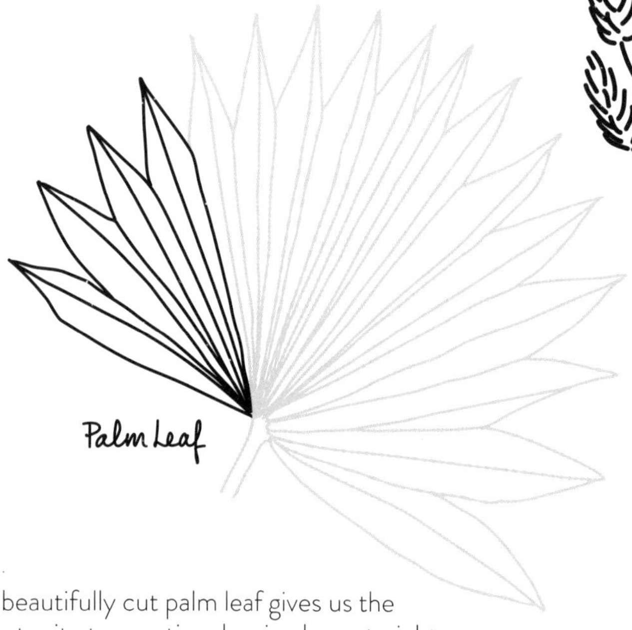

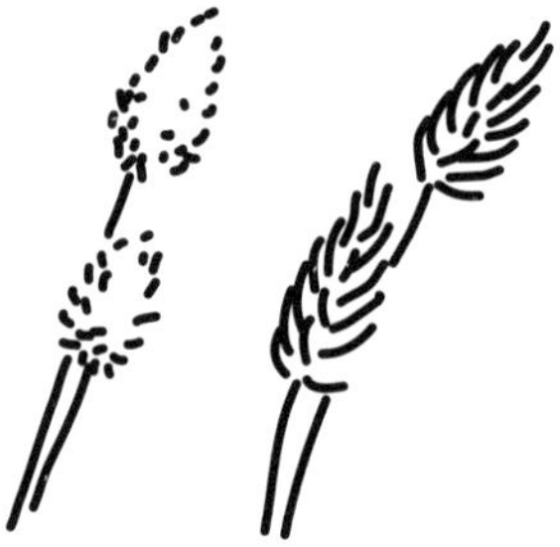

This beautifully cut palm leaf gives us the opportunity to practice drawing long straight lines. Take a deep breath before every line and clear your mind for a few seconds.

For the bunny tails and dried oat, layering the grasses by tucking one behind the other creates negative space around the flowerhead. This creates the illusion that the flowerheads are white.

HOW TO DRAW: Ranunculus (page 40; Ranunculus), Orchid (page 80; Anna's Bouquet), Leaves (page 52; Branches)

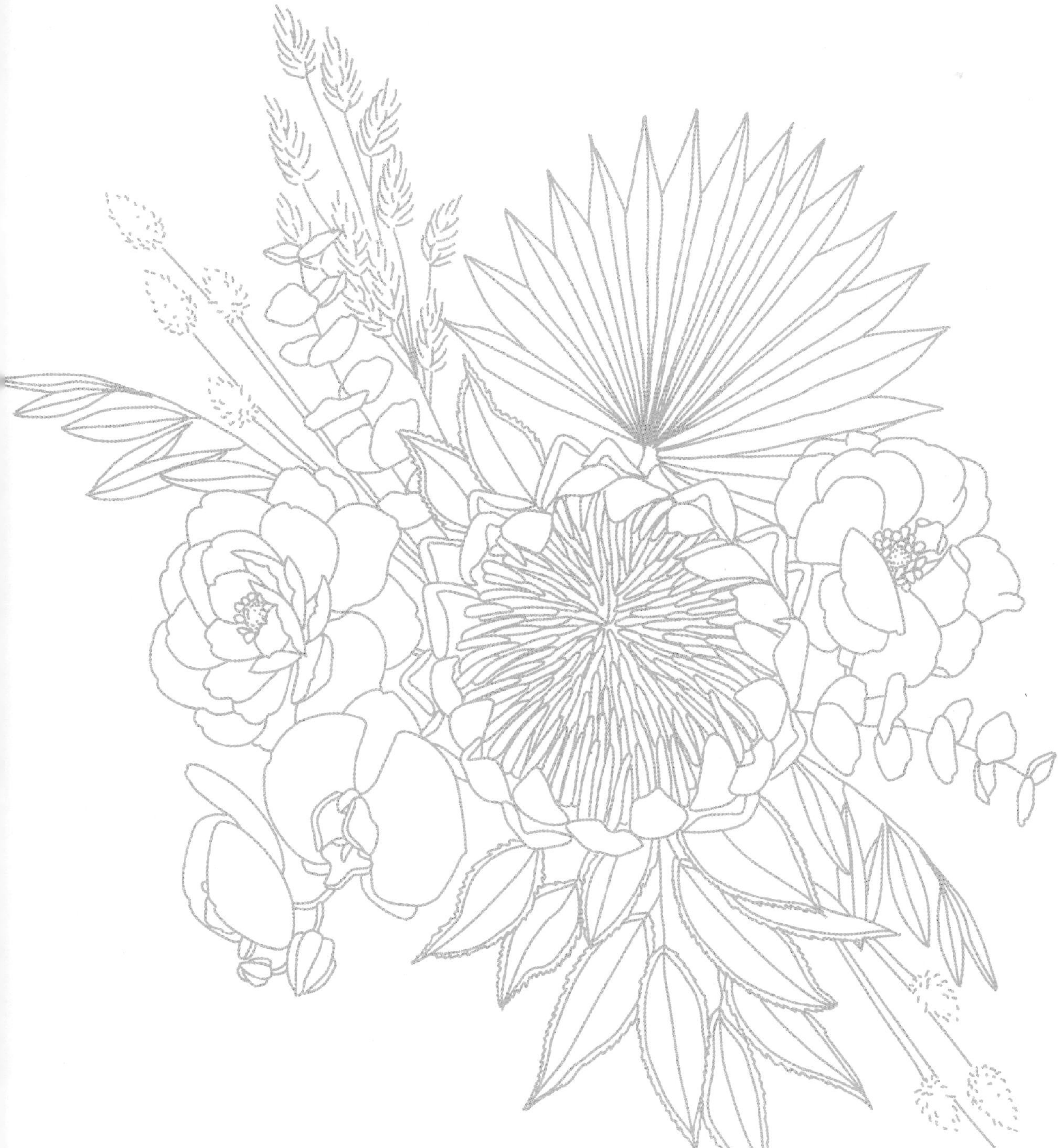

FOR HIM

What a dull stereotype that only women can love flowers. I am so happy to see more florists making bouquets especially for men too. I picked some of my favorite flowers, berries and foliage that I would choose for a masculine arrangement, either for a boutonnière or a loose bouquet as a gift for a friend. Would you also gift flowers to men?

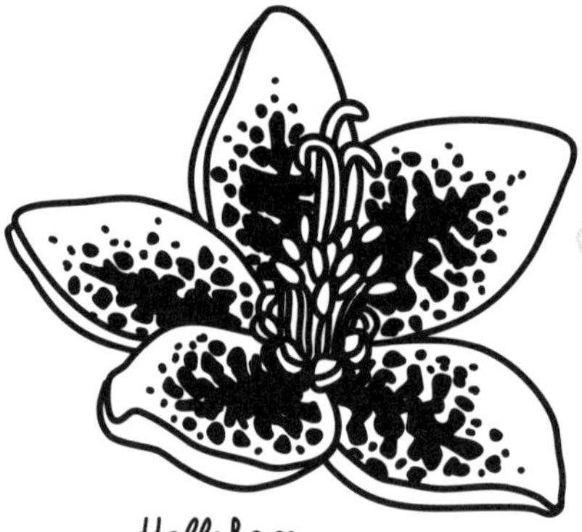

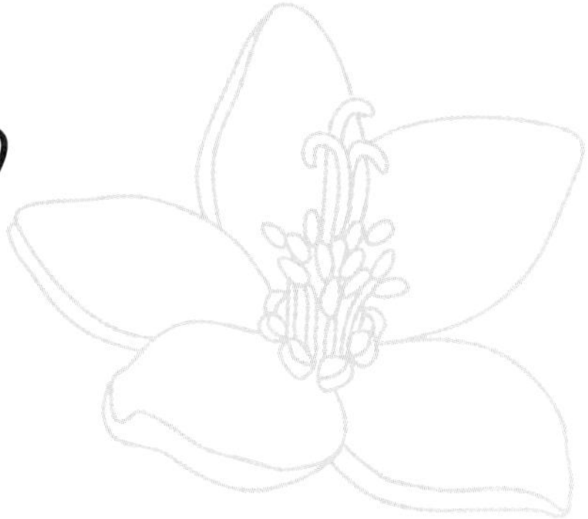

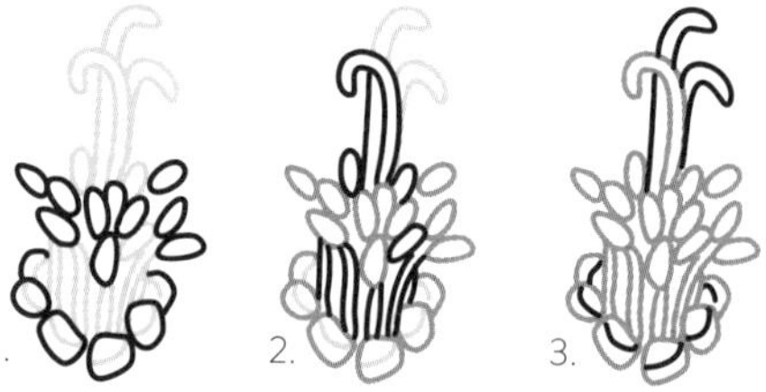

This hellebore has moody dark freckles, which makes it fit in the masculine group. Start with the center; add in the anthers and the little cups at the base. Not all anthers have a stamen here, so draw a few, making sure to leave some white area between them. After drawing all the outlines for the petals, add the freckles.

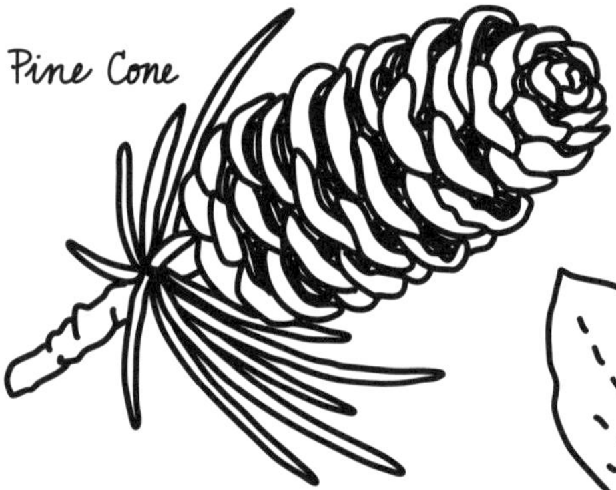

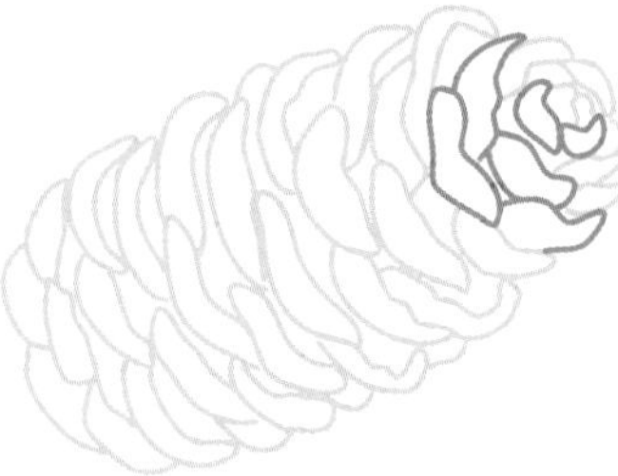

This pine cone looks almost like a flower. Start to draw its "petals" at the top and move toward the bottom layer by layer. Fill in the gaps between the "petals" with black. This will add the wow factor to the illustration.

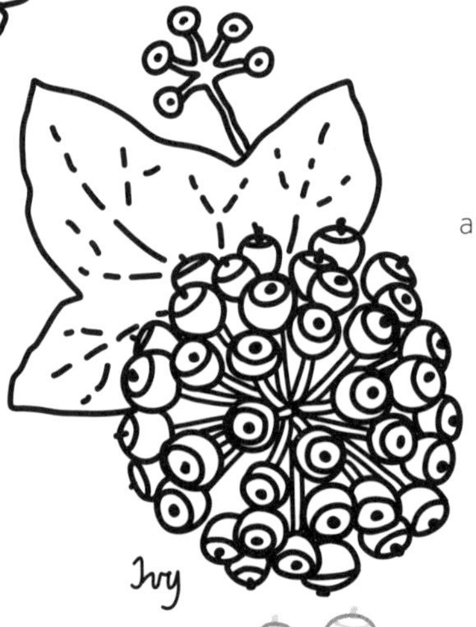

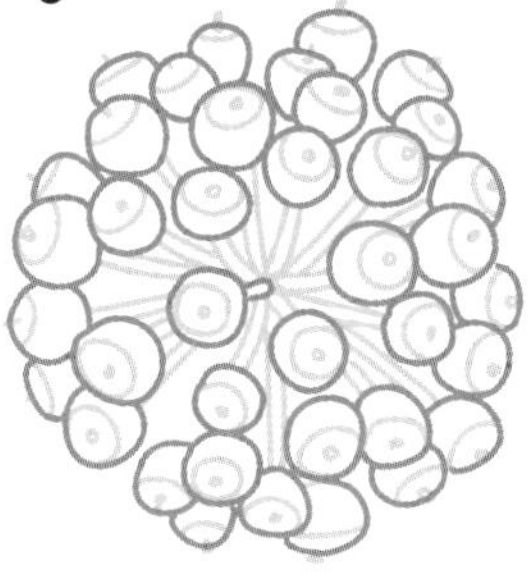

This is the fruit of common ivy, which I also think is on the moody side. Draw the outline of the berries first. Start at the center of the bunch and move outward. When working on the stems, start with the highlighted one in the center then draw the rest sprawling outward from that point. Finally, add the details on each berry.

HOW TO DRAW: Leaves (page 52; Branches), Waxflower (page 92; Greetings from Australia), Fritillaria (page 100; Showered in Purple)

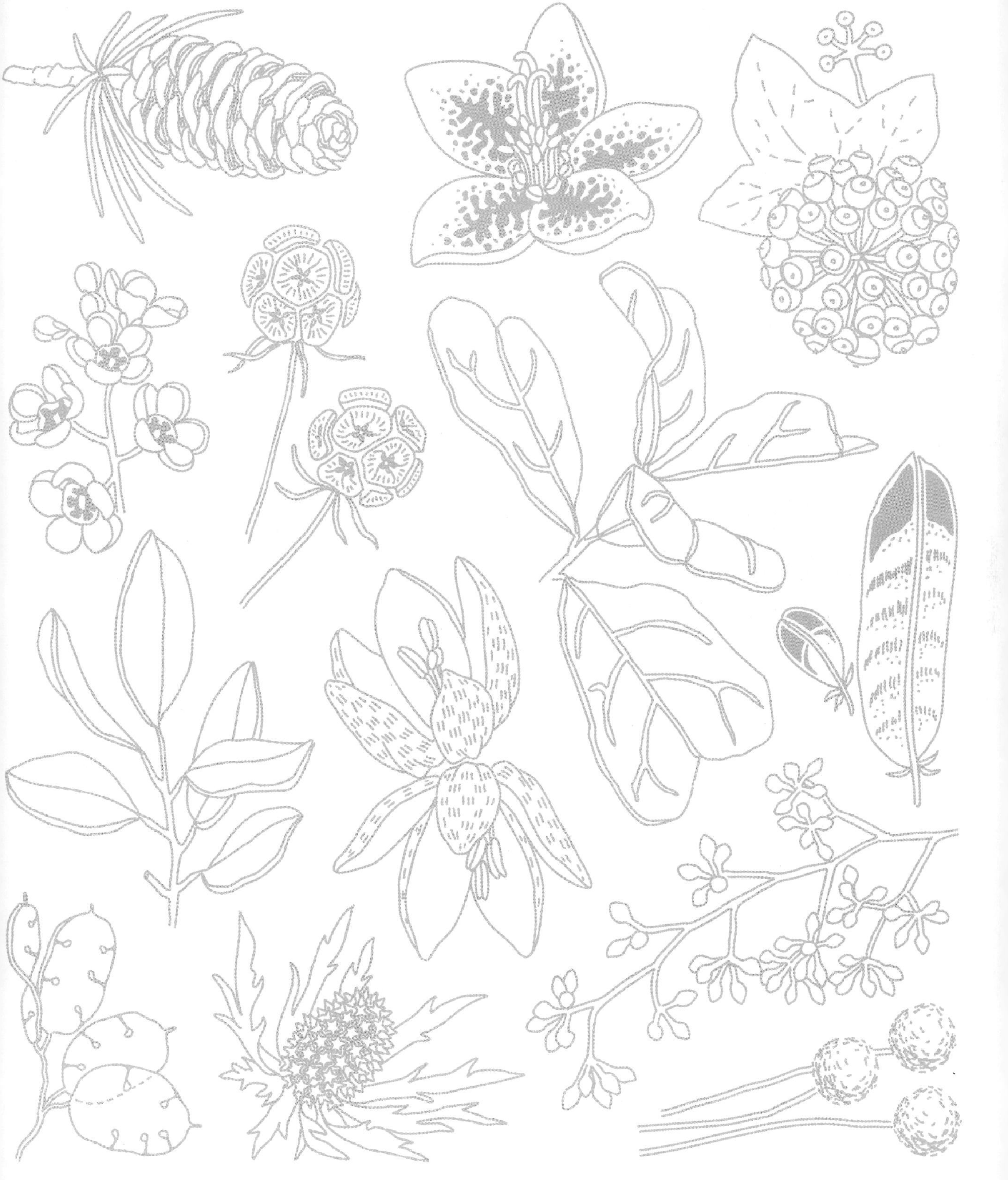

LUSH WEEDS

This illustration is inspired by an abandoned village garden, where nature takes back the space. Some species are left from the previous owner, but they assimilated already to the new wild family. This bouquet is more like an imaginary garden, with slight similarities to nature. Sometimes it is good to step out of the constraints of reality and play around with new creations.

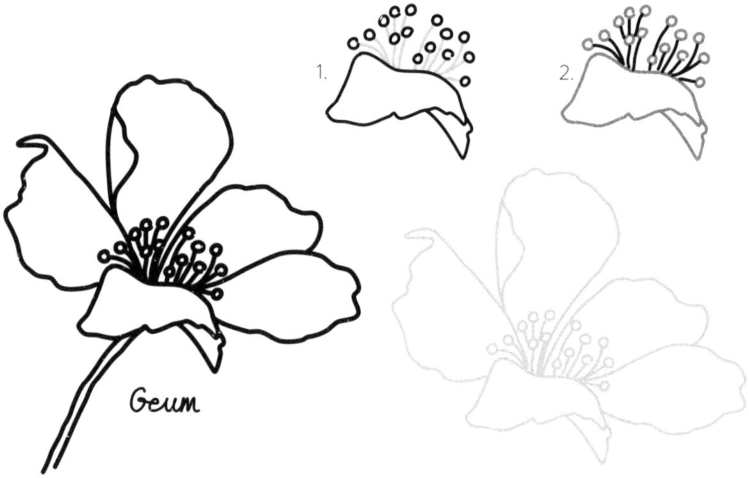

Geum has beautiful, ultralight petals, looking almost like it would be able to fly. Draw the tiny circles in the center first, but make sure they are big enough to have a small white space left inside. Try to draw each petal with one stroke to practice drawing smooth curves.

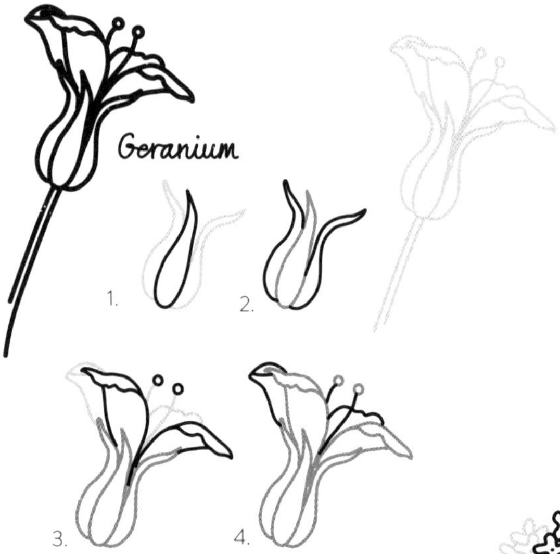

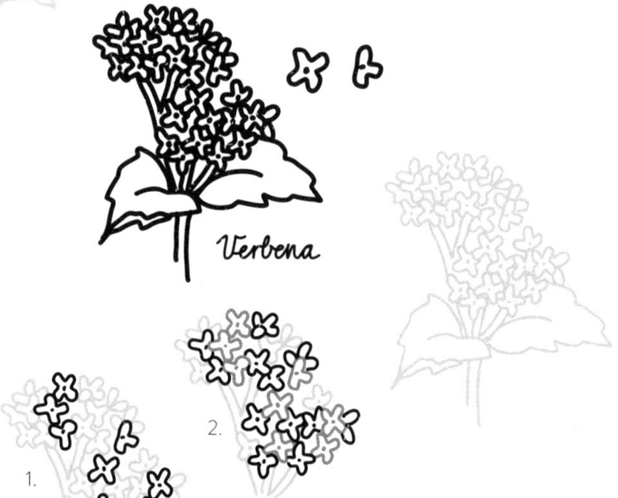

For the geranium, start with the sepals and add the petals afterward. The tiny anthers are circles, which I love to make big enough to leave a little white in the middle, similar to a bead.

This verbena-inspired flower has several layers of mini flowers. They're made of a simple dot and three or four childish petal shapes. The key to an advanced look is layering. Start with the fully visible flowers and work backward from there.

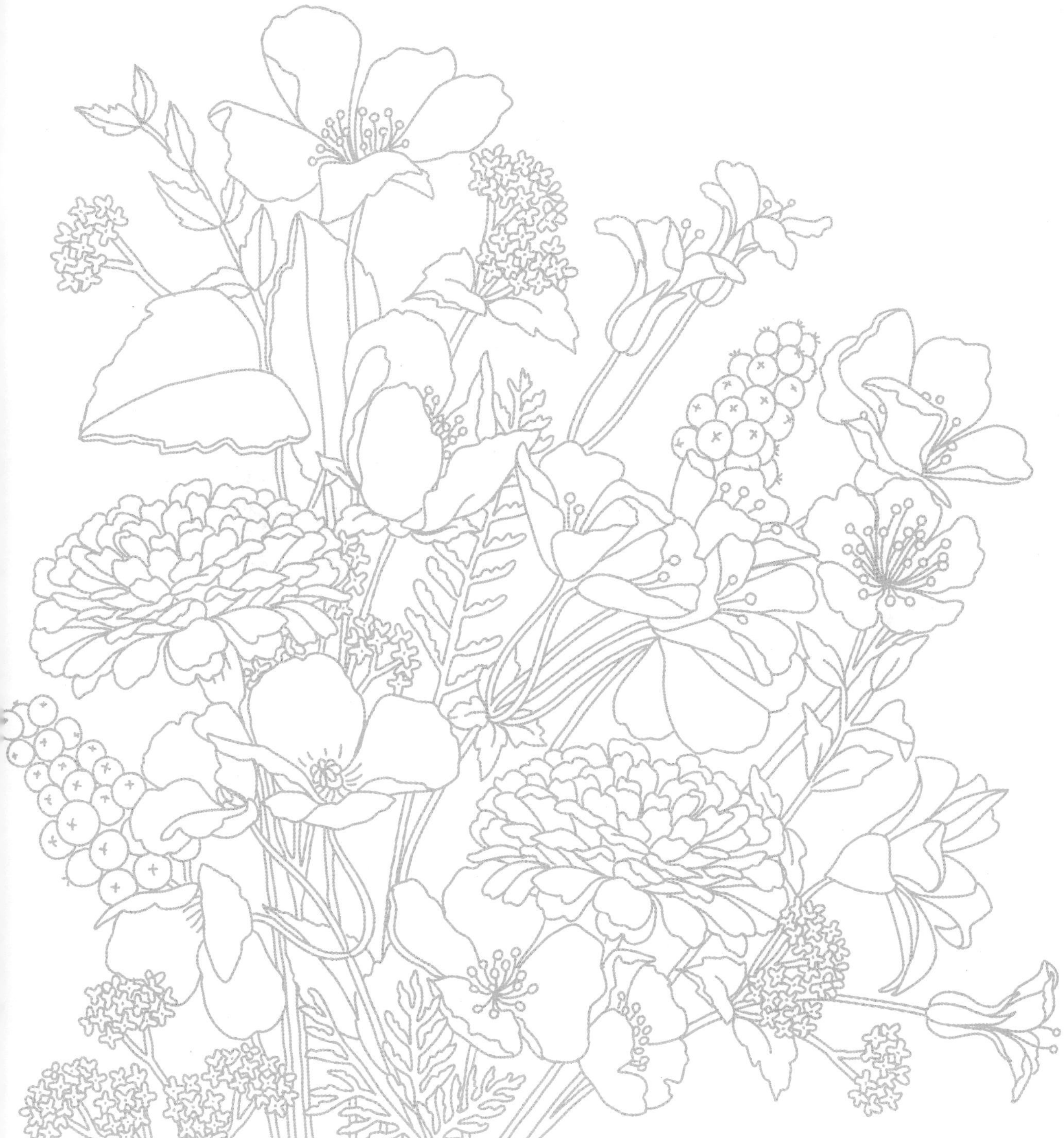

ROMANTIC WREATH

When I hear the word *romantic*, garden roses and hydrangea immediately come to mind. However, to be honest, I am not that romantic. Astrantia flowers tilt back the balance with their spiky petals and that beautiful central universe. Open garden roses have a beautiful center as well, and drawing all the anthers and stamens requires attention. So does the astrantia's center. Let your mind shut out the world and get into a relaxed, focused state.

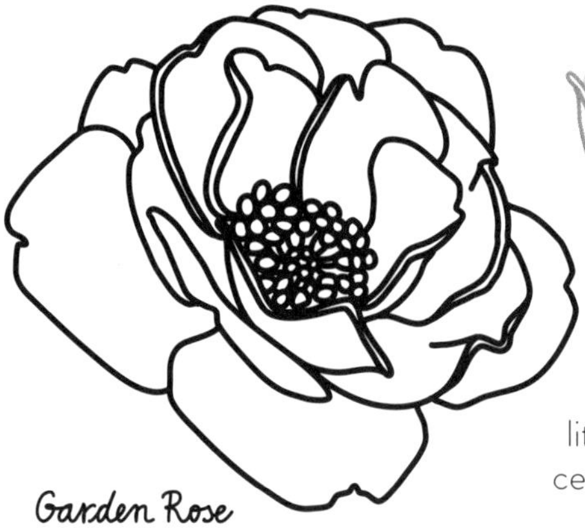

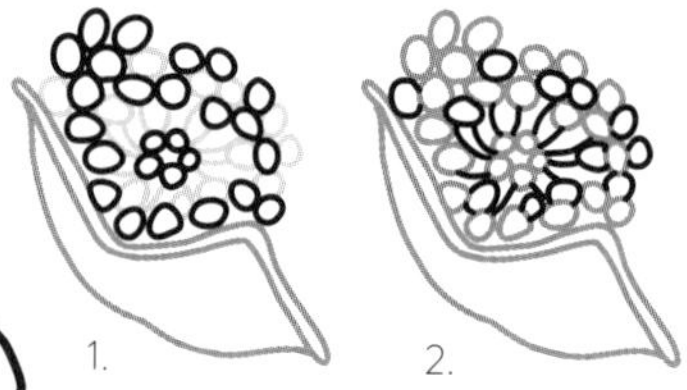

For the garden rose, draw a little cluster of five circles in the center. Then start to build up the ring of anthers around it. Start with the fully visible ones and tuck some underneath. Then, draw in a few stamens.

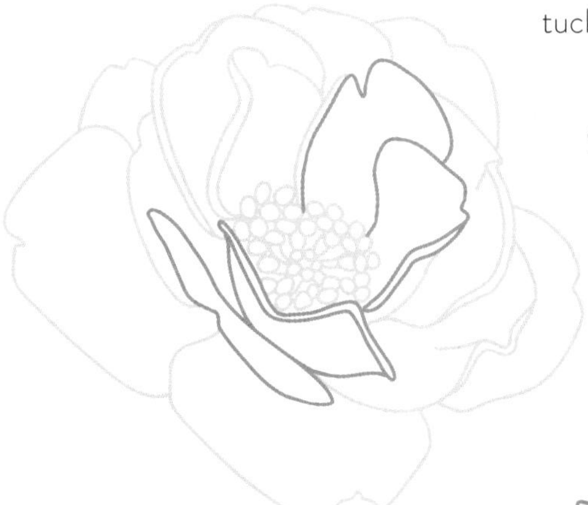

Some petals have a visible edge, illustrated with a parallel line. Try to draw the parallel line as narrow and even as possible.

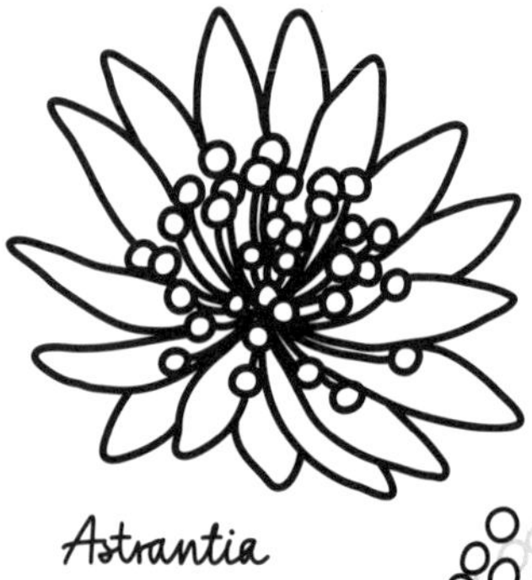

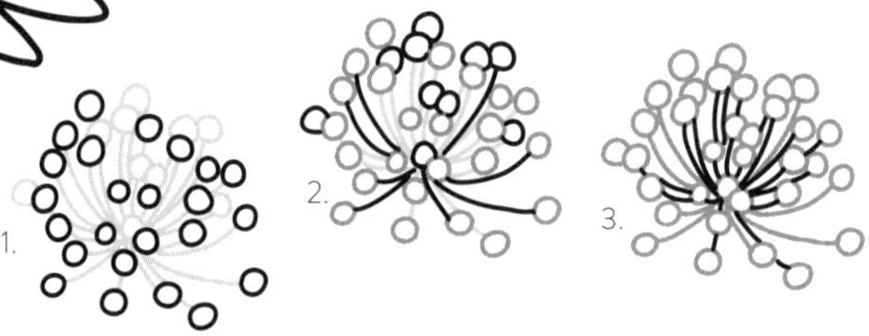

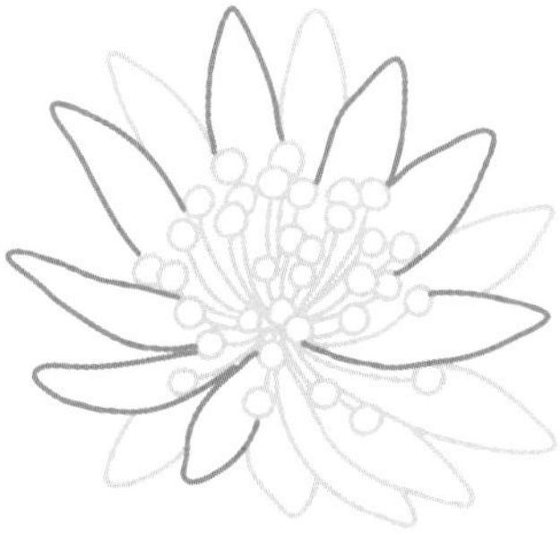

For the astrantia, I always leave some free areas for the stamens between the anthers. This creates the illusion of a full dome. Also, not every anther has to have a stamen. Try to avoid having the stamens merge together. Keep in mind that the stamens start at the same point at the center, even if they are hidden.

HOW TO DRAW: Leaves (page 52; Branches), Hydrangea (page 36; Hydrangea)

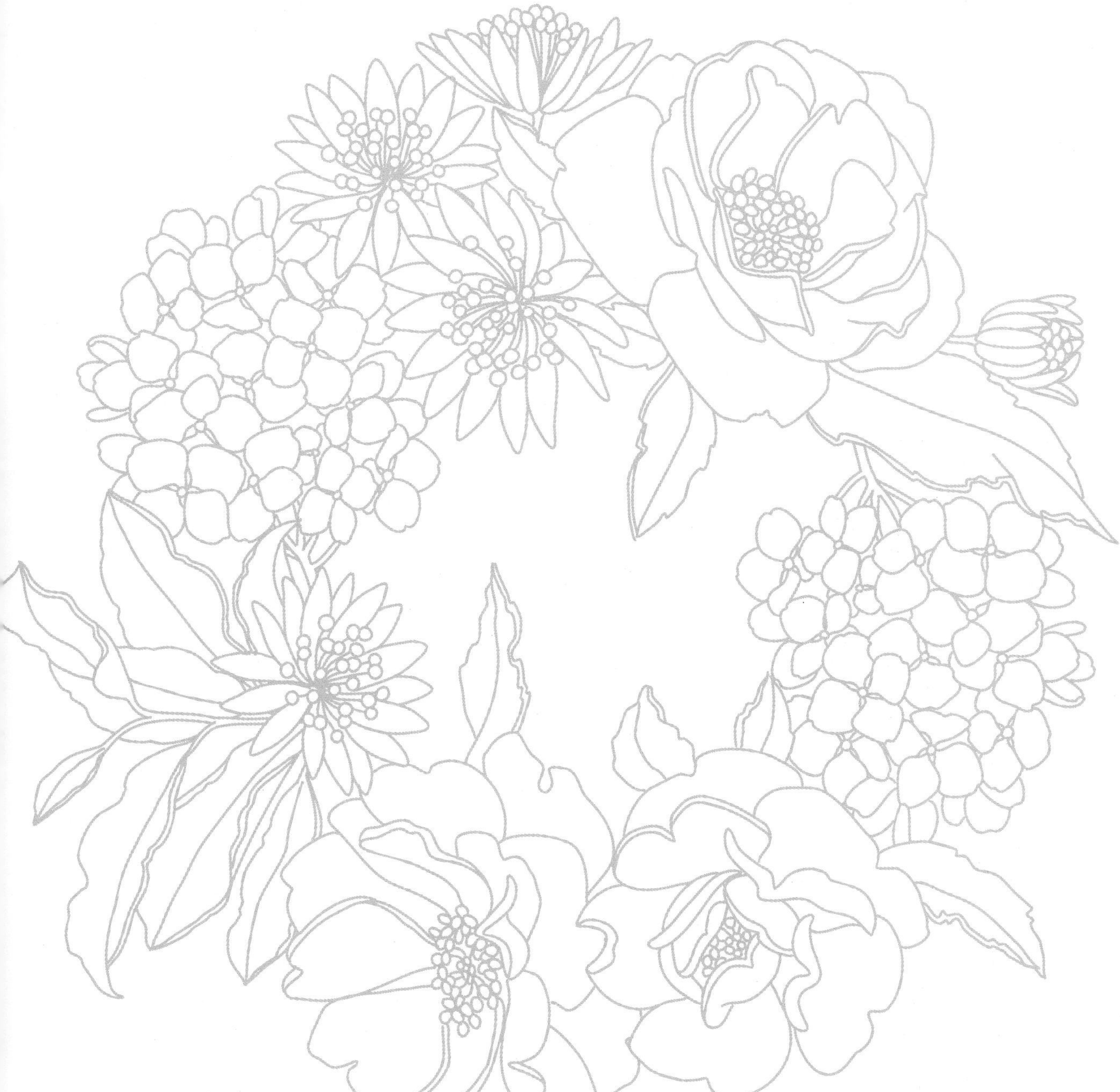

CAMELLIA GARDEN

Whenever I sit in a waiting room, I grab my phone and search for images of Japanese floral arrangements. It clears my mind in a minute and flies me to another universe. The simple beauty and clarity of lithesome and graceful flowers creates a unique impression. While you are working on the smooth curves of this illustration, let yourself soak up some of its lightness.

Camellia has several layers of beautiful round petals, illustrated with parallel lines at some points to add even more volume to it. The central part is a dense bunch of anthers; follow the steps below for achieving the crowded look.

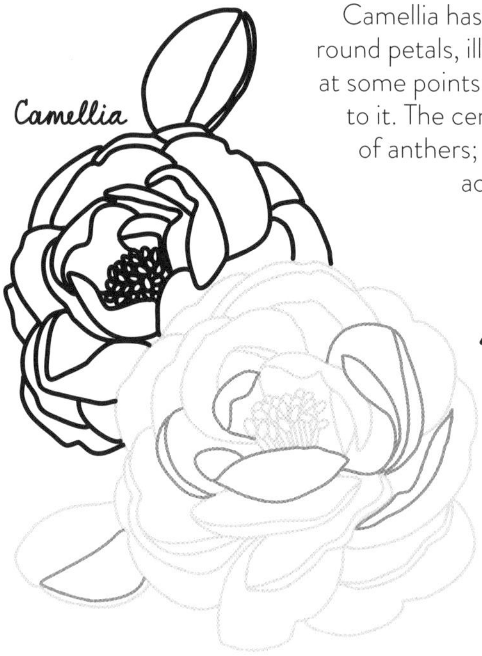

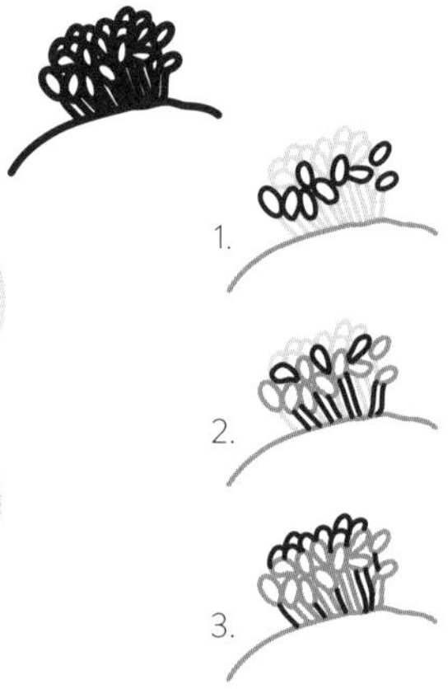

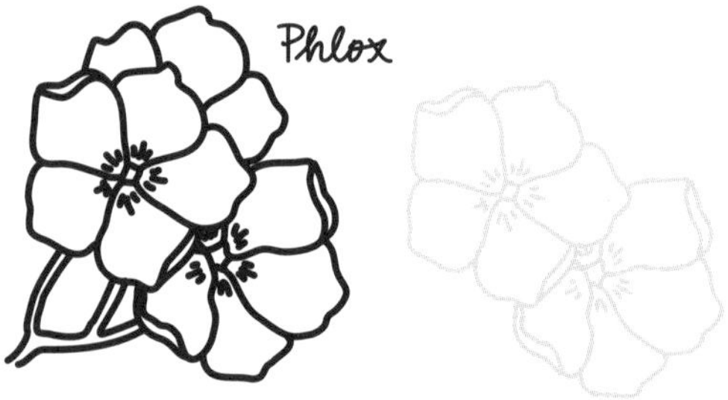

The dark center of lisianthus adds a little twist to this arrangement. Draw the anthers first, then add their stamens, which look like a starfish. Fill in the background circle with black and add short strokes around it like you would draw a sun. The petals are quite fringy at the edge, so trace them with a slight shakiness in your hand.

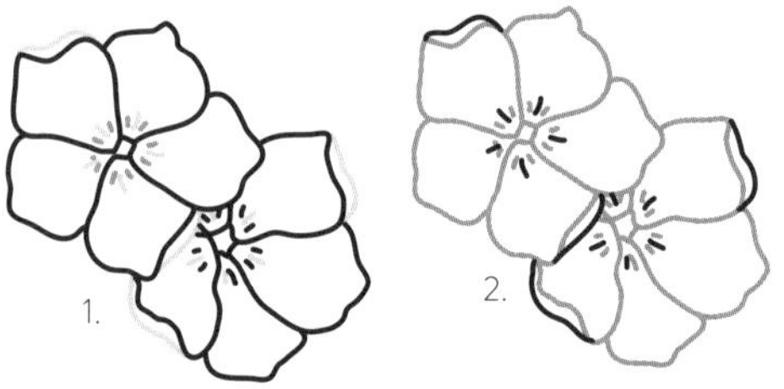

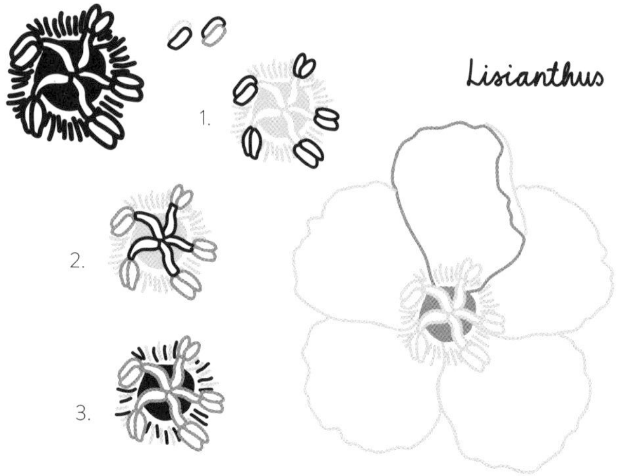

The five-petal flowers of phlox are really easy to draw. Be mindful of the layered look while tracing, and try to emulate the organic petal shape. Add some strokes around the center, which gives a unique element to this simple flower.

HOW TO DRAW: Bunny Tails (page 60; Boho Bouquet), Leaves (page 52; Branches)

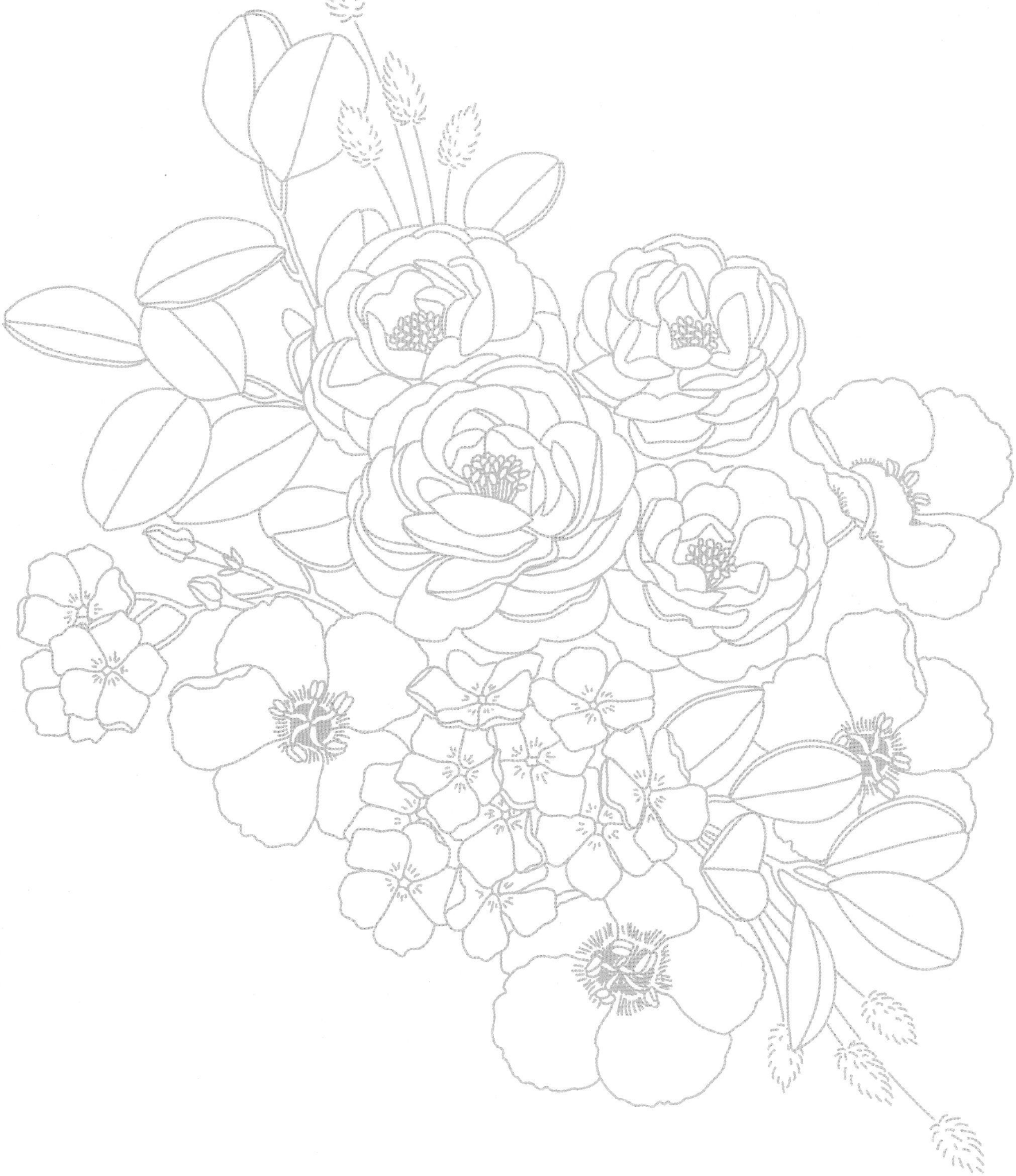

ROADSIDE TREASURES

This illustration is history. This is one of the first illustrations I drew when I started this whole journey of becoming an illustrator. And it is still one of my favorites. I picked these flowers on the playground while my son was having fun with the other kids. Isn't it a win-win situation? This is the sweetest little bunch with all my favorite wildflowers.

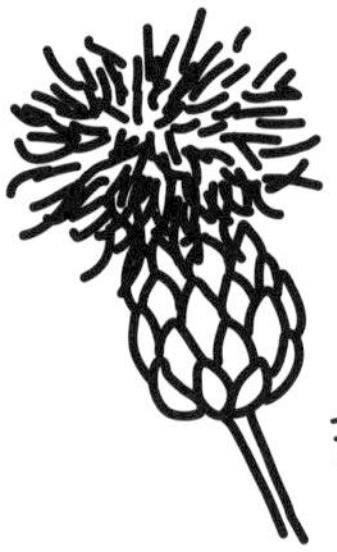

Field Thistle

The messy head of the field thistle might look a bit confusing, but the only trick to master it is to draw the first layer of the hairs pointing to the center. The second layer can be more random, weighing more on the bottom area. Build up the body from the bottom to the top to get a clean look.

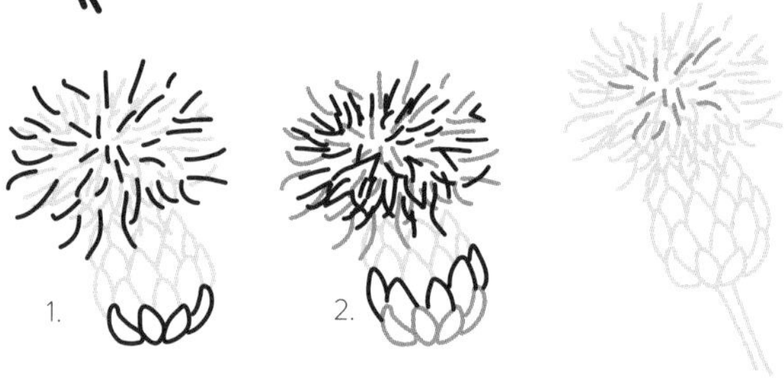

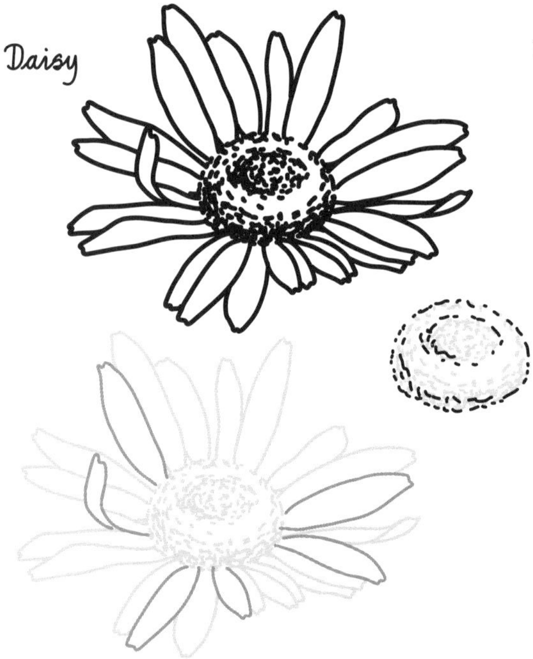

The lovely Queen Anne's lace is a dream. The tiny flowers are really simple—just three small dots sitting atop an oval. The only thing to focus on is the intersections, which gather the little stems. Make sure to start the stems from the same point.

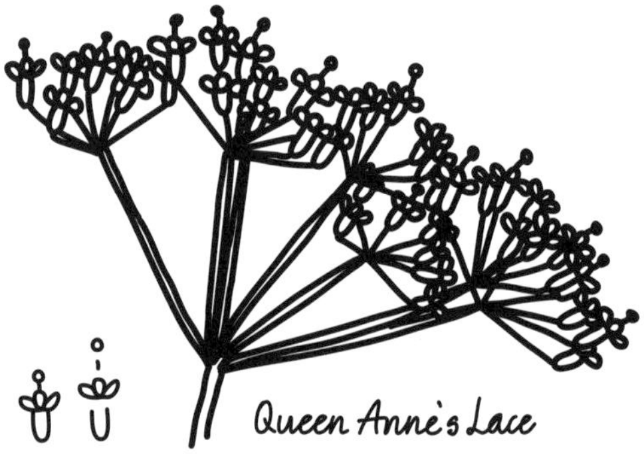

The magic of this wild daisy is the organic flow of its petals. The lower petals are shorter because we see the daisy from an angle. Be careful to keep the layered look of the petals by first drawing those in full view then tucking others behind them. The dome has a valley in the middle. Build up the darkest areas with mini strokes or dots.

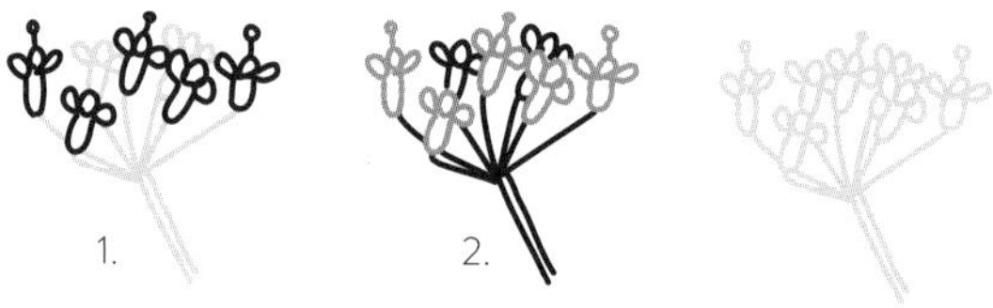

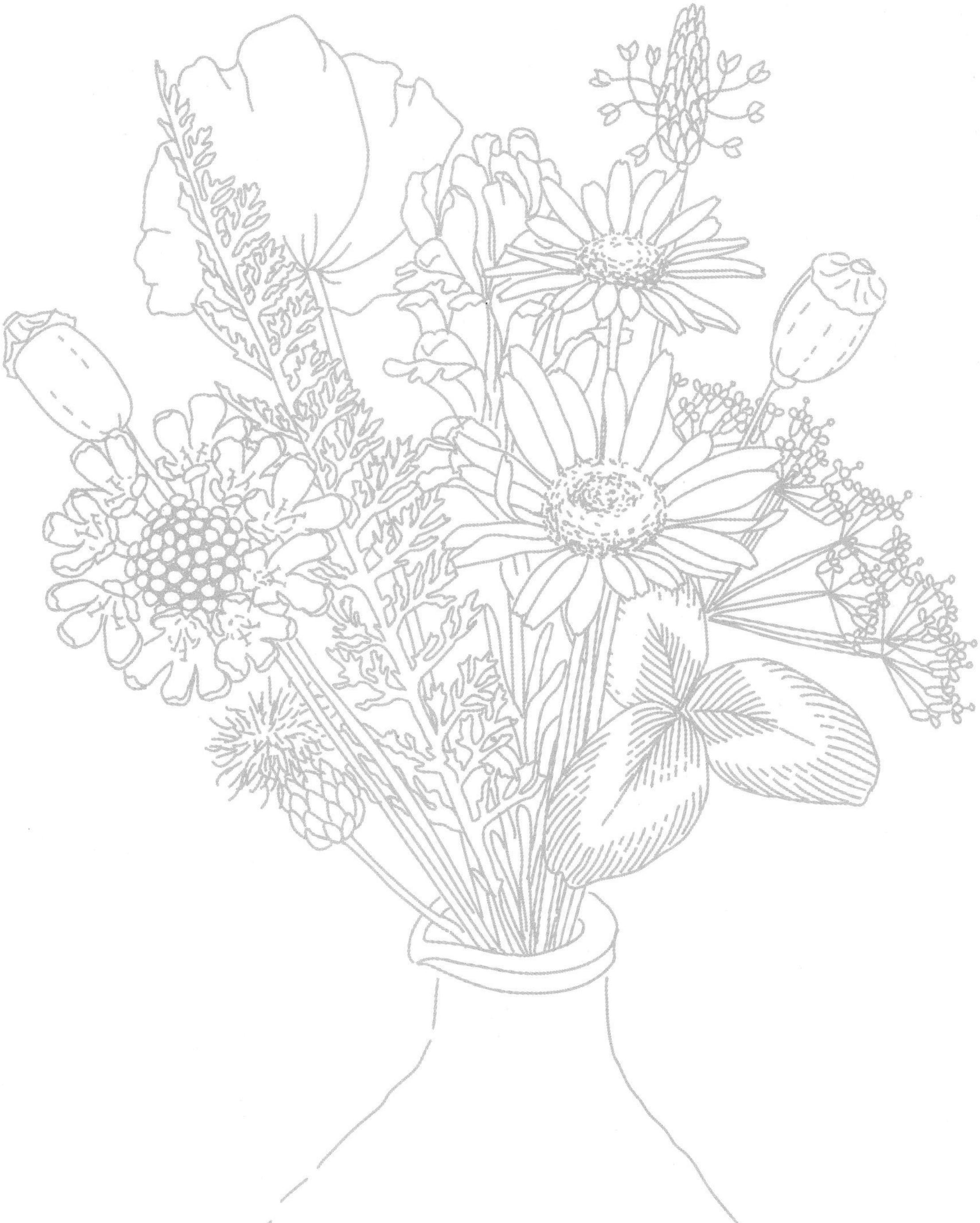

FOR MOTHER'S DAY

When I was a child, I used to live in the suburbs, where several empty lots were around us. I had a little crew, and we played a lot on the street. When Mother's Day came, we went on an expedition to these empty lots and we picked huge bouquets of lilacs. Then we visited every mother and grandmother on our street. Lilacs remind me of the excitement of these expeditions and the joy on the faces of those who received our bouquets. I hope you also travel back in time to a good childhood memory while working on this illustration.

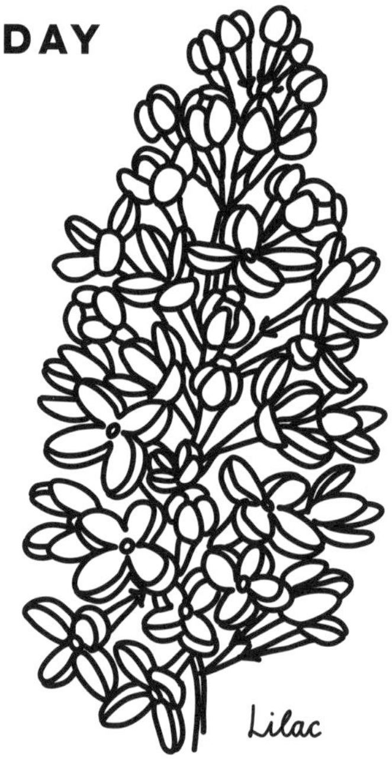

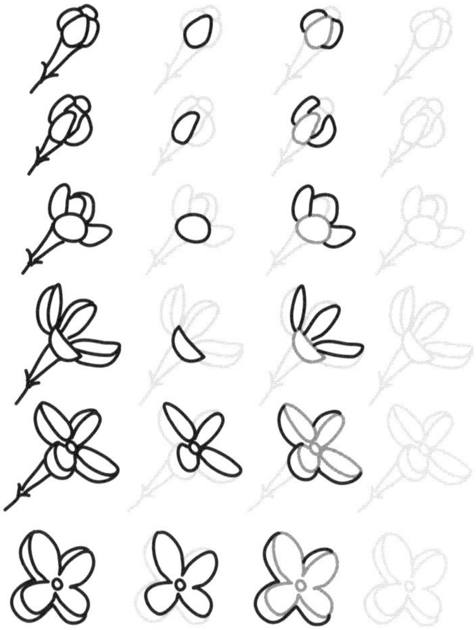

In the lilac, you can see the range of forms from bud to open flower. Start drawing the four-petaled flowers that face front and are fully shown. If the center of the flower is visible, start with that.

Primrose makes this bouquet stand out with the contrasting dark spots. First draw five heart-shaped petals, then add a double edge where the petals are visible from the side. Fill in the dark spots by drawing strokes in a spiral, connecting them all until no white remains.

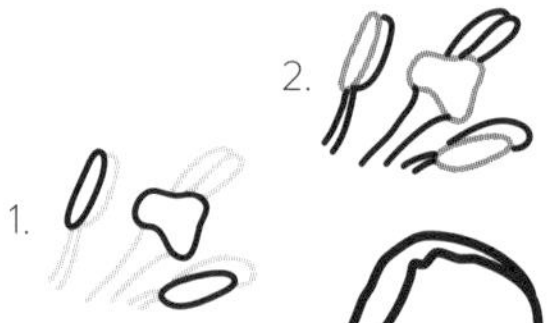

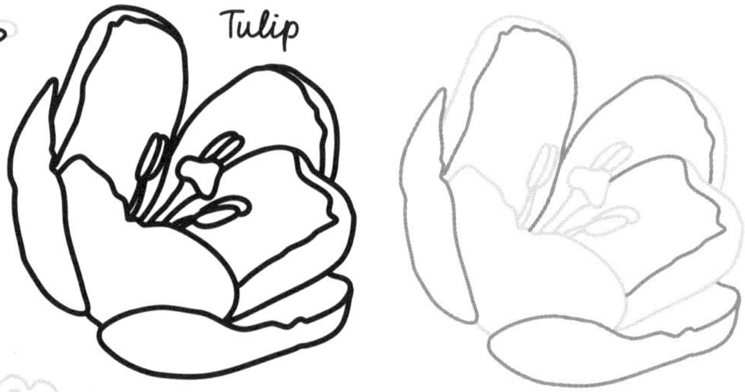

Drawing a tulip with lines is challenging, because the simple-yet-bent petals are hard to capture, but double lines at the edge of the petals give them body. The anthers are built up from two ovals, one tucked behind the other.

HOW TO DRAW: Grasses (page 82; Quince Blossom), Leaves (page 52; Branches), Peony (page 24; Peony)

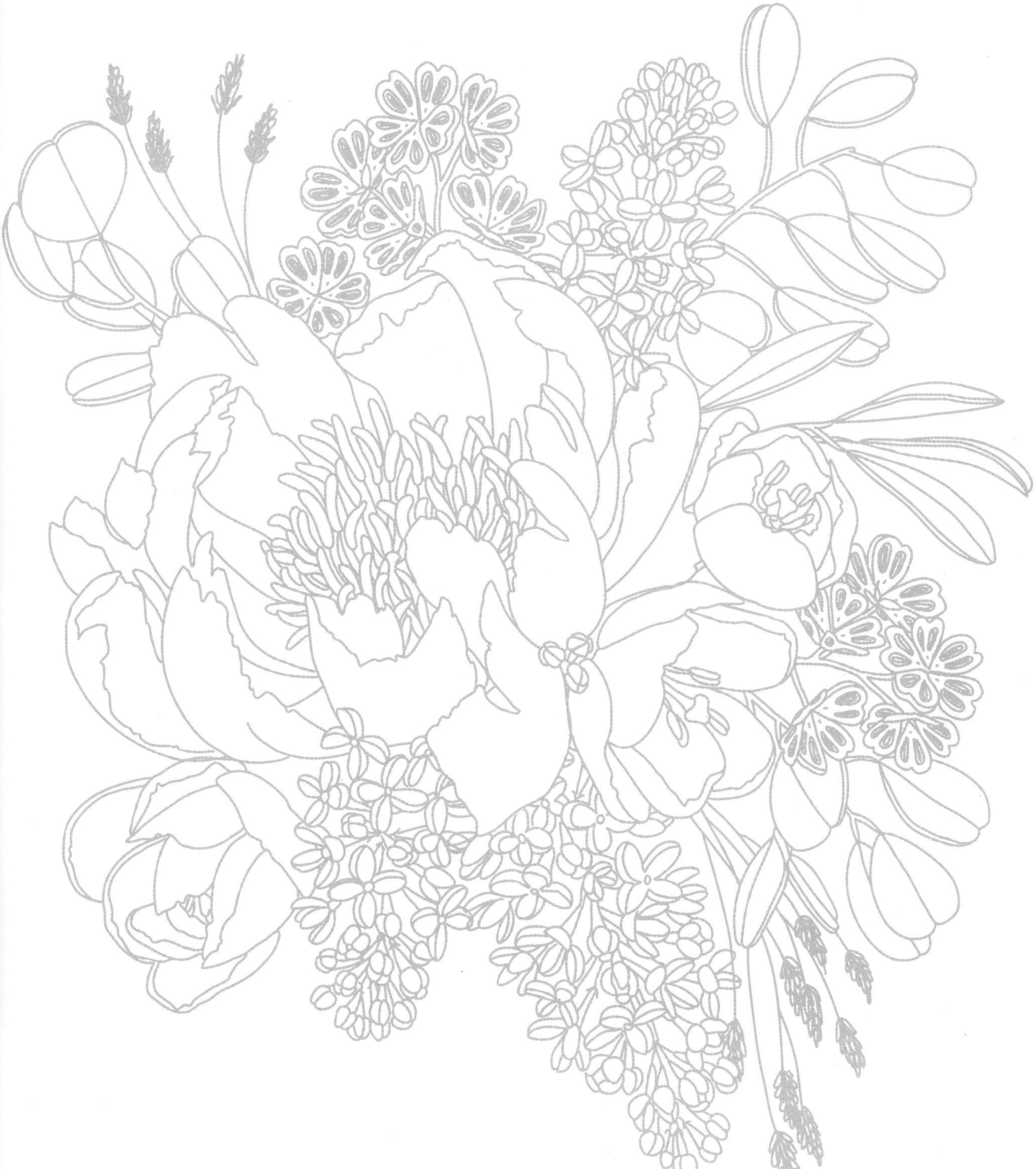

A BOUQUET WITH SASS

This bouquet is lively, bold and full of spirit. It's cheeky in the best sense of the word. The unearthly snapdragon with its interesting pattern and bubbly shapes plays the beast above the lush feminine softness of dahlia and the masculine, angular dogwood. The two helenium aunties look at the scene from above with all their love. They are surrounded by soft greens and tiny hearts. What a nice dramedy.

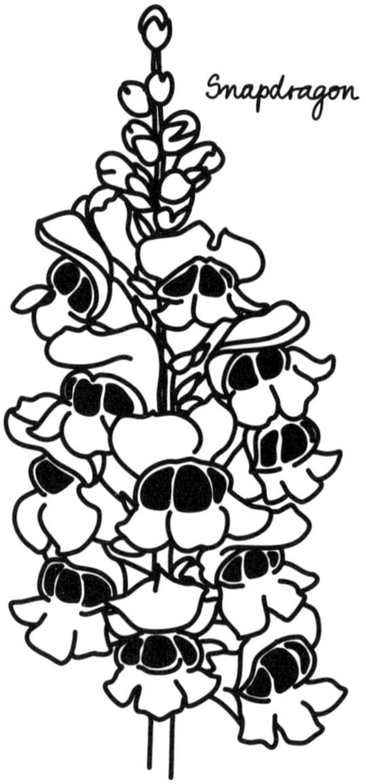

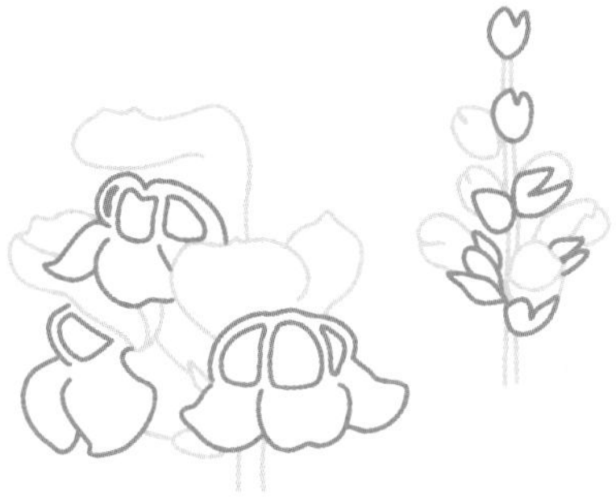

Snapdragon is a mystery. It has so many different faces, but a trick to drawing them all is to break down each structure into three components. It has a bubble in the center with the dark pattern on it. There are three petals below, looking like a mythical beard. And finally there is a big wing above all, which could make the whole thing fly away.

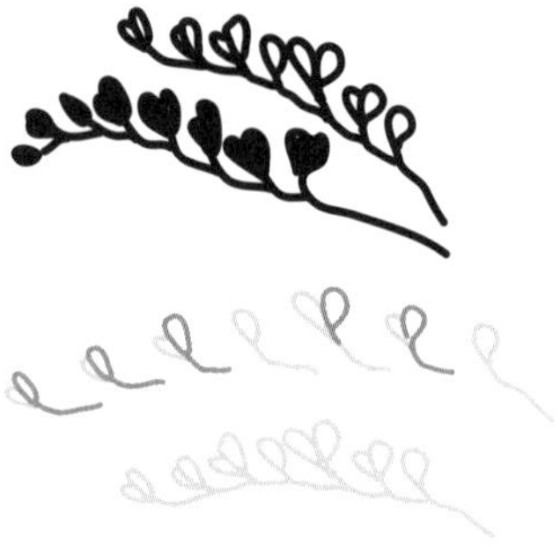

This imaginary greenery is built up from tiny heart balloons. You can fill them in or leave them as just outlines.

Helenium has extra ruffled petals looking like a soft silk skirt. Start by drawing the top petals. Each petal is separated in the step-by-step illustration to help you decide which line belongs to which petal. The central dome is almost a full sphere. Draw short strokes and dots in a cluster to create the shadow for a three-dimensional look.

1.

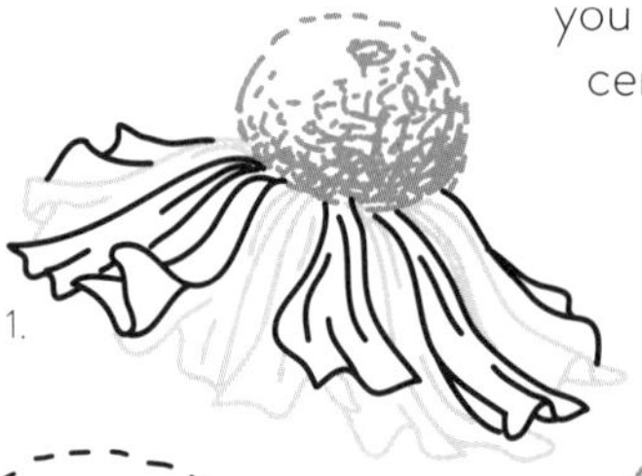

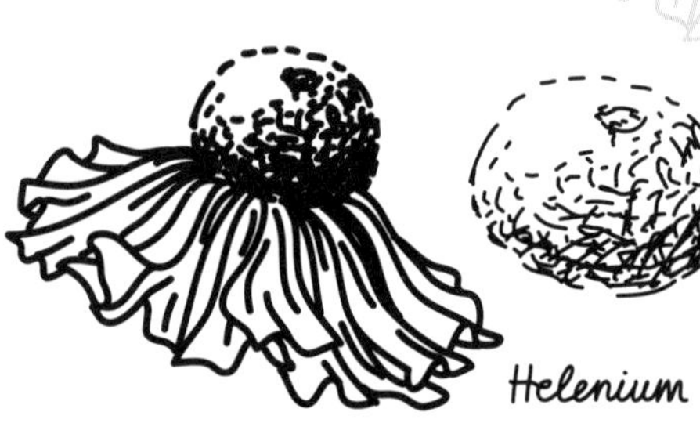

2.

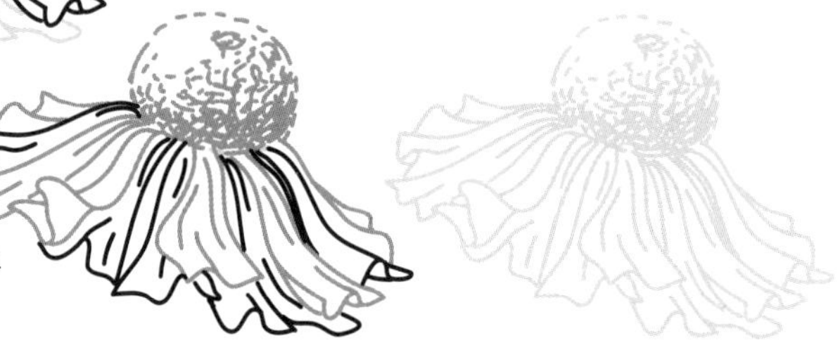

HOW TO DRAW: Dogwood (page 76; A Stroll in the Park), Dahlia (page 28; Dahlia)

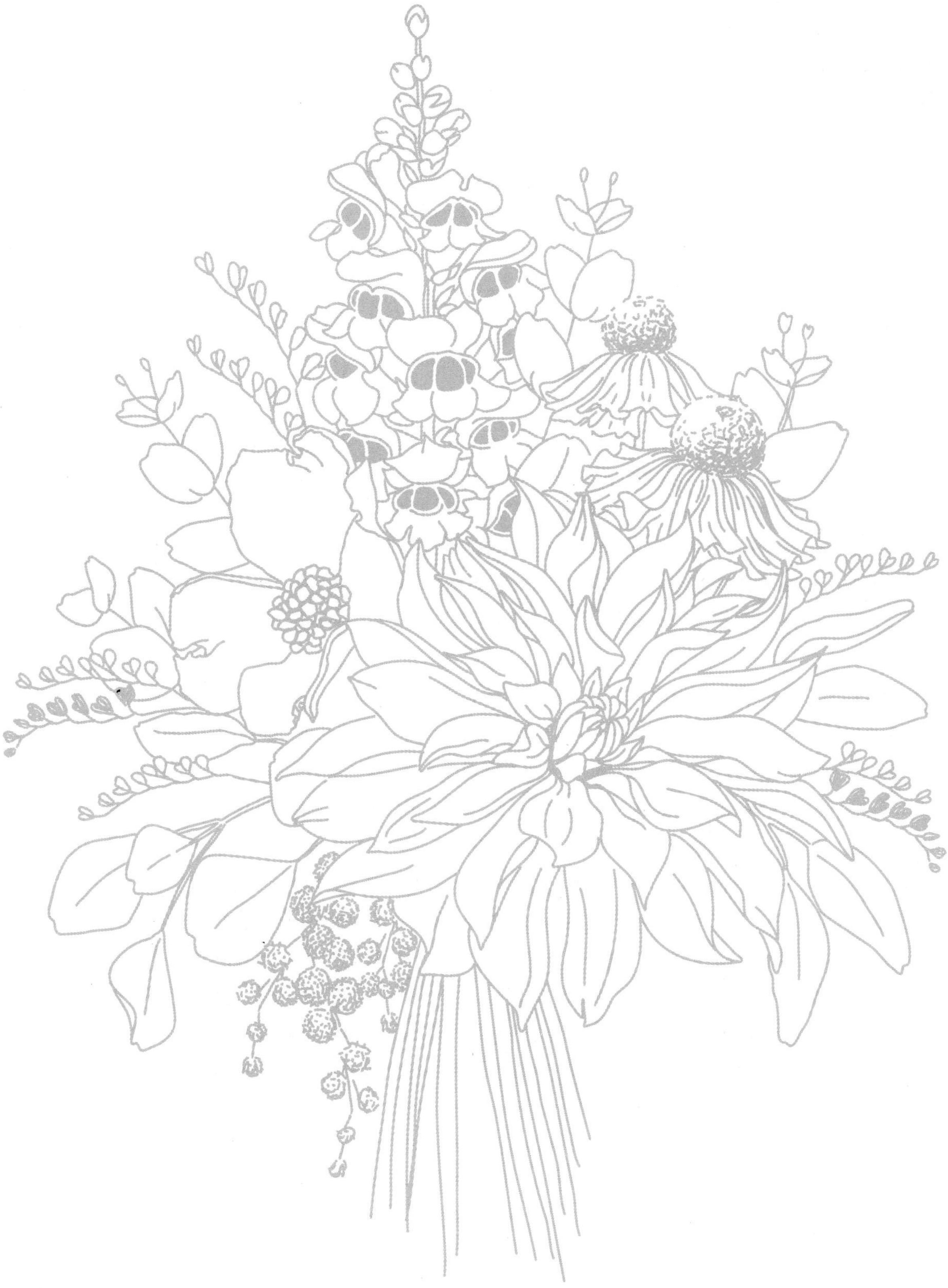

A STROLL IN THE PARK

When I was a child, I felt like I was on a treasure hunt when we walked in the neighborhood or even in a park. I wanted to pick all the flowers we walked by. As I got older, I learned that this is not the most nature-friendly behavior. So instead I bring you this imaginary table full of treasures laid out after a nice stroll in the park.

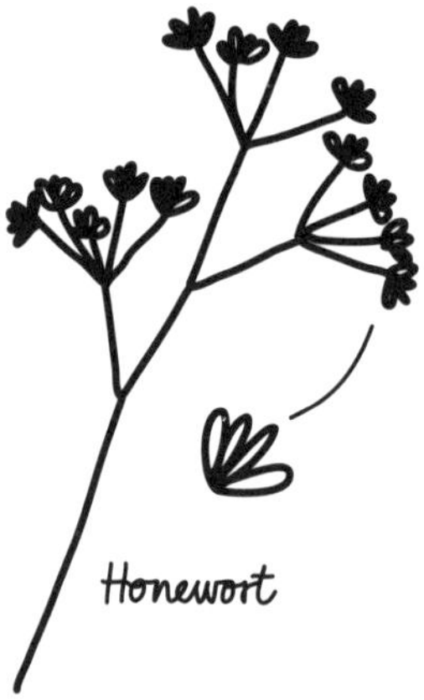

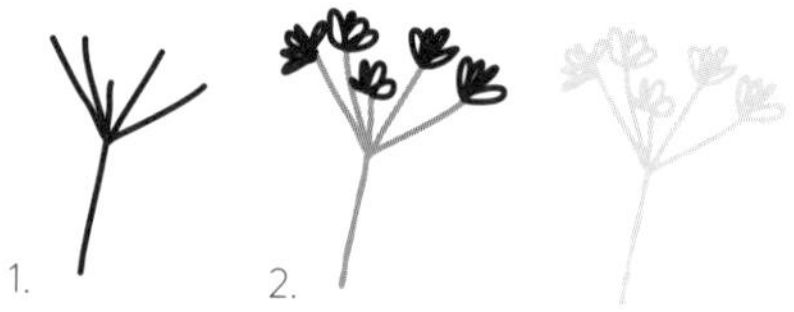

This grass—honewort—grabs the attention with its beauty and is so effortless to draw. The stems don't even have to be that straight, and the little pom-poms at the end can be totally random.

Bushes of dogwood are mesmerizing with all their gorgeous flowers. I hope you get lost in their beauty as you fill them in, just like you would if you were strolling by them in nature.

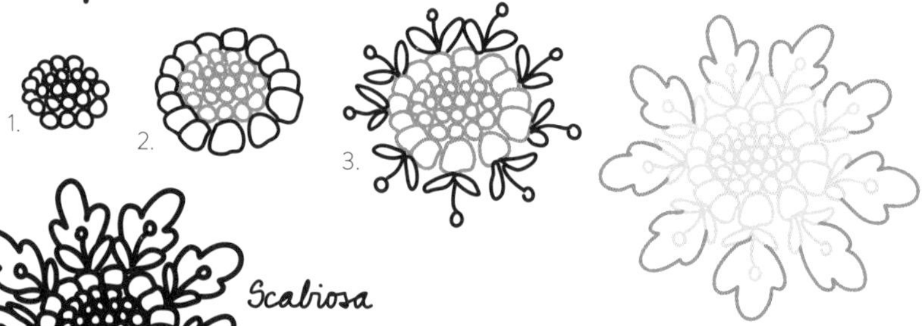

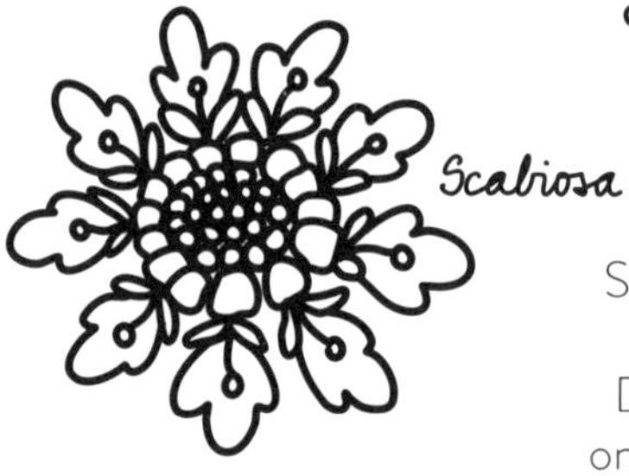

Scabiosa is built up from smaller and slightly bigger buds and a ring of opened flowers. Draw the central buds first, then the bigger ones around them. Draw two ovals sprouting from each bud, then draw an anther between each pair. Finish up the flowers with their big bulky petals.

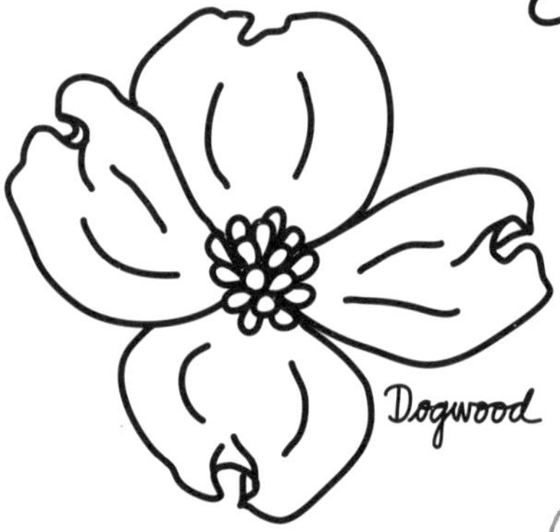

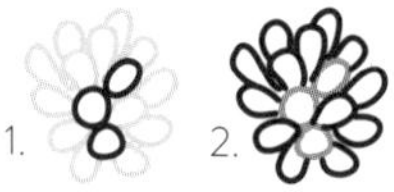

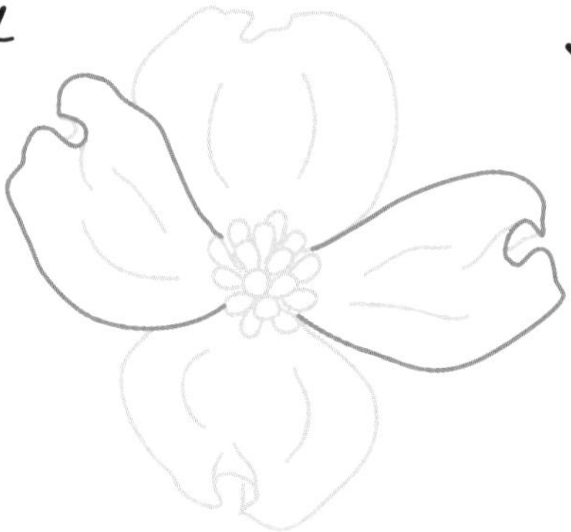

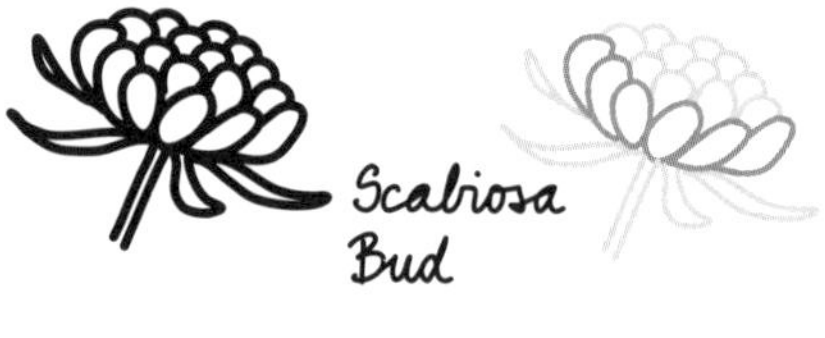

Dogwood has four quite simple petals, except the tip looks like it has a bite missing from it. Draw each petal in threes: smooth side, middle bite, other smooth side. The central part is a dense dome of teardrop shapes. Start with the ones that look like a circle and continue toward the edges.

The bud of the scabiosa is similar to the center of the dogwood. The only difference is the shape of the buds is oval, not teardrop-like. Start by drawing the row in the front and move backward.

SUN-KISSED AUTUMN

This bouquet encompasses the romance of summer and autumn. Wild roses bloom in high summer, while the chocolate cosmos and playful berries add an autumn spice to this composition. All of the elements have different densities, from the fluffy light roses to the dark spots of the cosmos. This is the perfect recipe for a beautiful illustration.

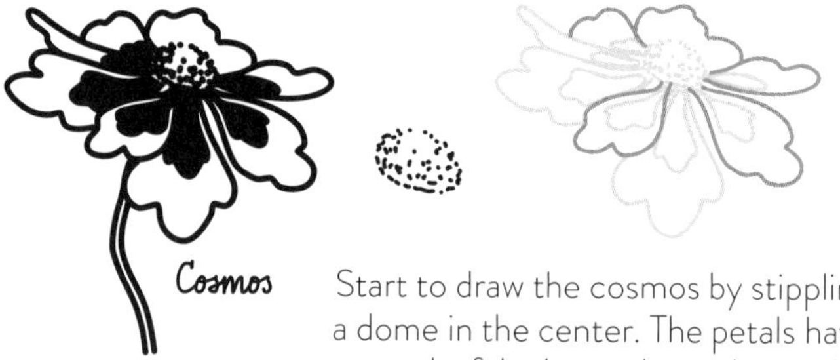

Start to draw the cosmos by stippling a dome in the center. The petals have a playful edge, a shape that is also echoed on the dark areas close to the center. Be sure to leave a thin white line at the edges of the petals, to keep them separated.

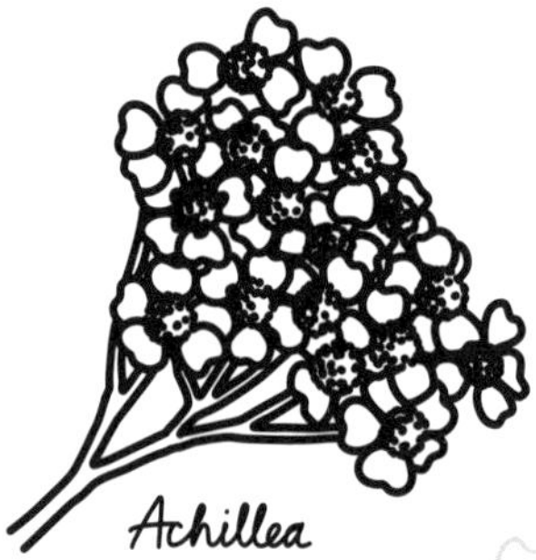

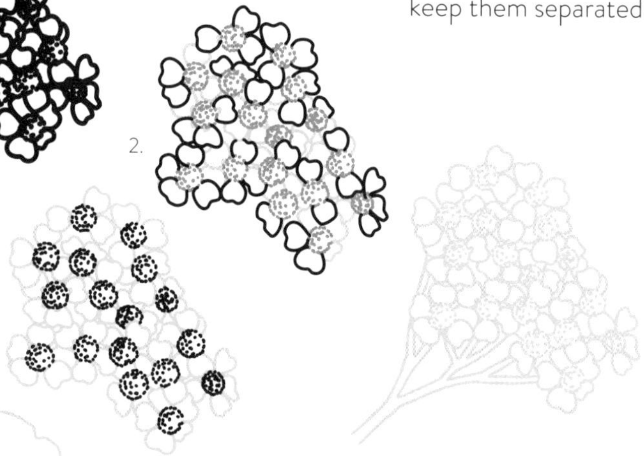

Achillea is beautiful with its wonderfully dense, tiny flowers. Start drawing the center of each flower with stippling. Draw the heart-shaped petals in several layers, starting with the ones that are fully visible and working backward from there.

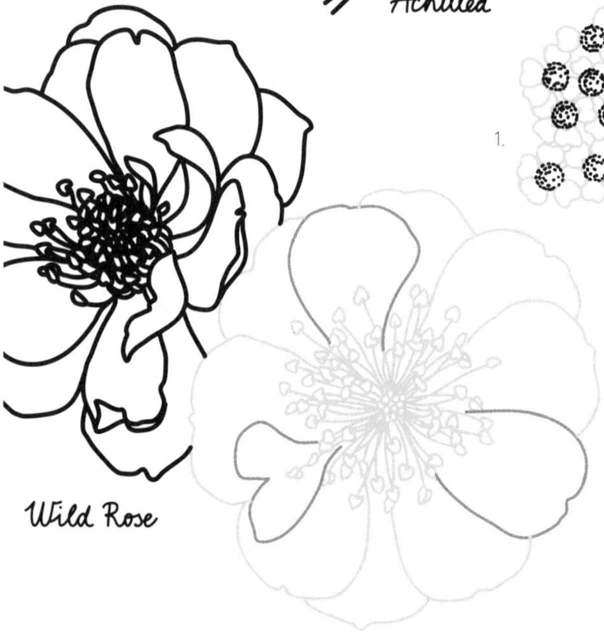

These wild roses are full of love. Both the anthers and the petals are heart shaped. The center is really dense, but try to avoid having your lines run together.

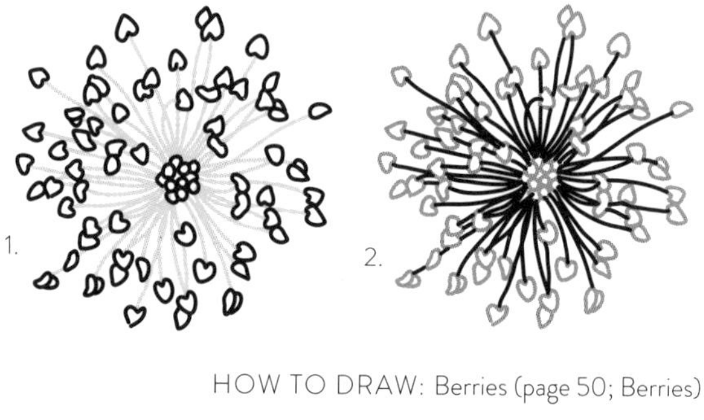

HOW TO DRAW: Berries (page 50; Berries)

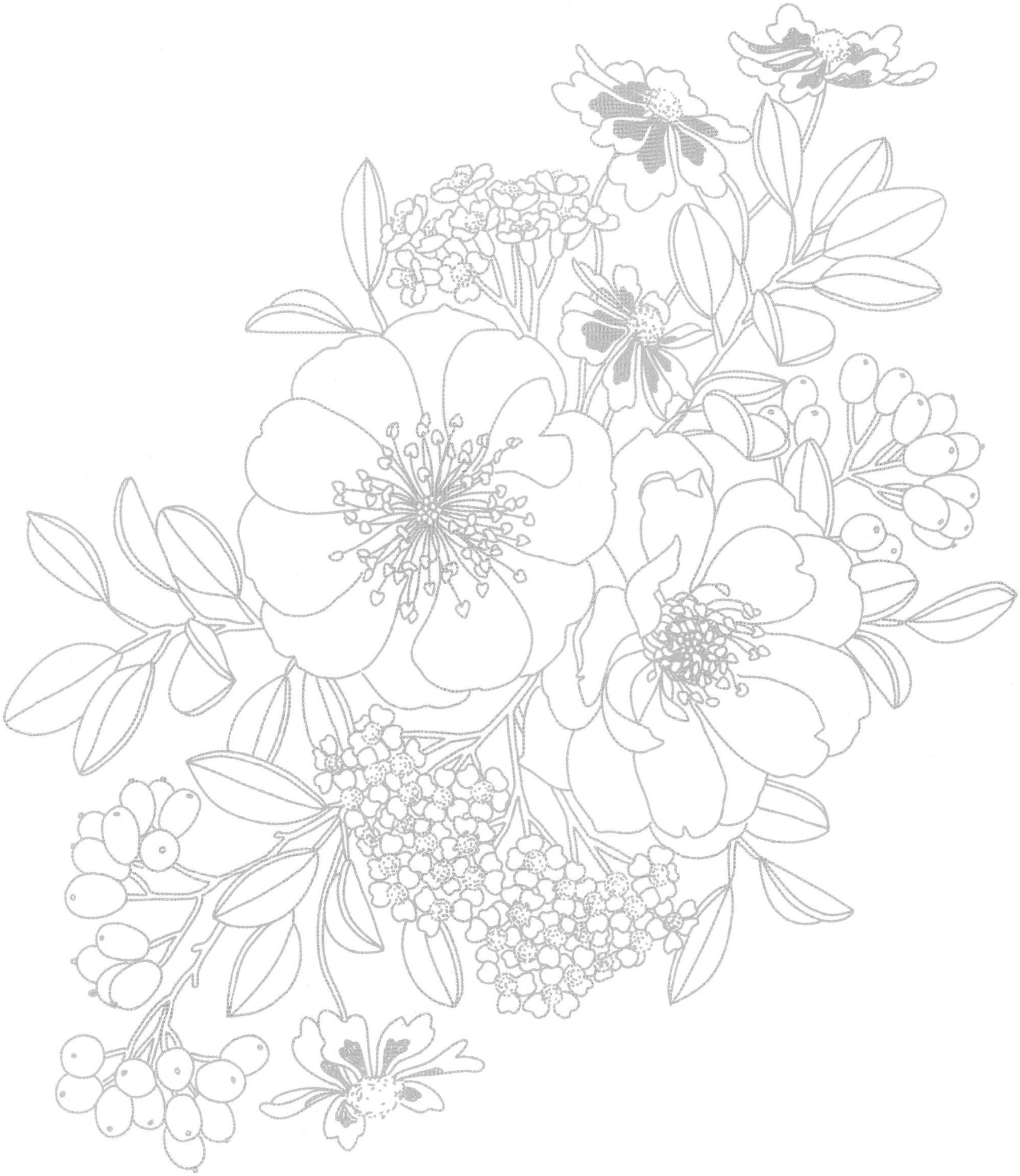

ANNA'S BOUQUET

Yes, this is it: my bridal bouquet! I wish I could show you those beautiful colors! It was a bit on the moody side, with red and purple anemones, burgundy orchids and deep mauve waxflowers and carnations, lightened up with soft and fluffy white ranunculus and silver brunia balls. It was a masterpiece for me. Maybe you'll want to add some of these colors to your illustration when you're finished?

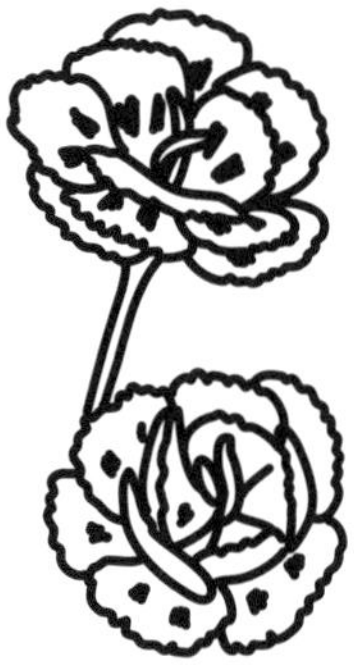

Carnation

Mini carnations have two spikes in the center that cross like an X. Make sure you leave some white space between the edges while you outline them. The petals have the characteristic sawlike edge, which is a nice practice for fine motor control. Add in the black spots as a final detail.

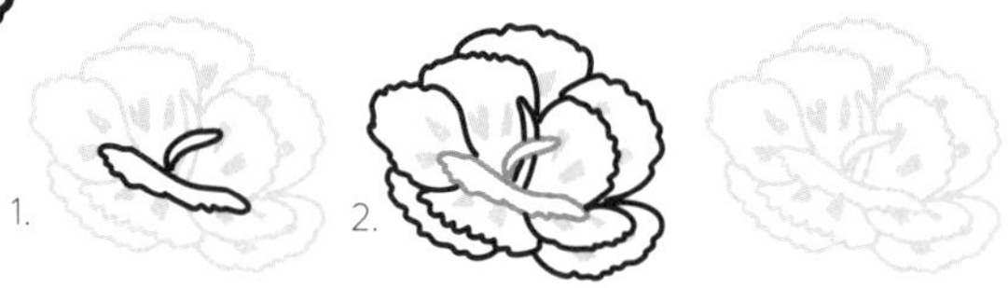

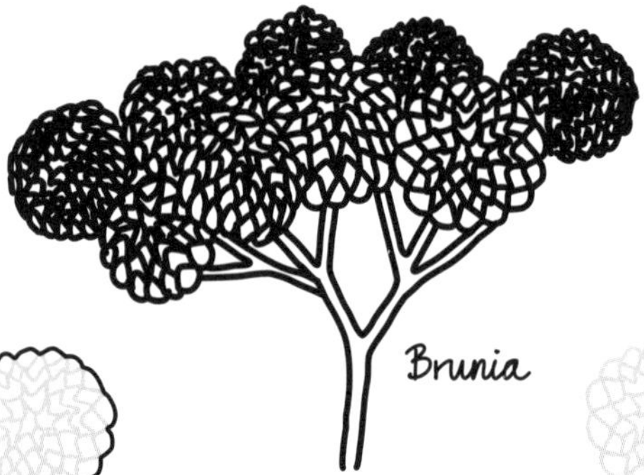

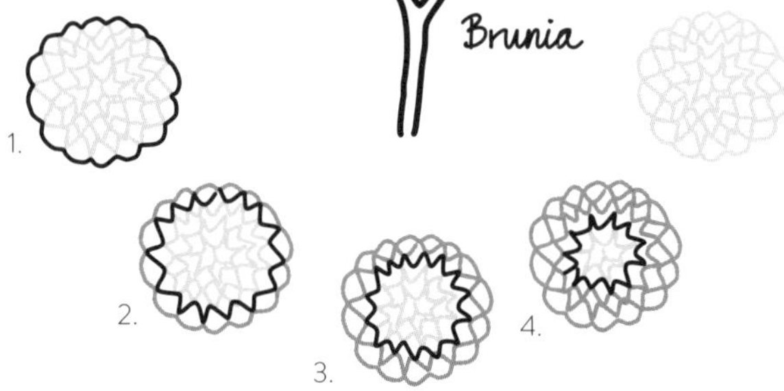

Drawing an orchid is all about capturing the central body. It has three wings hugging around the anthers. I left some light areas at the edges to make sure the shape is recognizable. The freckles add an extra effect to this flower.

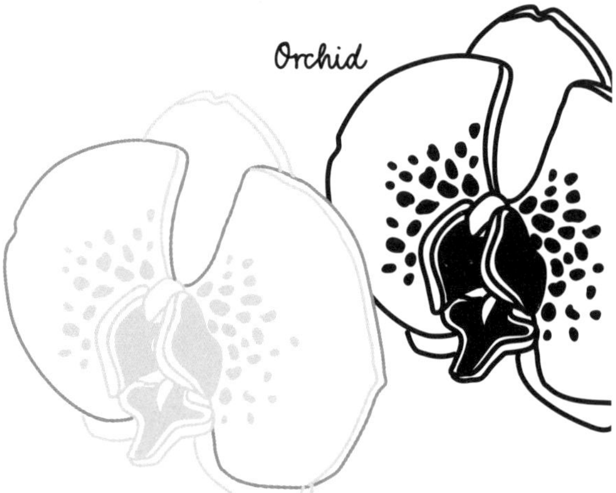

Brunia balls are rich in detail. The back ones are so dense that the lines are even hard to see. The best way to capture that detail is with random zigzag lines. But the closer ones have a fun structure. Start from the outside. The first circle is bulky, and the inner ones are zigzags. Make sure the zigzag in step 2 meets the valleys of the bulky outline. This creates the outer "petals" of the ball. Then fill the inside with rings of zigzag circles.

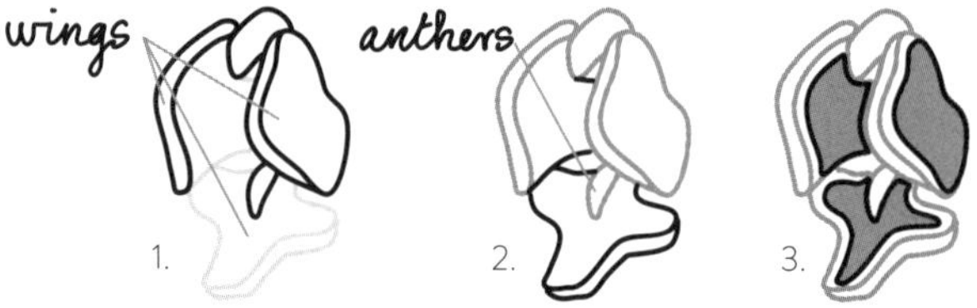

HOW TO DRAW: Anemone (page 26; Anemone), Waxflower (page 92; Greetings from Australia), Ranunculus (page 40; Ranunculus)

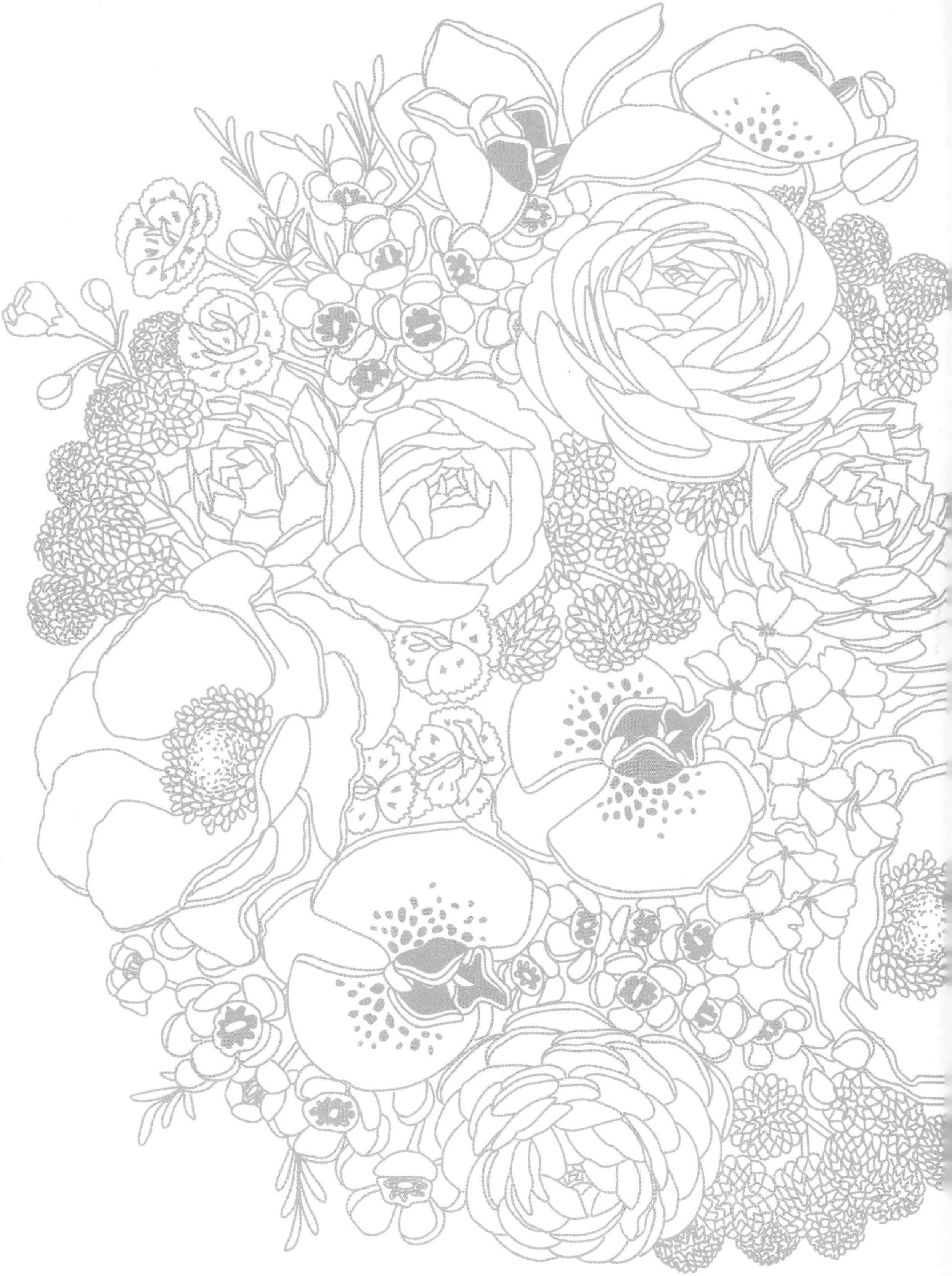

QUINCE BLOSSOM

This bouquet with blooming Japanese quince blossom is inspired by an annual early spring treasure hunt I never miss. The bright red flowers of quince are one of the first spring flowers in my neighborhood, so they are the first to ease my hunger for fresh blooms after winter. During these treasure hunts, I instantly feel a boost from these aesthetic bombs. Same goes for the wonderful peonies I gifted myself a few years ago.

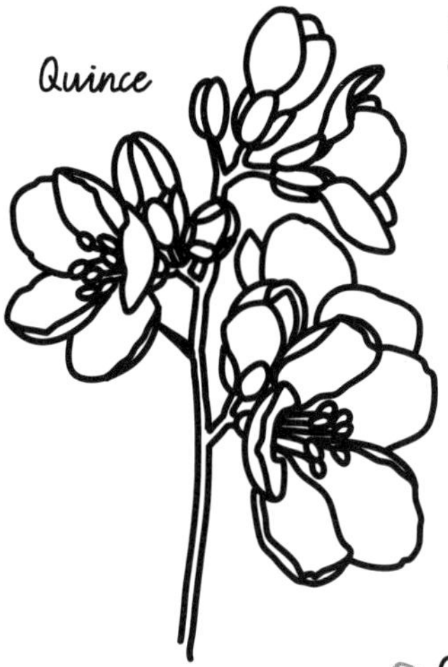

The quince blossom has flowers at different stages, from full buds to semi-opened buds to open flowers. Start with the open flowers. First add the anthers and petals underneath the bunch, followed by the stamens and the rest of the petals. Move back from there. Outline every bud and flower, then add the branches. Draw them parallel and narrow.

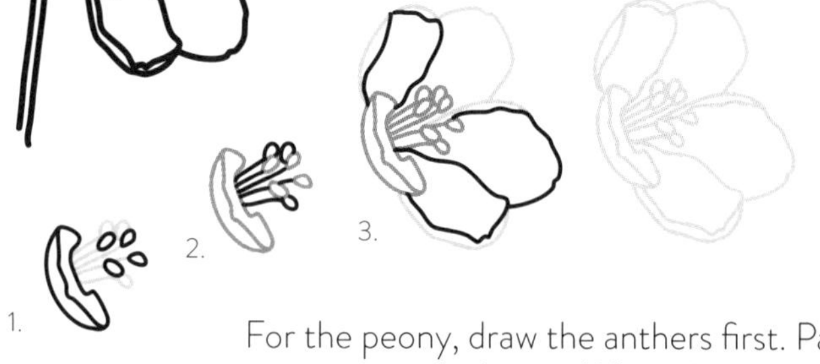

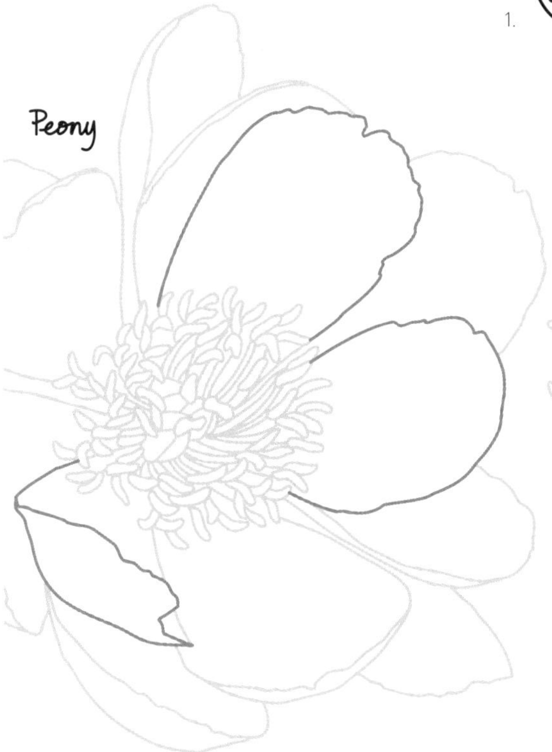

For the peony, draw the anthers first. Pay attention to the layers. When drawing the stamens of the anthers, always leave a little space between the two strokes. Then finish the flower with its luscious petals.

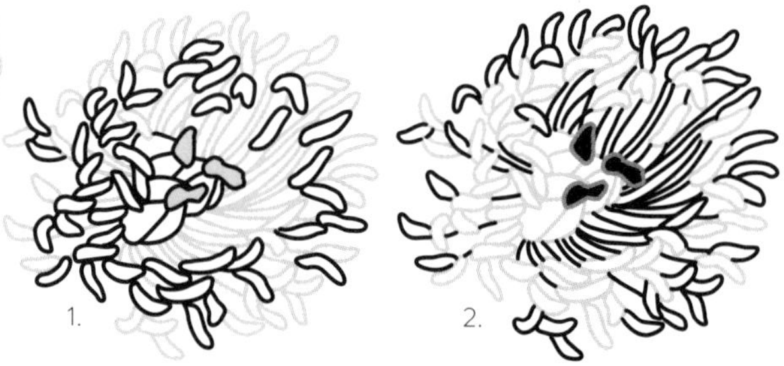

For the grass, draw some layers of zigzags, getting smaller toward the top.

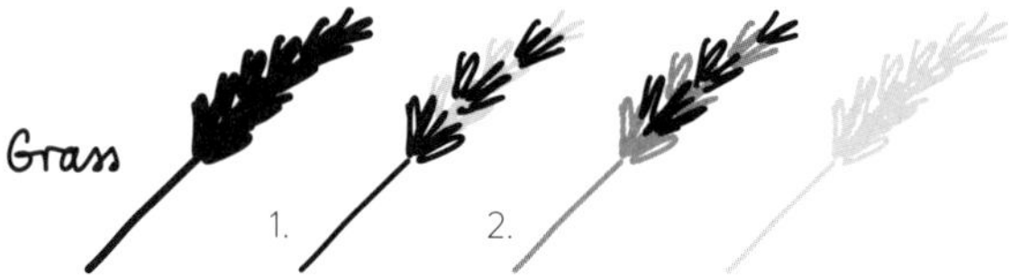

HOW TO DRAW: Leaves (page 52; Branches)

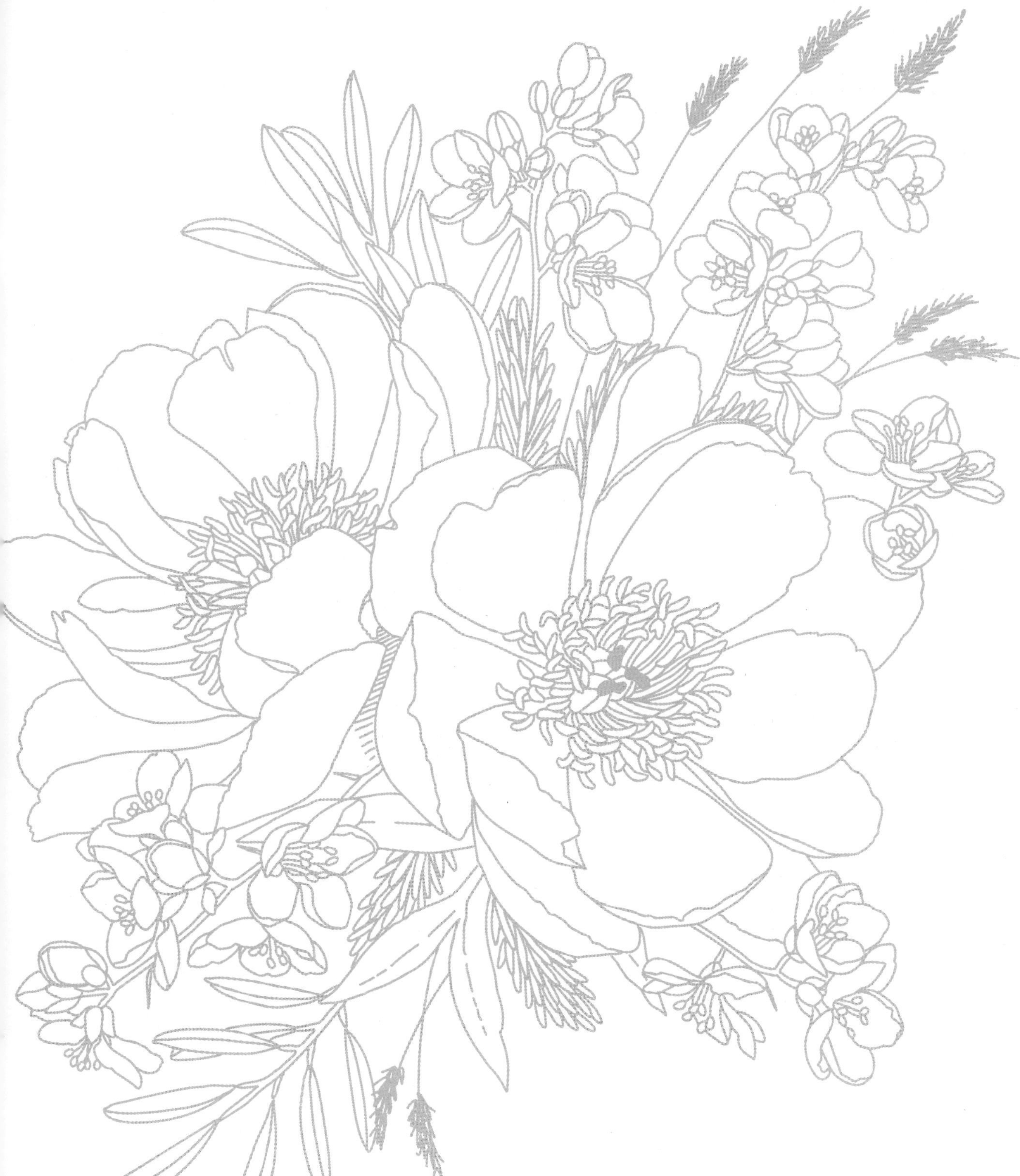

WARM SUMMER DAYS

No doubt summer is the high season for enjoying the blooming flowers in nature. I take photos of flowers everywhere—in front of the post office, at the park and during a walk. Usually my camera is full of floral photos from May to September. And I love to scroll through them later, even jumping back to previous years.

I made this arrangement referencing some of these photos. The wonderful thing is that these flowers fly me back to those warm summer days whenever I am working on them.

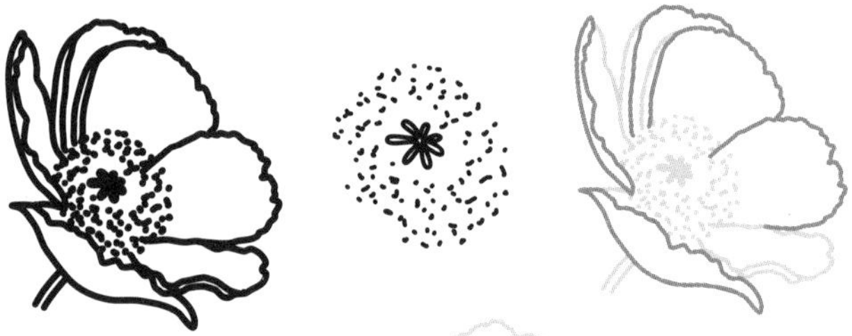

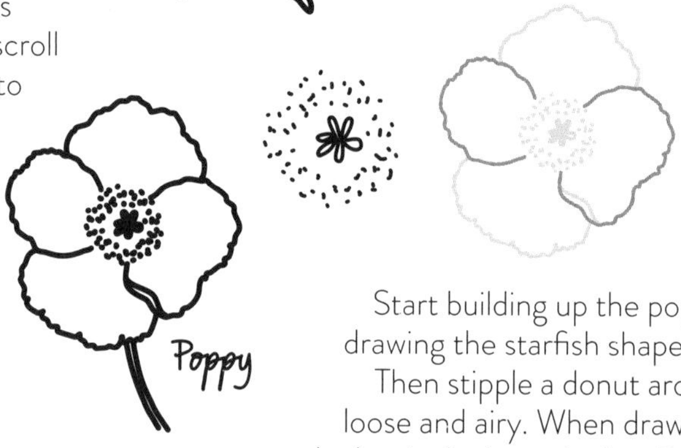

Start building up the poppy flowers by drawing the starfish shape in the middle. Then stipple a donut around it; keep it loose and airy. When drawing the petals, the key is the jagged edge. Draw lightly and create slightly shaky lines. It makes the illustration delicate and imitates the rich folds a poppy petal naturally has.

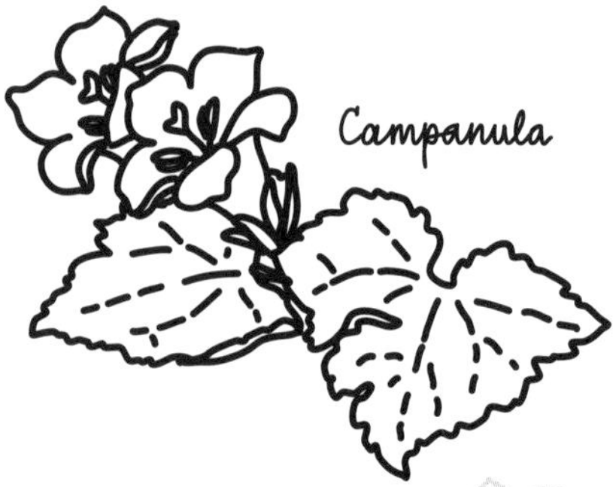

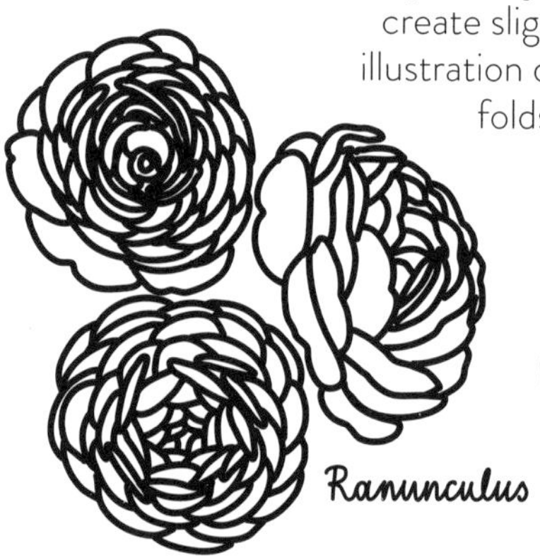

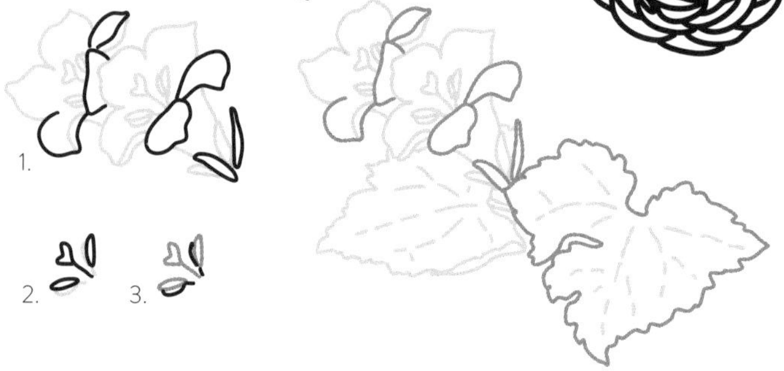

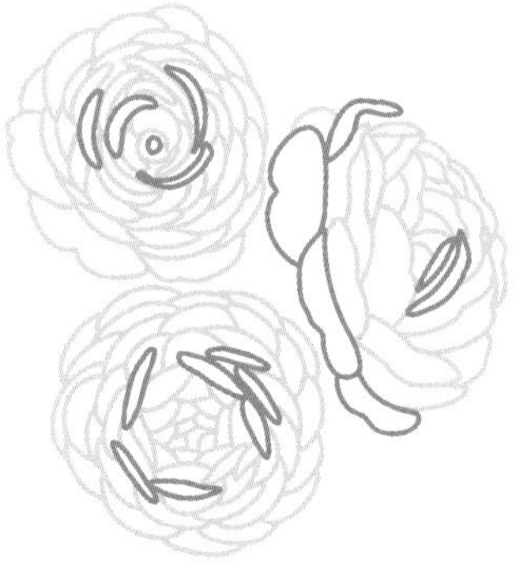

These little ranunculus heads have tons of petals. I highlighted some cigar-shaped petals that can act as starting points. Then move in a spiral and draw semicircles in several layers.

Campanula, or Canterbury bells, are so joyful. Start with their front petals, then add the anthers followed by the rest of the petals and the leaves.

HOW TO DRAW: Peony (page 24; Peony), Sunflower (page 38; Sunflower), Leaves (page 52; Branches)

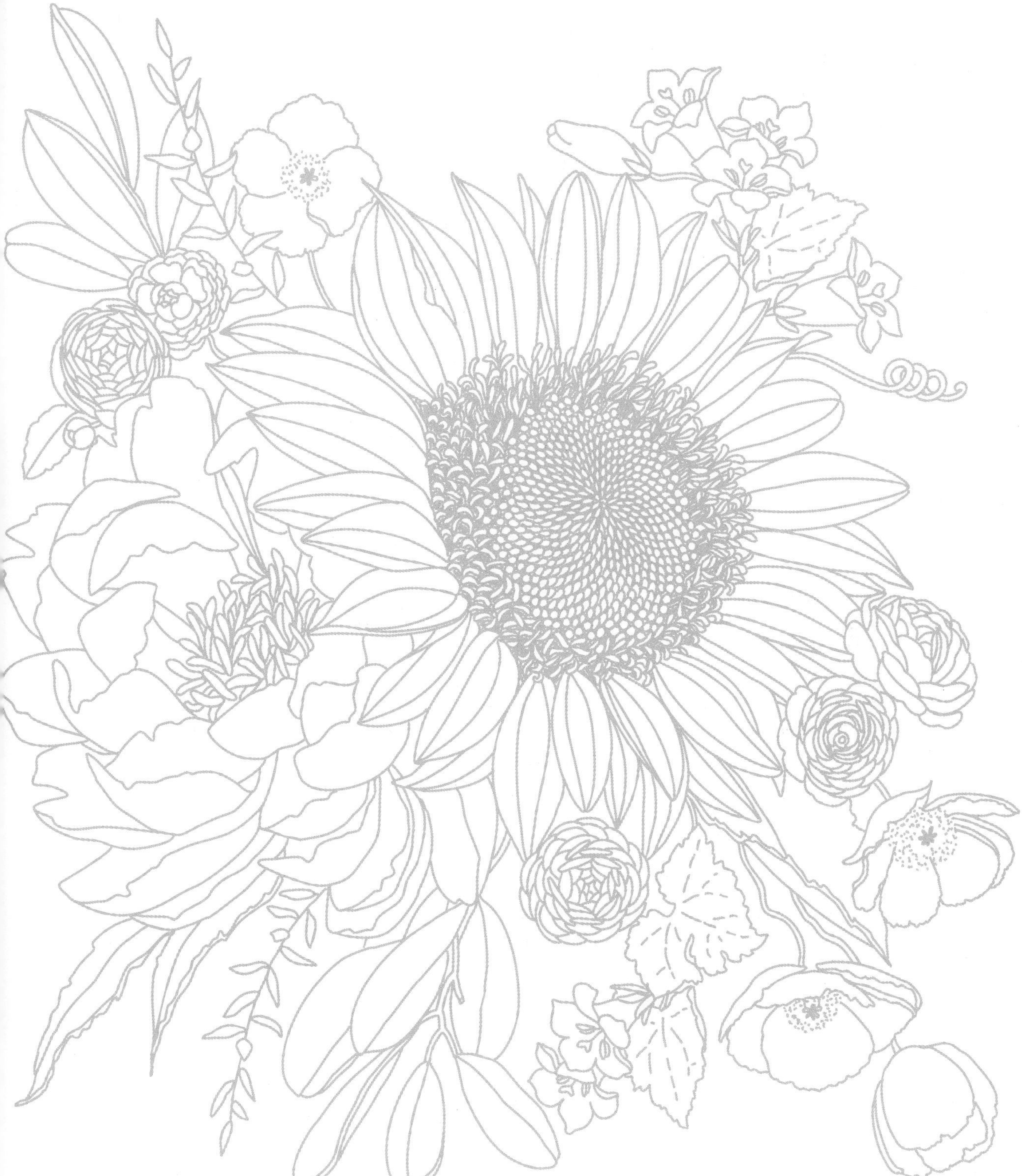

A BRIDE'S BOUQUET

When I think of a bridal bouquet, this combination appears in my mind. This is the perfect blend of romance and elegance with an essential pinch of playful and wild elements.

I love the contrast of textures between the lush petals of the anemones and the dense, spiky body of Veronica spiced with the dark spots of the berries. The even texture of the hydrangea serves as the perfect canvas and makes the other elements glow even brighter.

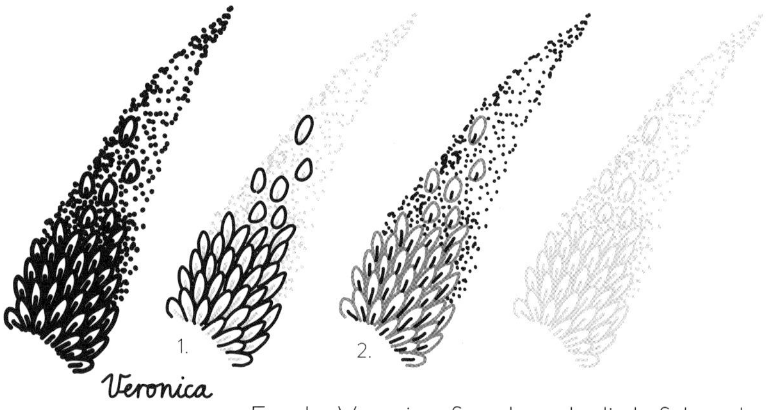

For the Veronica, first draw the little fish scales starting at the bottom, then add a stroke in their centers. To define the shape of the spike, put down some dots at the edge. I like to add a shadow on one side of the spike to make it pop. Draw more dots on that particular side.

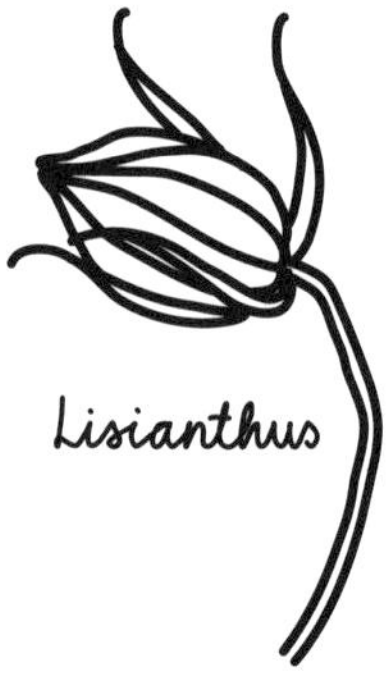

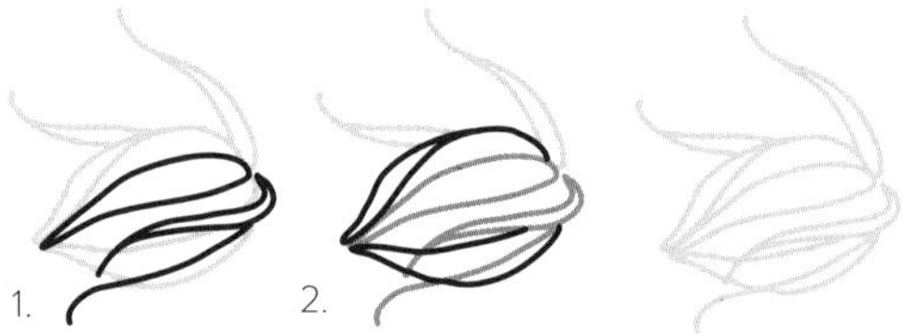

The long spiky leaves make this lisianthus bud stand out. Make sure to draw them nice and curvy.

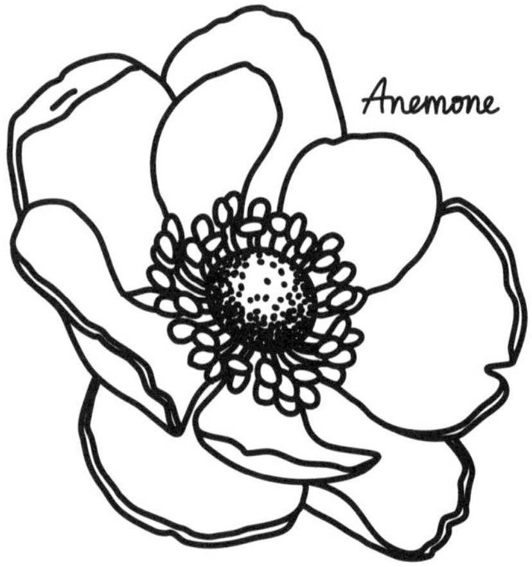

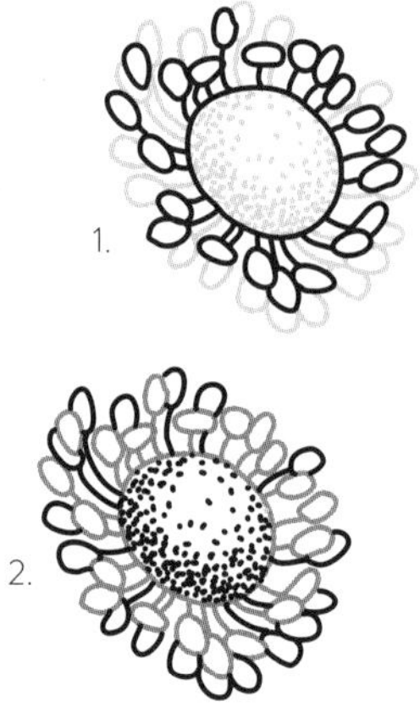

For the anemone, start by outlining the anthers. Pay attention to the order of the layers. Some are fully visible and others are partially hidden. The stamens are laid down evenly and have a slight curve. When stippling the central dome, I like to move my pen in a spiral motion around the dome and leave the highlight area white.

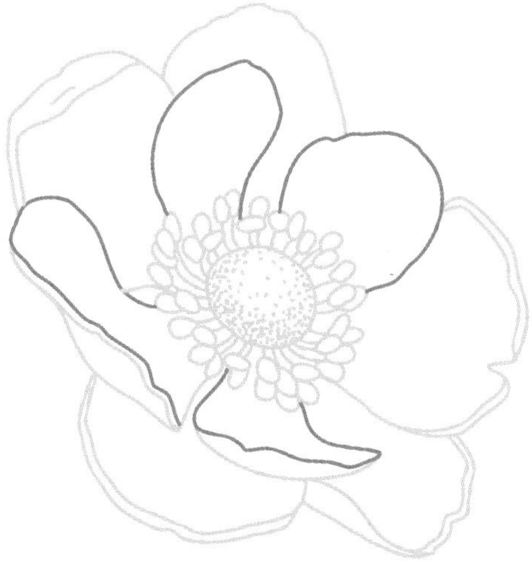

HOW TO DRAW: Hydrangea (page 36; Hydrangea), Leaves (page 52; Branches)

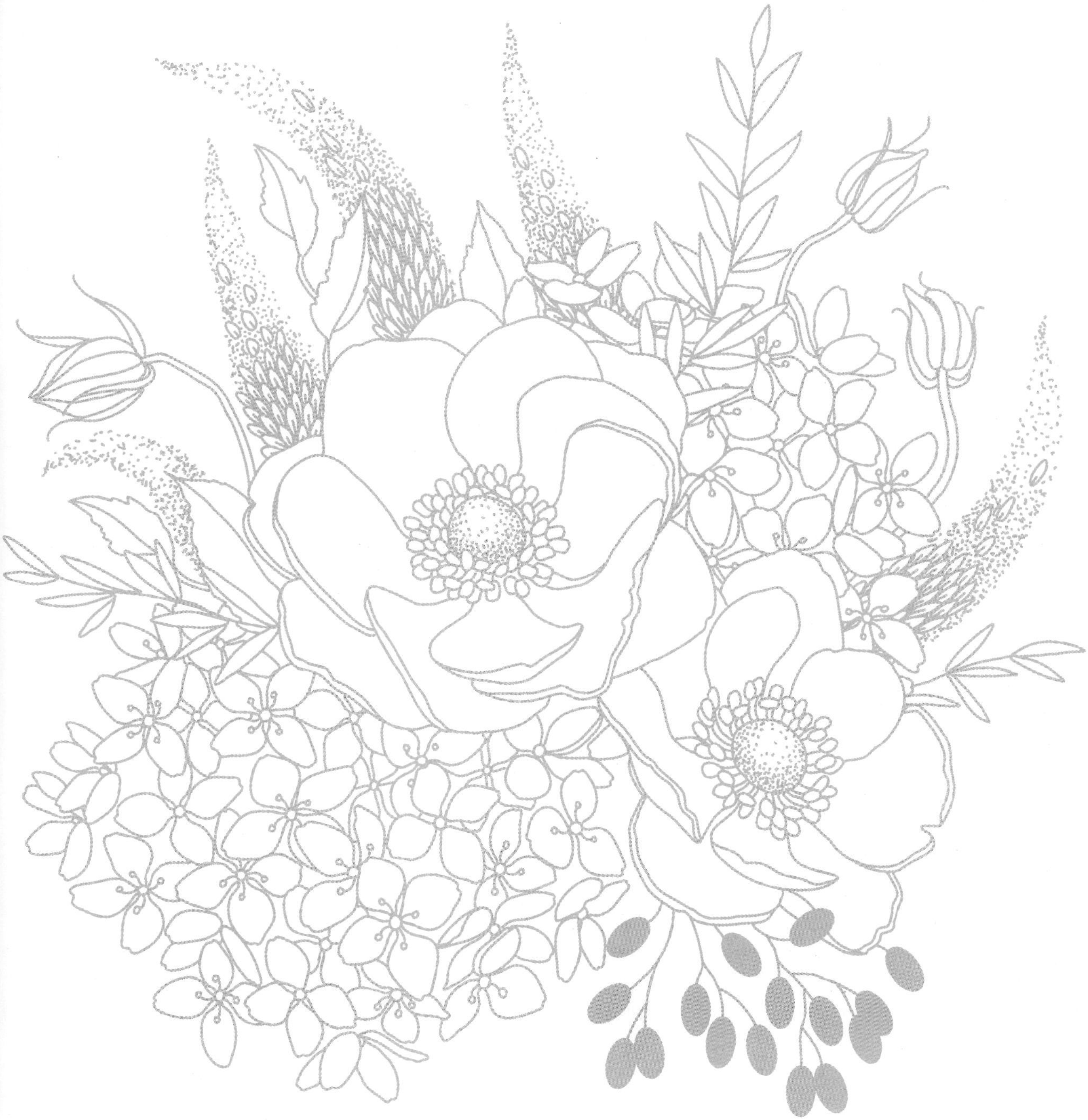

WILDFLOWER MEADOW

When I started my illustrator Instagram page, I needed topics to draw. I used to go for a walk and pick all kinds of wild-growing flowers and grasses that we usually don't even recognize. This served as a constant source of subject matter and inspired my all-time favorite illustrations. Organizing delicate wildflowers in beautiful compositions is pure joy. I hope working on this illustration will take you on a joyride too.

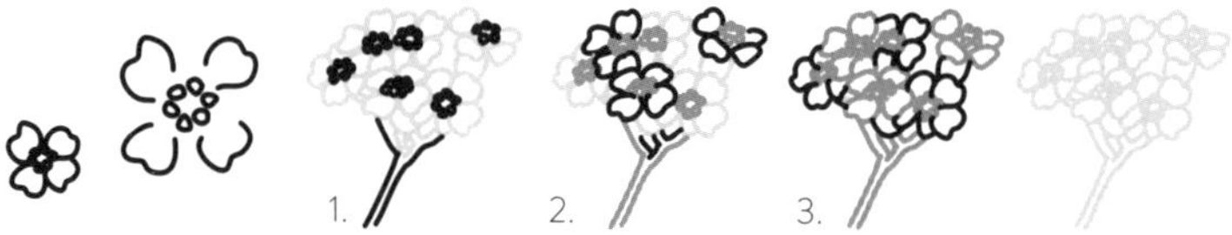

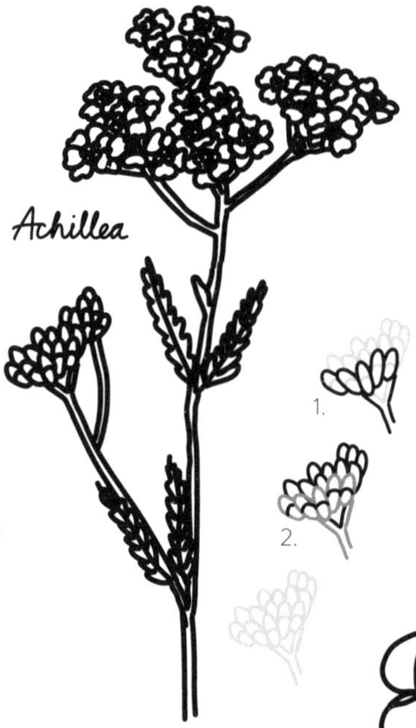

The densely spaced petals of achillea might be intimidating at first, but the flower is built up from very basic shapes: tiny dots in the middle and four heart-shaped petals. Layer them on top of each other. The leaves are also highly detailed. Draw the vein first, then use a single wiggly stroke to draw the edges. The buds are made up of ovals split by a half circle.

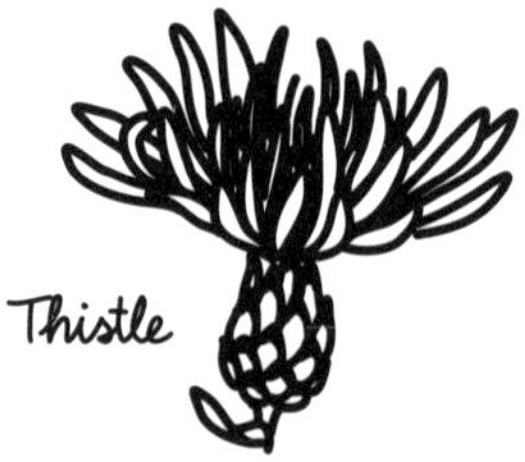

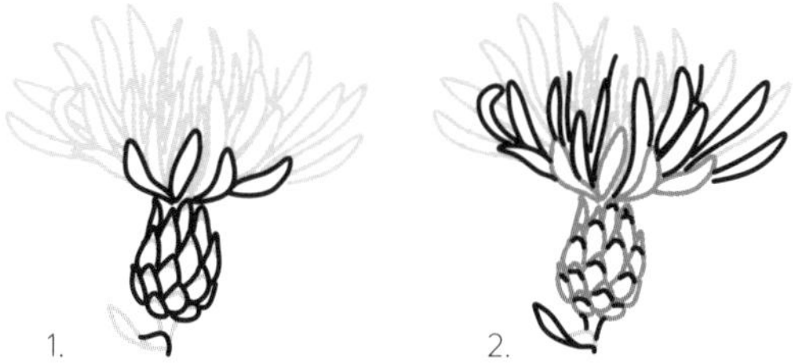

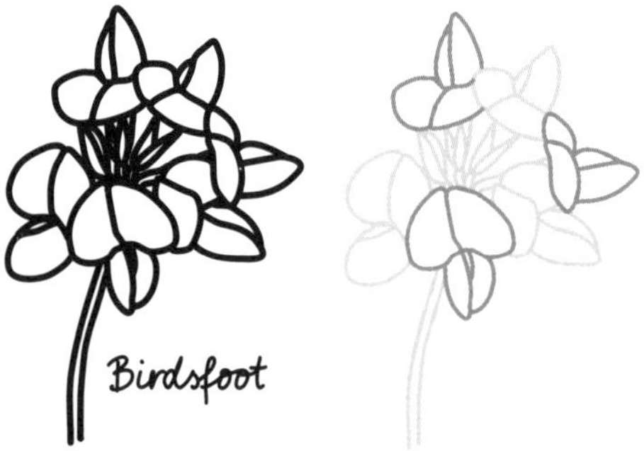

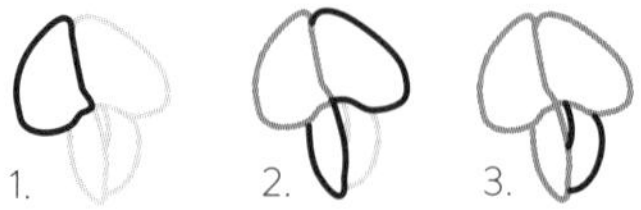

Thistle has a delicate pom-pom of beautiful narrow petals. Start to draw some in the foreground, then add some spikier ones in the middle. The base has scales, similar to the scales of a fish. Adding an extra stroke on the top of each little leaf on the base brings this illustration to the next level.

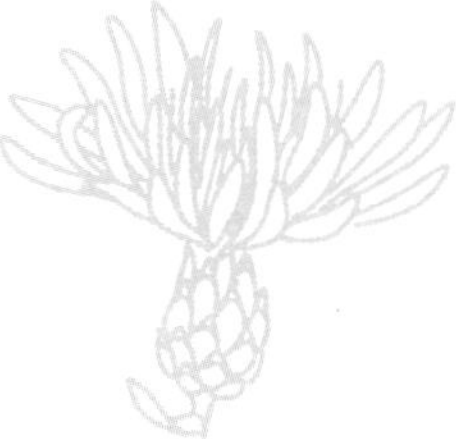

I love to draw the unique birdsfoot flower. The four lip-like petals are really simple and look stunning. As they are growing in a bunch, they form a ring around the stems. Start by drawing the petals, then move on to the stamens.

HOW TO DRAW: Poppy (page 22; Poppy), Daisy (page 70; Roadside Treasures)

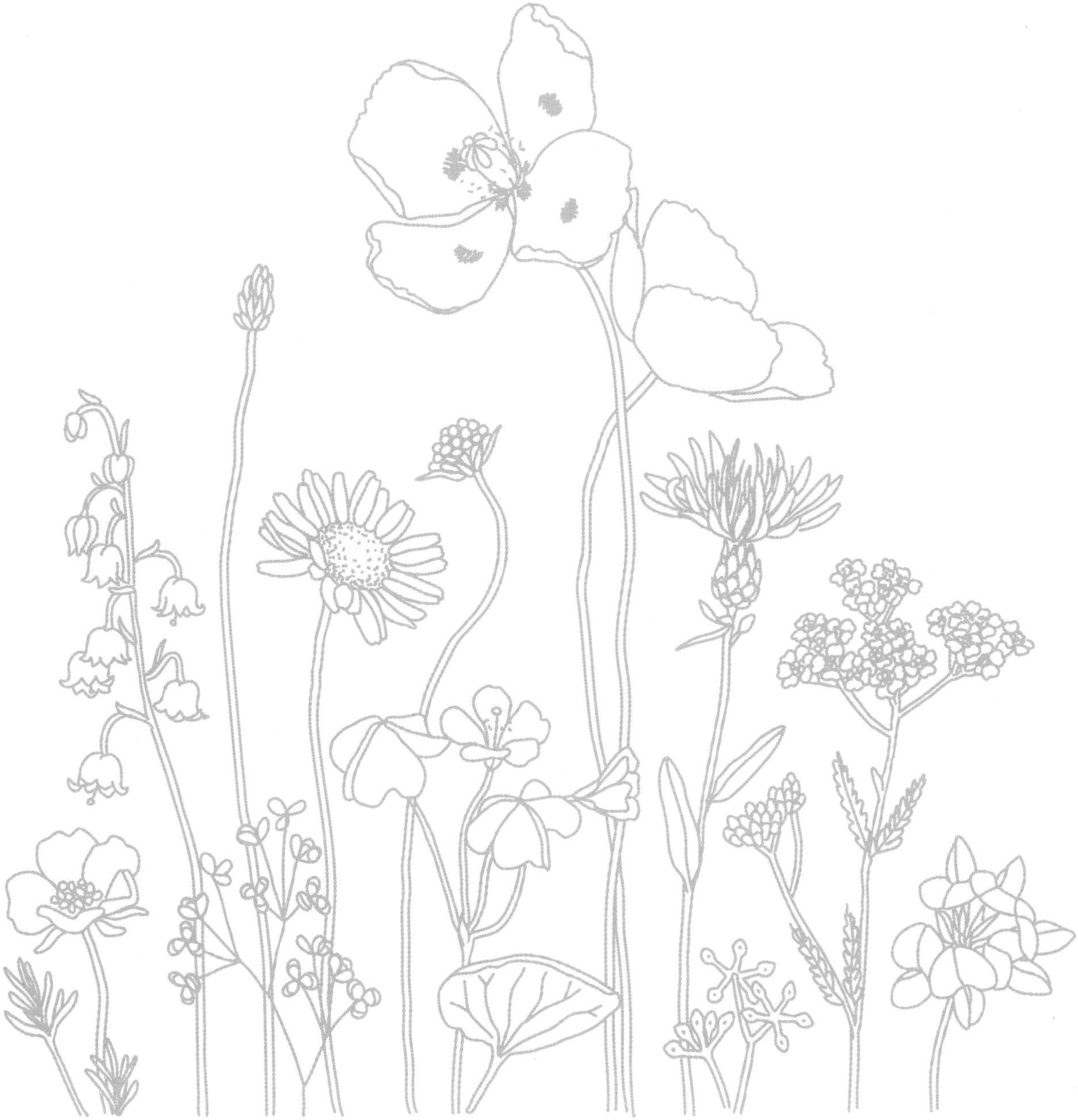

WINTER WONDERLAND

A few years ago I saw a Christmas wreath with a beautiful white magnolia. I had never seen this flower in such a festive vibe, but I immediately held it in my heart. The soft curves of the huge porcelain-like petals are pure elegance. The spiky pine branches and small berries serve as a perfect background and make this elegance shine really bright.

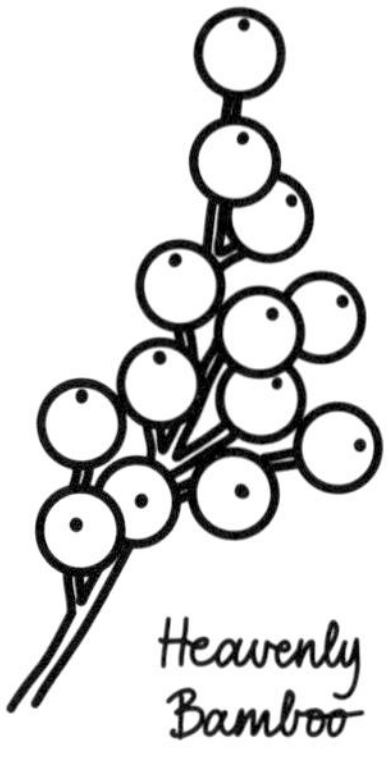

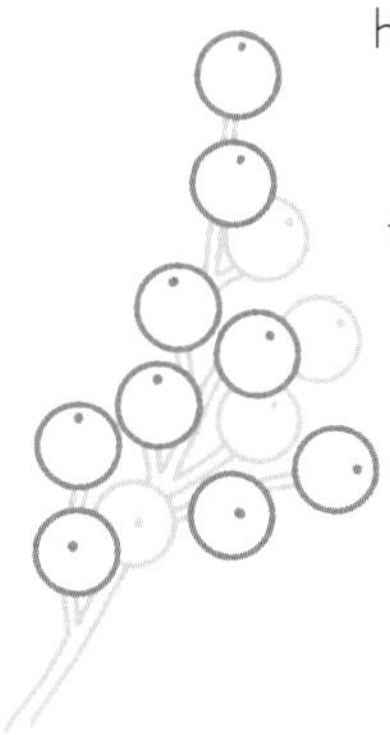

Drawing stunning berries, like this heavenly bamboo, comprises two things: beautiful circles and layering. Start with the fully visible berries, then add the rest in the background.

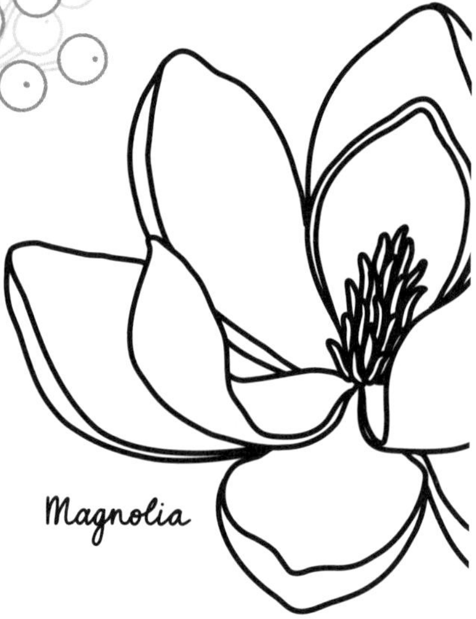

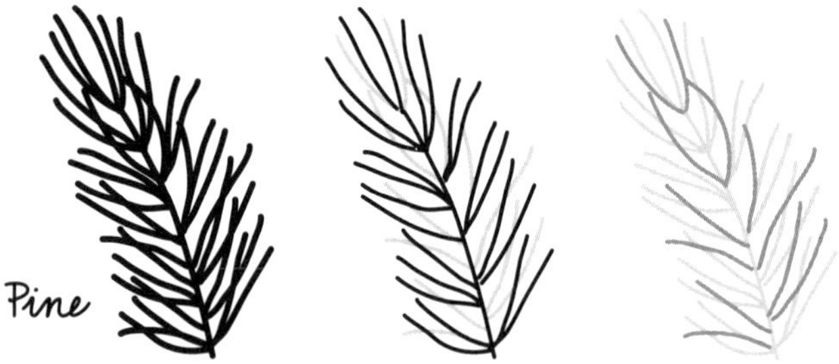

For the pine, start with the central line, so you know where to stop the needles. Then draw single or double needles on each side. The trick to achieving a realistic result is to place needles crossing on top. This makes the real magic.

To illustrate the body of the magnolia petals, draw double edges. Draw the two front petals first, then move on to the center, which is built up from slightly bent spikes in several layers. Start at the bottom and move upward.

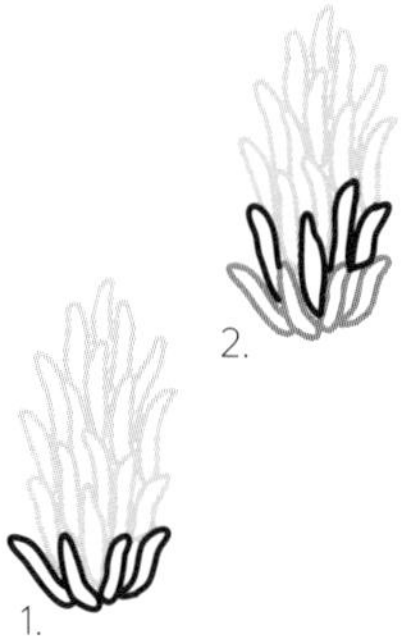

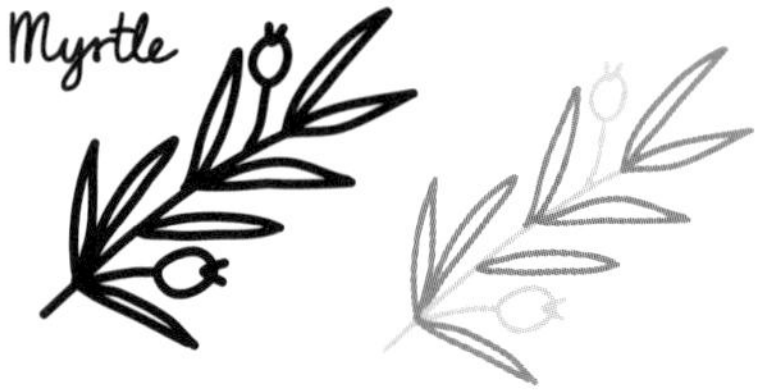

For the myrtle, use the opposite order. First draw the needles, then the branch. Add the berries at the end.

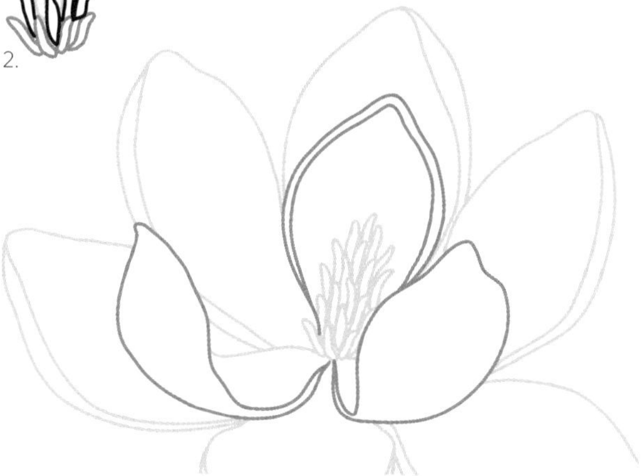

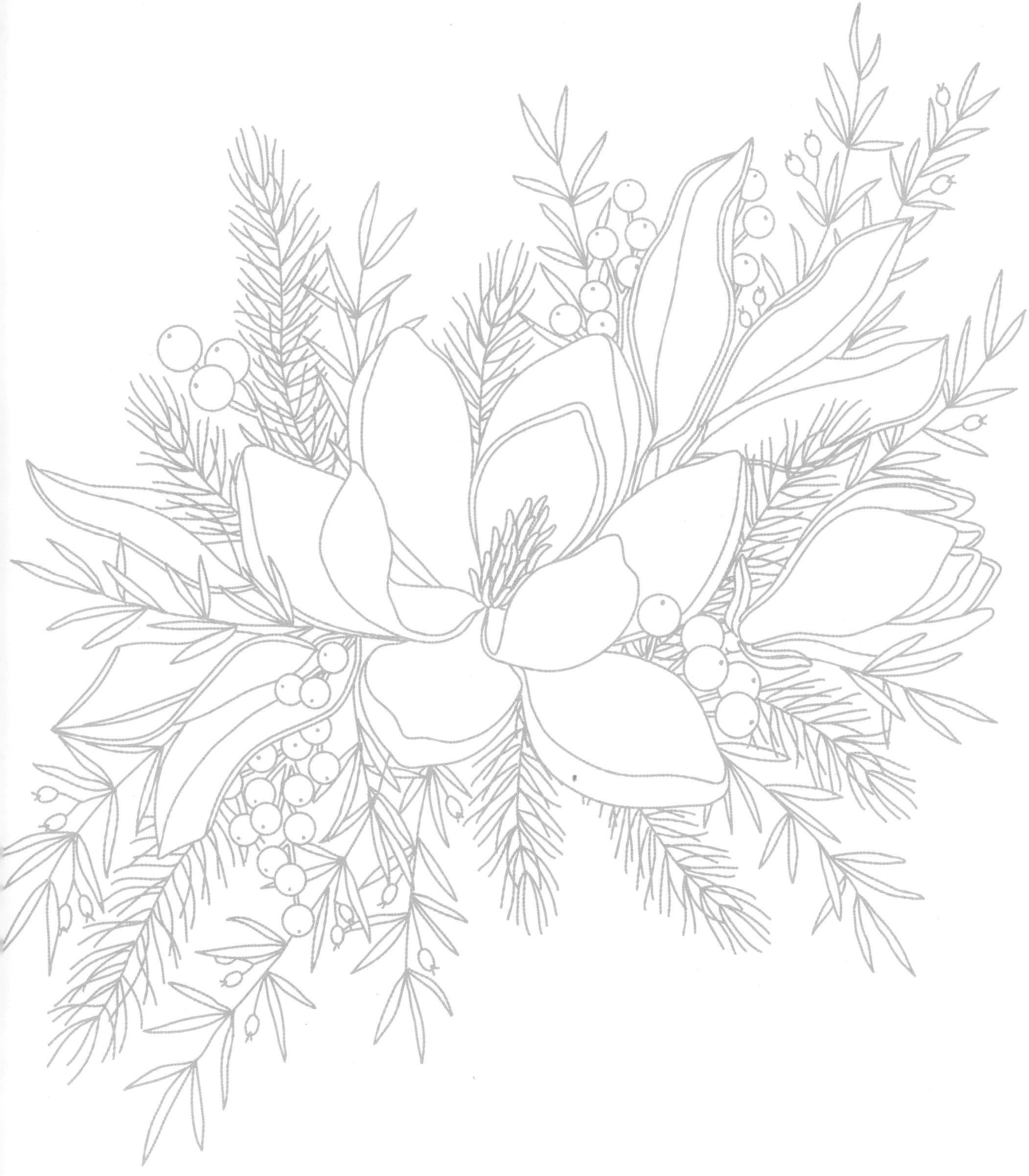

GREETINGS FROM AUSTRALIA

Protea, waxflower and kangaroo paw are spectacular Australian flowers. And they look stunning together. The dense spiky petals of protea, the round porcelain-like petals of waxflower and the long narrow stem of the kangaroo paw bring a variety of textures and sizes.

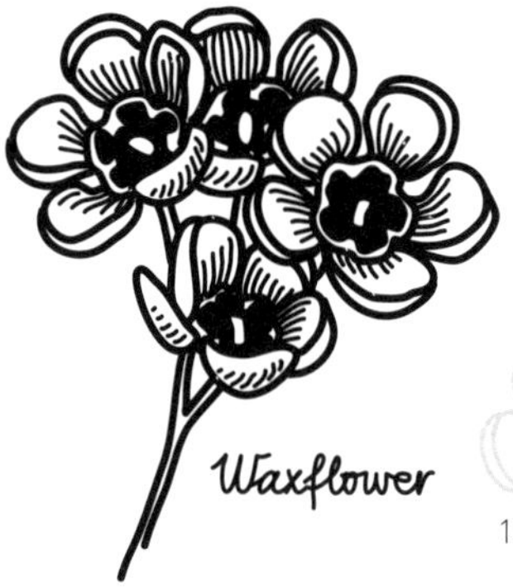

For the waxflower, start with the loose flower shape in the center. Draw a parallel line around it. Color in the center shape, making sure to leave a light spot in the middle. The petals are round and have a double edge from almost every angle.

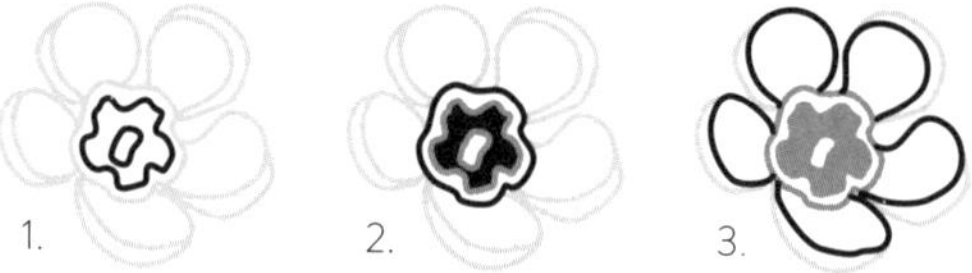

Get lost in the diverse shapes of this edgy illustration. This drawing has a lot of shading, but relax and take a deep breath—you got this! Create your own shading for this illustration in the Shading Templates on page 113.

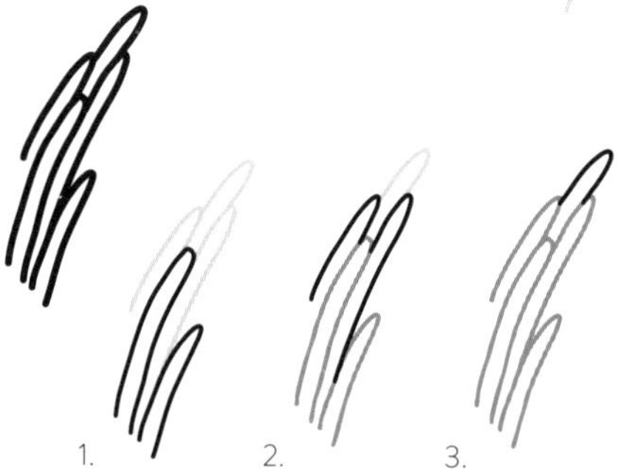

The dense inner world of protea might look intimidating, but it is all built up from upside-down U shapes with long legs. The key is the direction. They are all pointing toward the center point. The petals are densely shaded. Apply an extra layer of shading at the darkest areas.

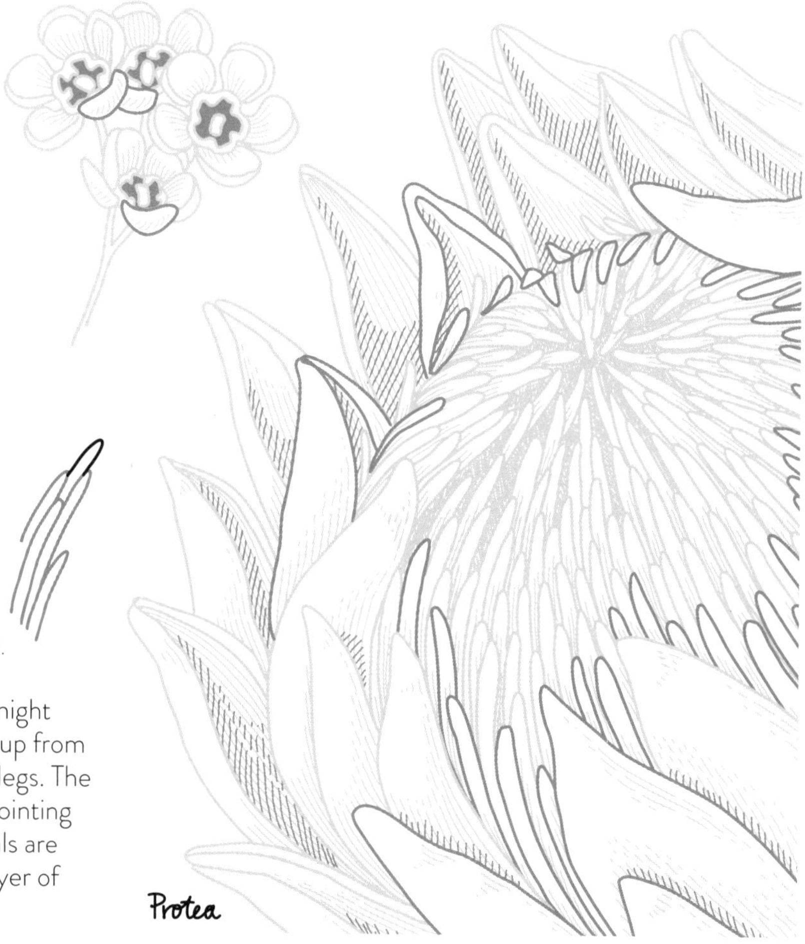

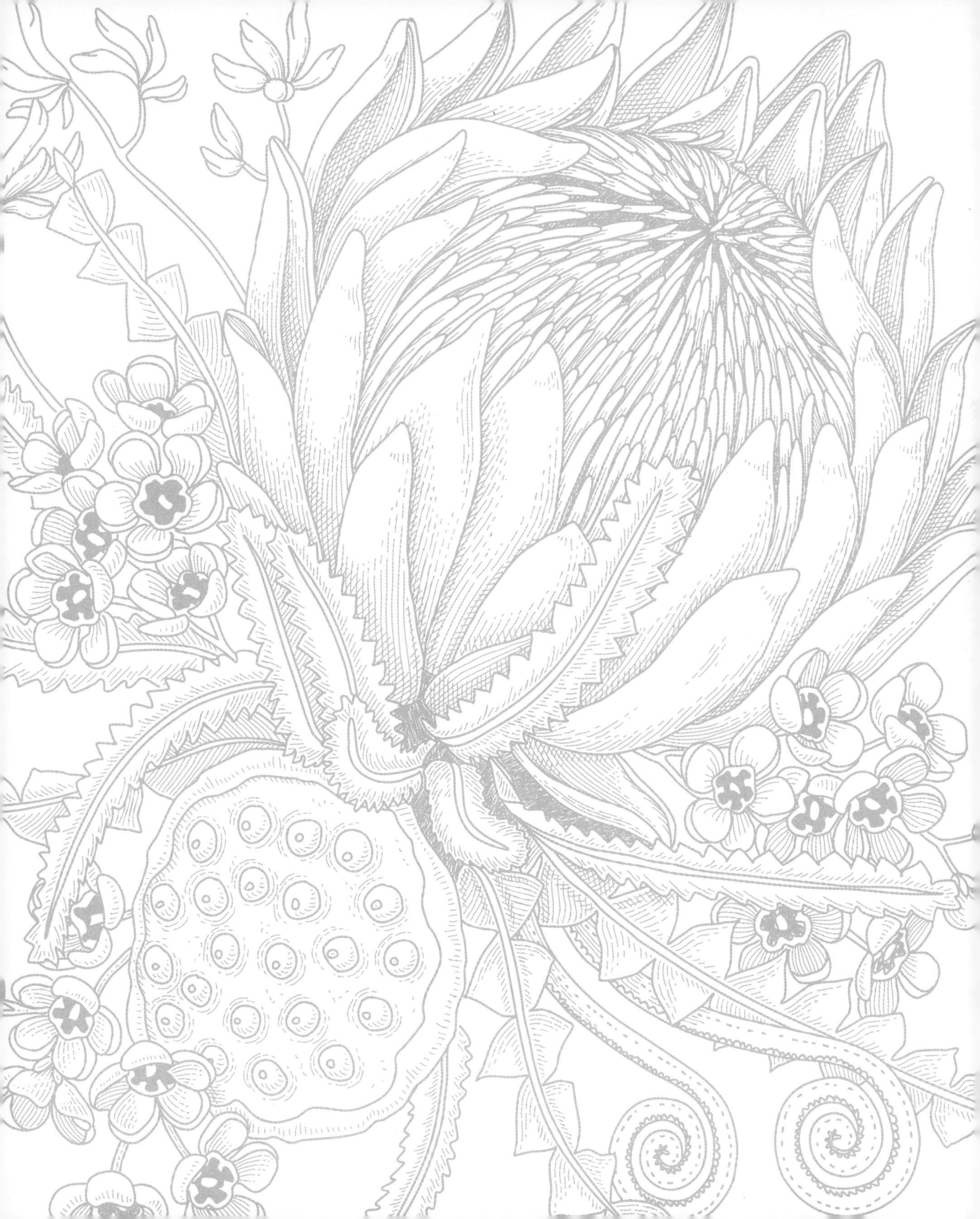

PICKED FROM THE GARDEN

My parents have a little garden, and I have already shown you some of my mom's beautiful blooms. But my father also has his hands dirty every weekend taking good care of his favorites. I decided to dedicate an illustration to these beauties too, including the fast-growing kiwi tree, with its showy flowers, and the shy mimosa plant, which closes its leaves if you touch them. I mixed in my personal favorite of their garden: the dreamy Japanese anemone.

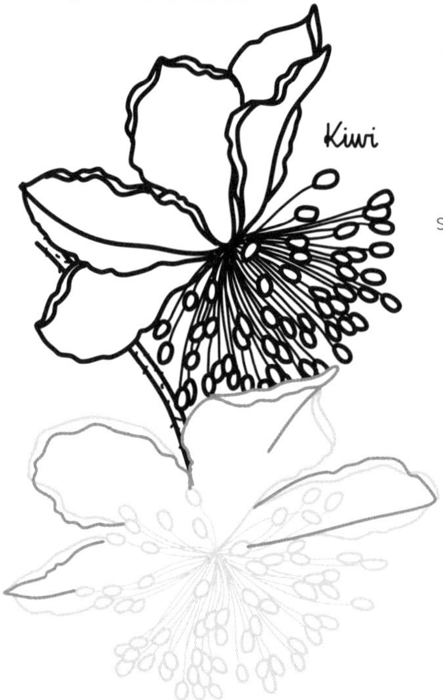

Kiwi blossom has tons of anthers. I wanted to highlight them, so I drew as many details as possible. First draw the anthers that are fully visible—they are oval. Then add the ones in the background. Use a thin pen to draw the stems. Make sure they all start at the same point in the center.

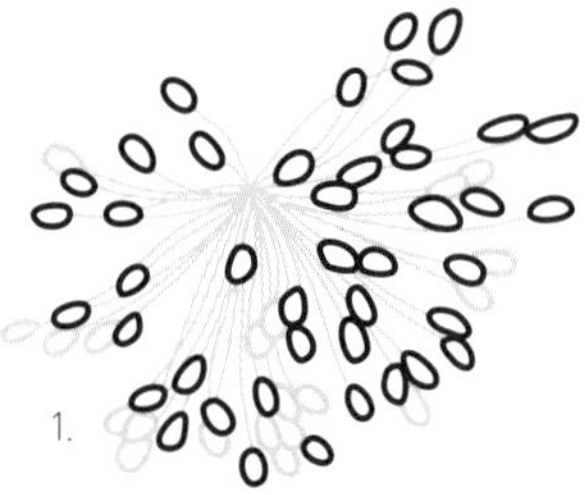

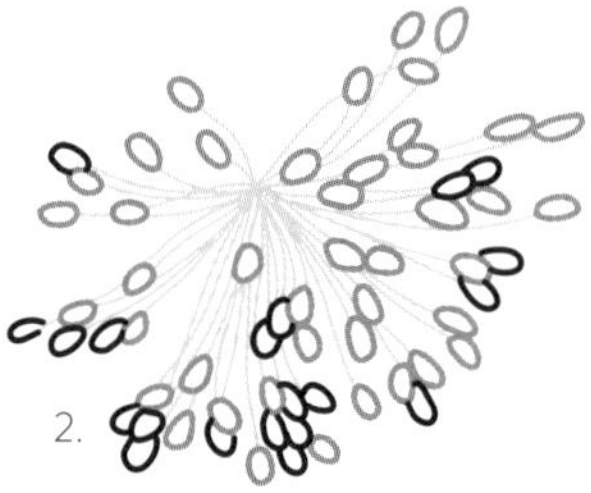

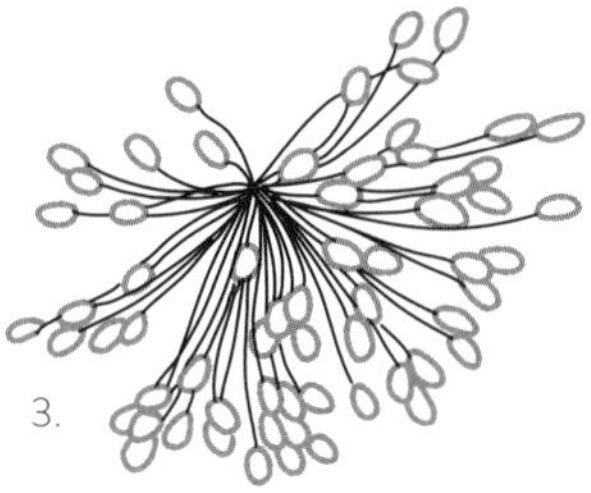

Mimosa closes its leaves when touched. This illustration shows the open state. Draw the branch first to know where to start the cigar-shaped leaves.

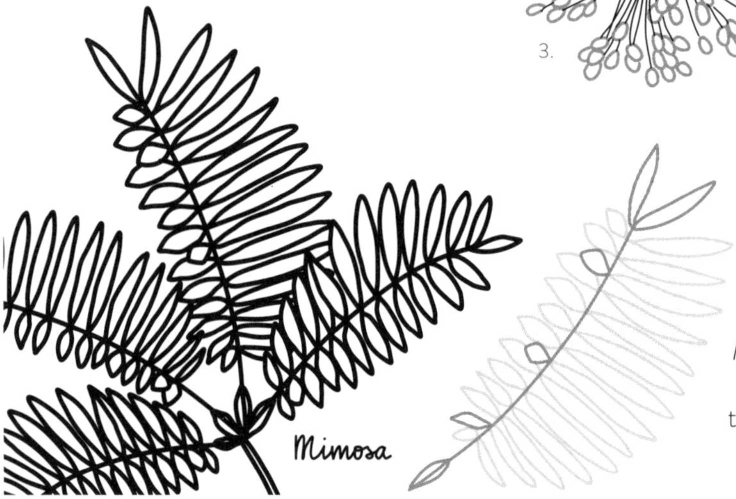

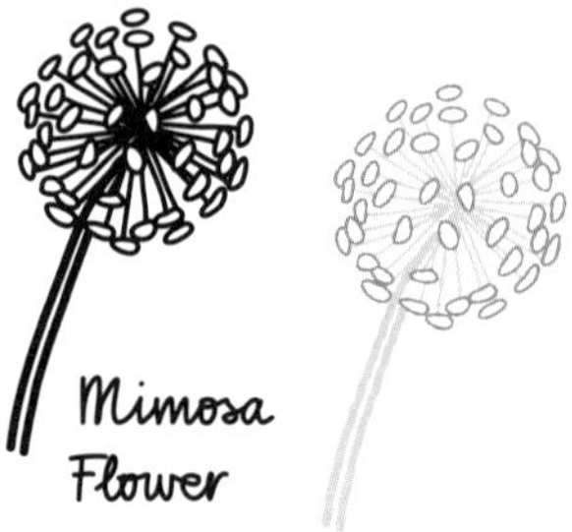

Mimosa flower is a little universe similar to the center of the kiwi flower. Use a thin pen to draw the small oval dots first and then add the stems in the background.

HOW TO DRAW: Anemone (page 26; Anemone), Tendrils (page 30; Passionflower)

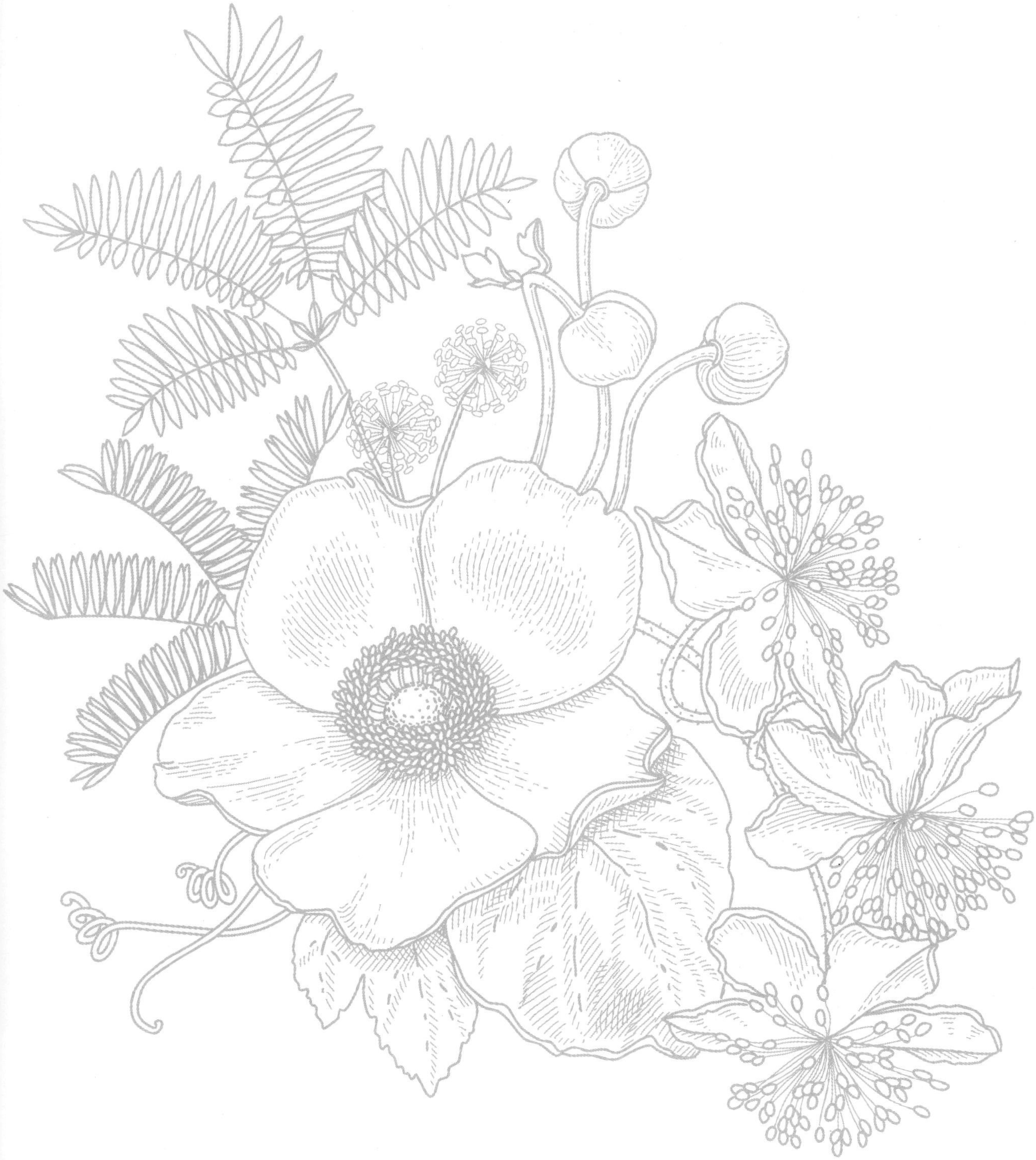

FOXGLOVE WITH PEONY

The suburbs I live in have manicured gardens and lawns, but there are still some old-world "peasant" gardens full of beautiful flowers in the summer, where such treasures as the breathtaking foxglove can be seen. This bouquet brings back the scent of these richly blooming gardens for me.

Prepare a cup of tea with a fruity-flowery scent and get lost in the details of this project.

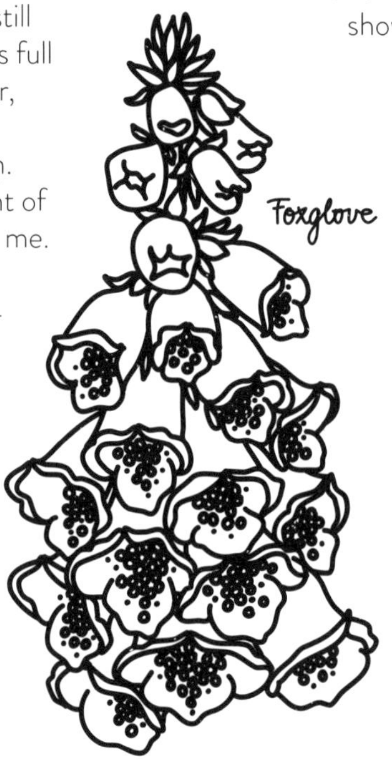

Each flower on the foxglove stem has two upper lips and a lower petal to start with. The body is mostly hidden, but the playful pattern of circles on the inside of the petals steals the show anyway. Draw them just big enough to leave a bit of white in the centers.

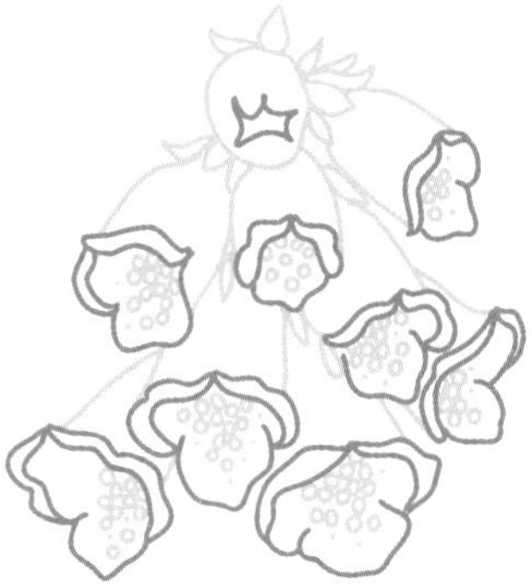

Start drawing the peony at its center. Build up a dense wreath of simple oval anthers around the three pistils. The edges of the petals are rich in divots, which hold a lot of information about the shape. Grab a thin pen and add the evenly spaced shading lines. Add an extra layer of shading to deepen the shadows.

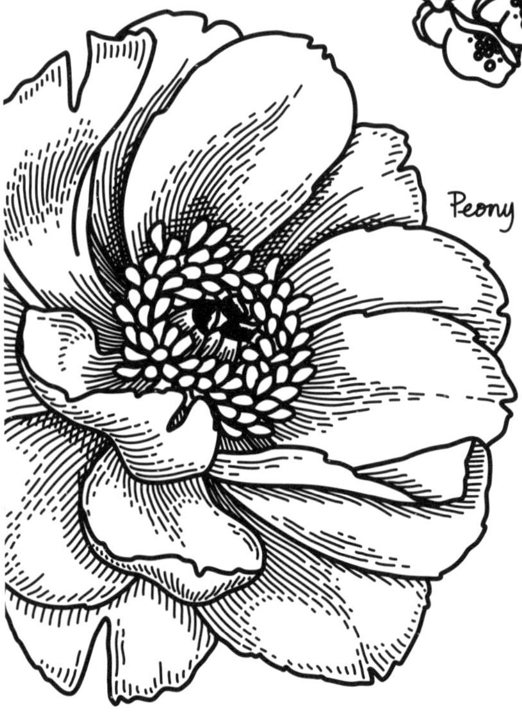

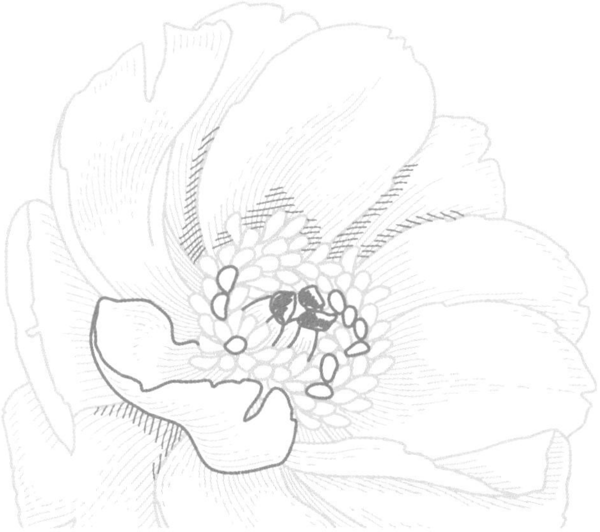

HOW TO DRAW: Grasses (page 82; Quince Blossom), Chrysanthemum (page 46; Chrysanthemum), Leaves (page 52; Branches)

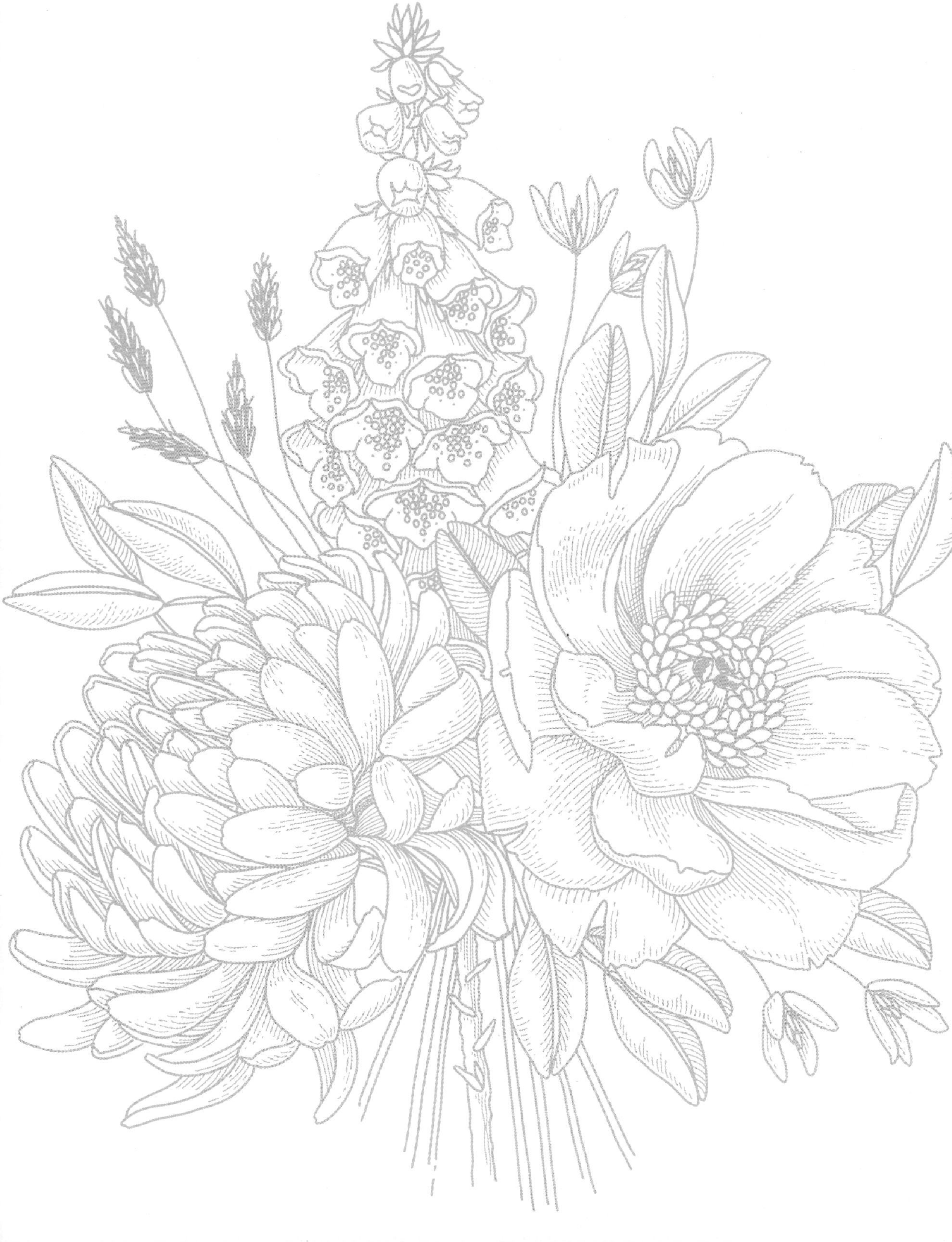

PURE BEAUTY

This illustration defines pure beauty for me—as you can tell by the name. If you asked me what kind of bouquet I would like to get, this would be my answer. It is full of texture, luscious petals, interesting details and unique flowers. I hope this will be as fun to trace as it was to design. Create your own shading for this illustration in the Shading Templates on page 115.

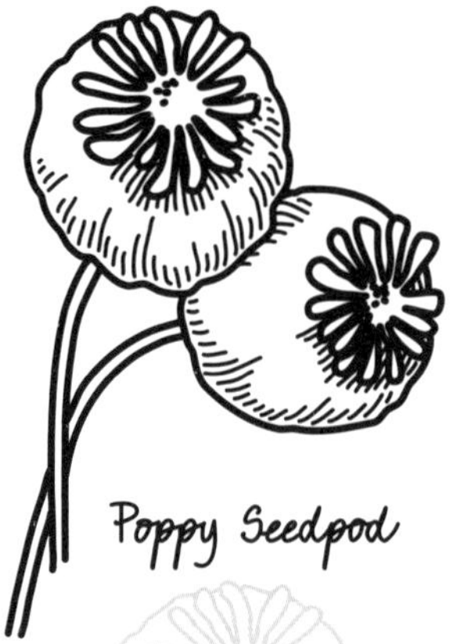

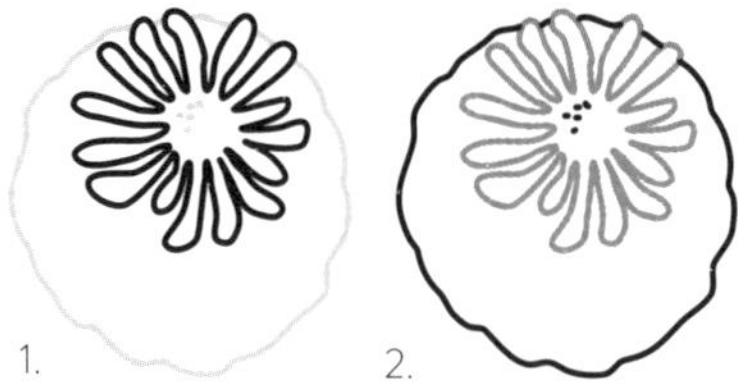

Poppy seedpods are the hero of this composition. Start with the beautiful organic shape similar to a star. Add a few dots in the upper left corner of the star, and draw the body last with a slightly uneven line.

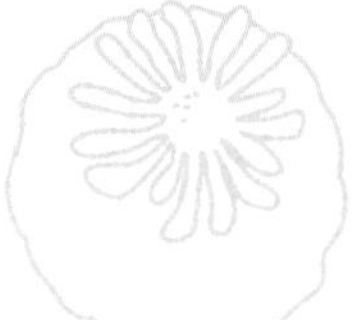

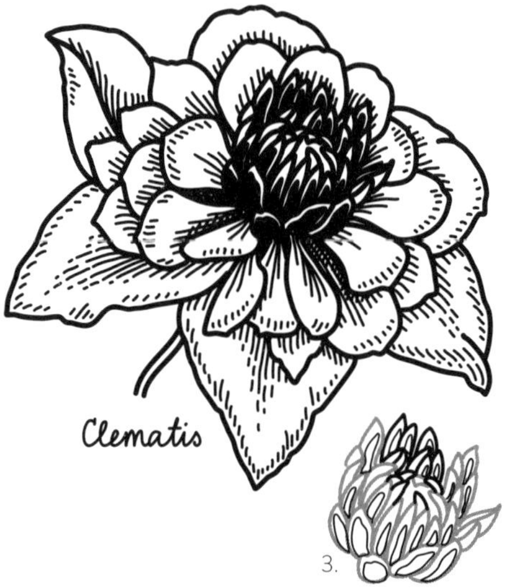

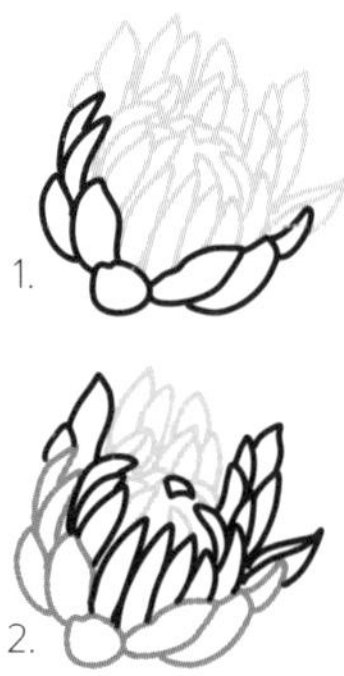

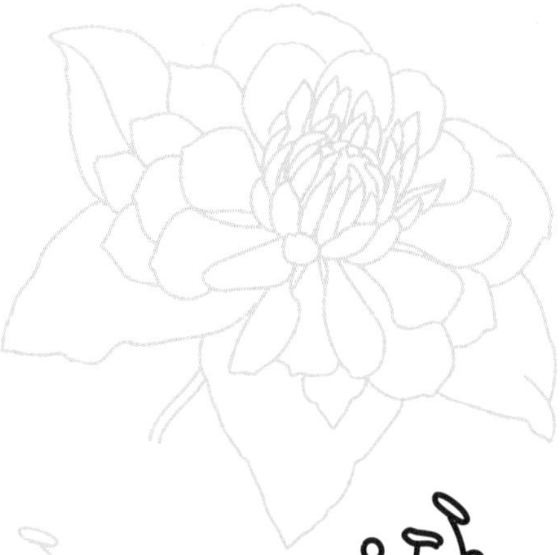

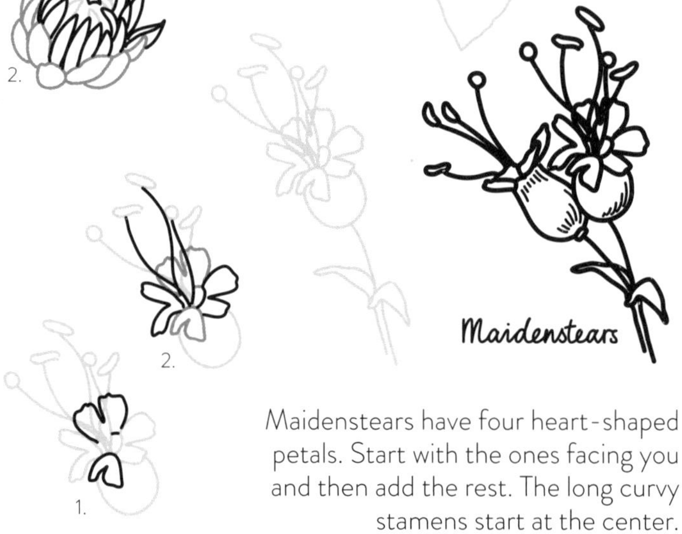

The center of this clematis is still a bit closed. Start with the front petals of the closed part and tuck the next layer of petals behind them. The black pattern on these petals starts with a thin outline, leaving a narrow white gap along the edges. Fill in the pattern carefully. Then move on to the larger open petals.

Maidenstears have four heart-shaped petals. Start with the ones facing you and then add the rest. The long curvy stamens start at the center.

HOW TO DRAW: Zinnia (page 32; Zinnia), Phlox (page 68; Camellia Garden), Anemone (page 26; Anemone), Peony (page 24; Peony)

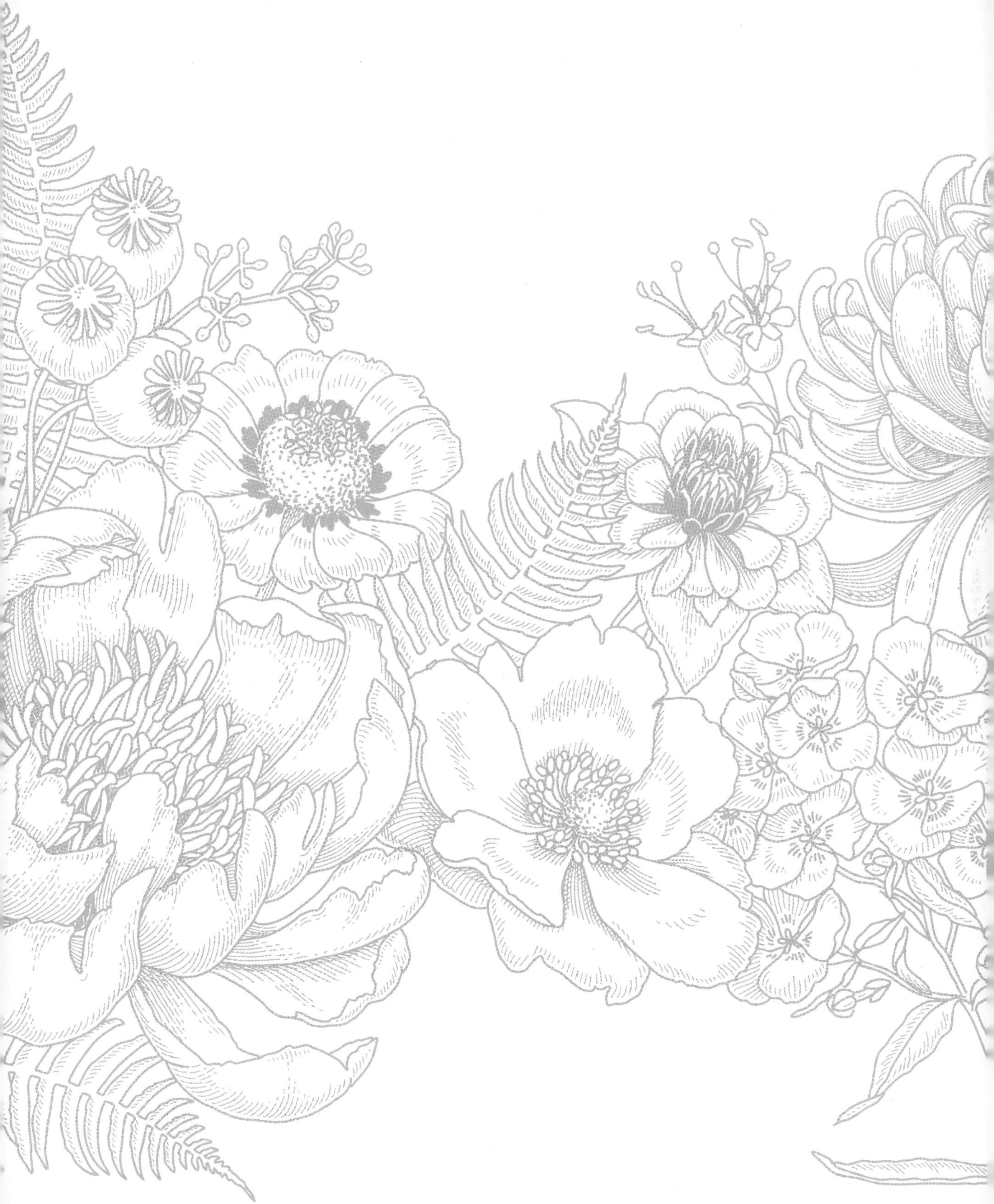

SHOWERED IN PURPLE

Clematis and fritillaria, also known as checkered lily, are being rediscovered as cut flowers. They elevate the look of any arrangement with their unique character. The simplicity of clematis's petals is beautifully balanced by the full bunch of stamens in its center. I love the playfully bending stems, which add motion to any composition. Fritillaria's checkered pattern is a brilliant eye-catcher. Create your own shading for this illustration in the Shading Templates on page 117.

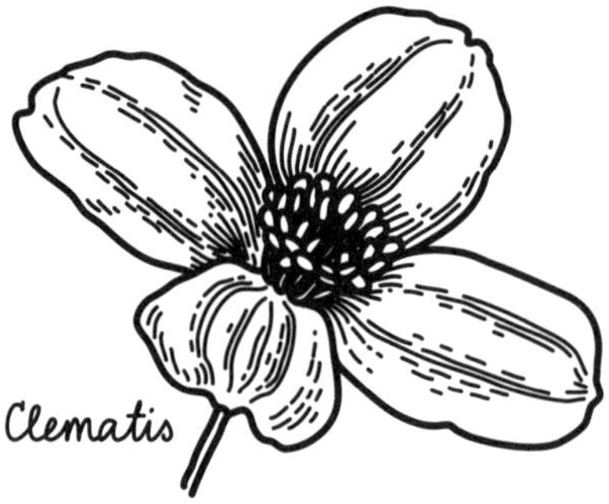
Clematis

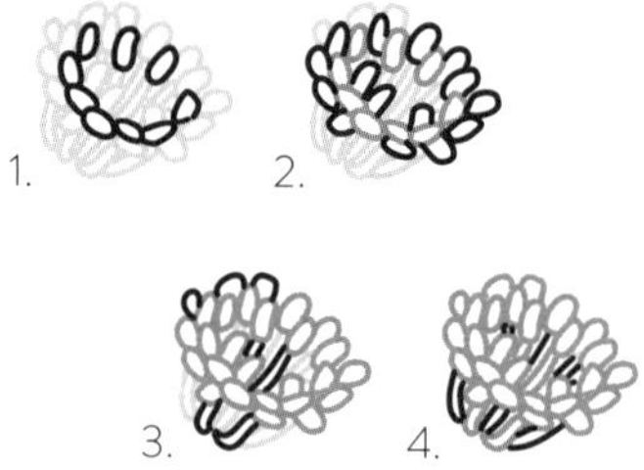

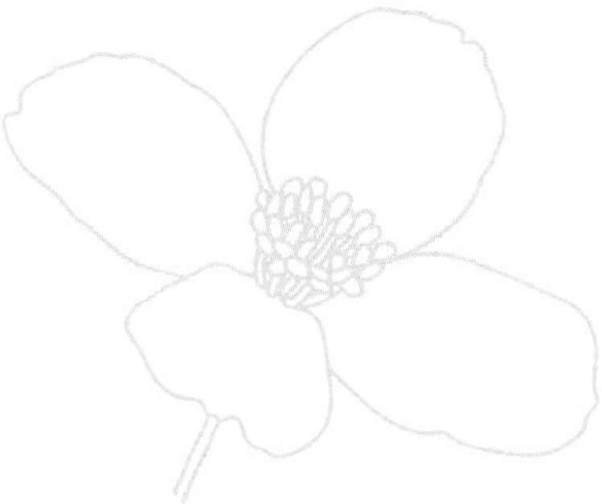

For the clematis, the trick to having a full bunch of stamens is layering. Draw in the wreath of anthers, starting with the ones that are fully visible, and tuck some behind them. The same is key for the stems. Draw two in the front, making sure you leave a tiny gap between the two parallel lines. Then fill in the rest. When you are finished with the outlines of the petals, switch to a thinner pen for the shading.

Start the fritillaria with its outlines (see a little tip for the anthers to the right). Then switch to a thinner pen and draw in the checkered pattern. To create the illusion of a bent surface on the petals, change the direction of the strokes in the checkered pattern.

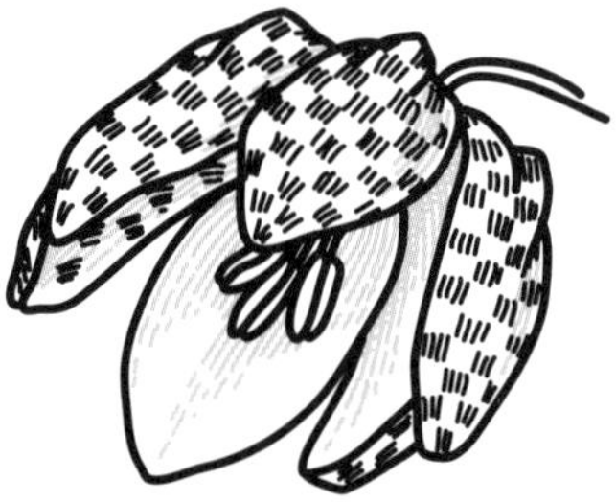
Fritillaria

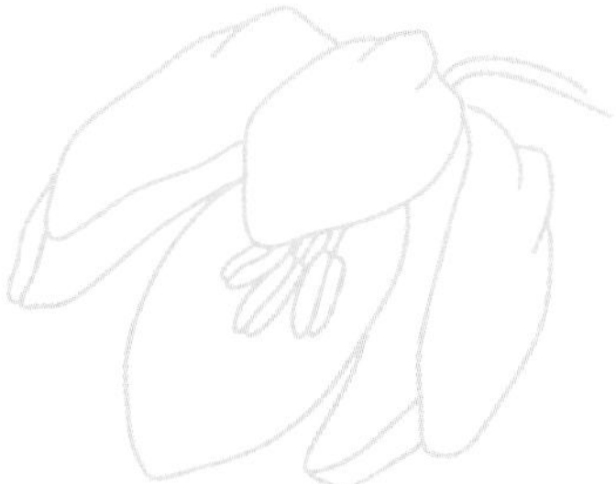

The next step is shading. A few shading lines are enough on the checkered surface. To create depth on the inside, add an extra layer of shading lines where the petals overlap.

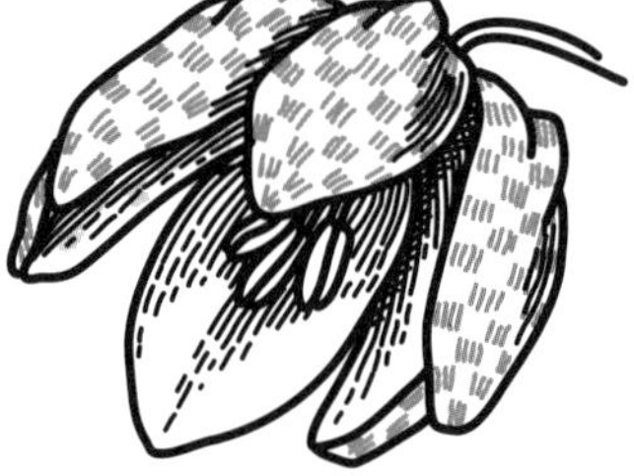

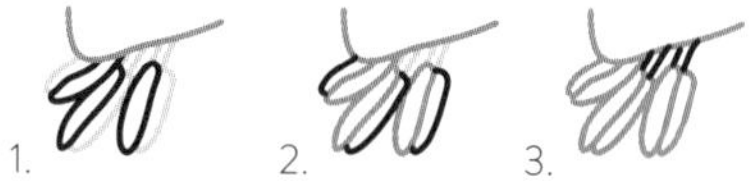

HOW TO DRAW: Peony (page 24; Peony)

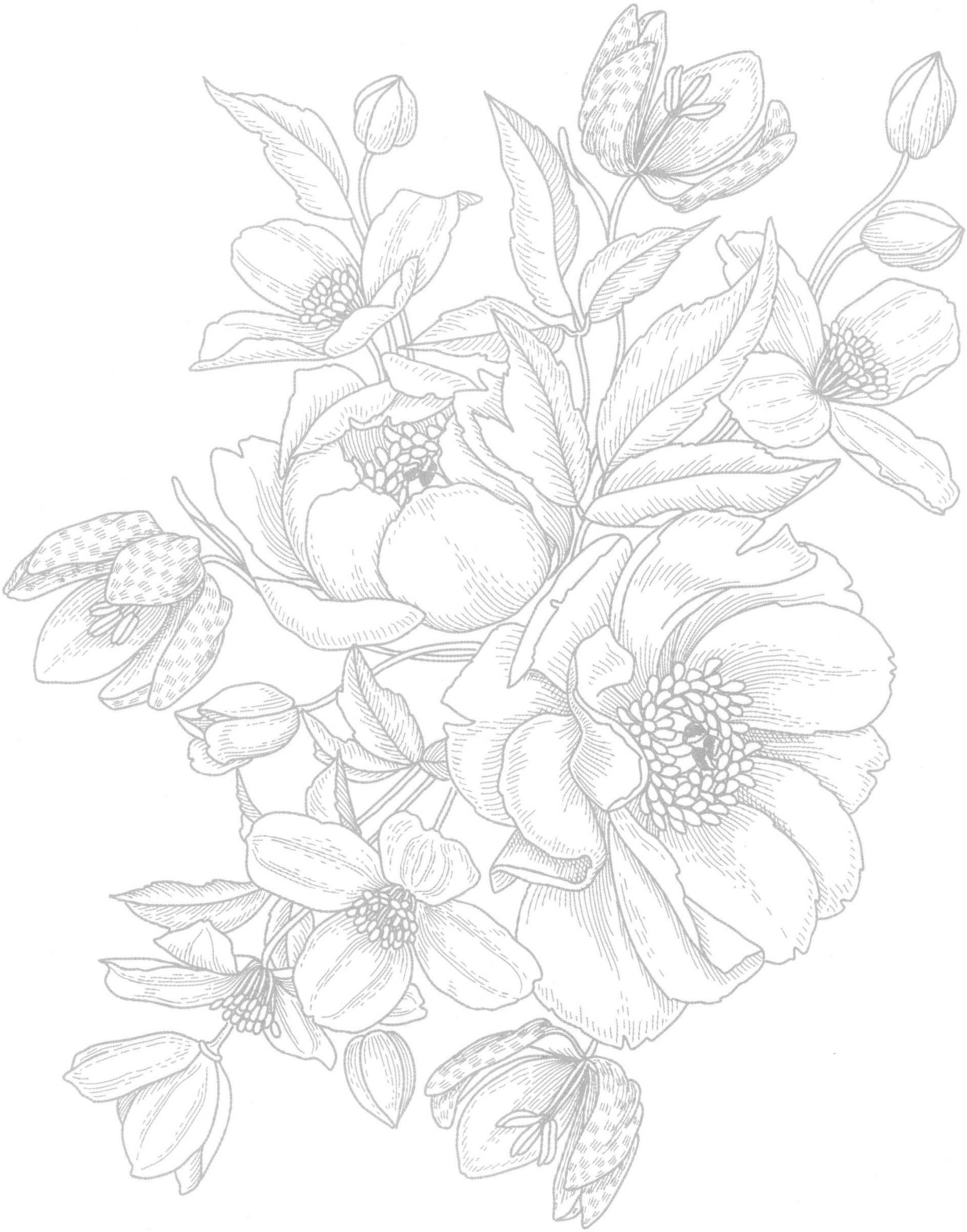

CHAMOMILE

Chamomile reminds me of my childhood because my mom made me chamomile tea when I had a sore throat. Although it really helped, I hated the taste of it as a child. Now as an adult, I have a better relationship with chamomile tea as well as green olives (which I also hated). I think drawing these lovely flowers helped with that. The center is really simple and for the petals, the more random the better. Create your own shading for this illustration in the Shading Templates on page 119.

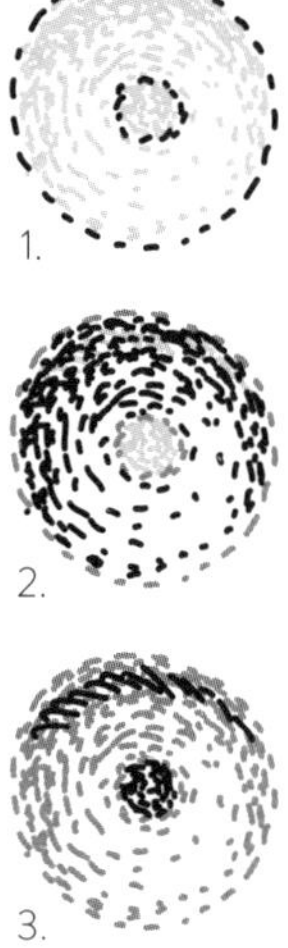

For the chamomile, start by stippling the edge of the center dome. To make it three-dimensional, make the dots denser on one side. For even more depth, you can also add extra shading lines toward the top. Finally, add the little hole in the center. For the petals, pay attention to the layers. Draw the fully visible ones first. Then add the lower ones.

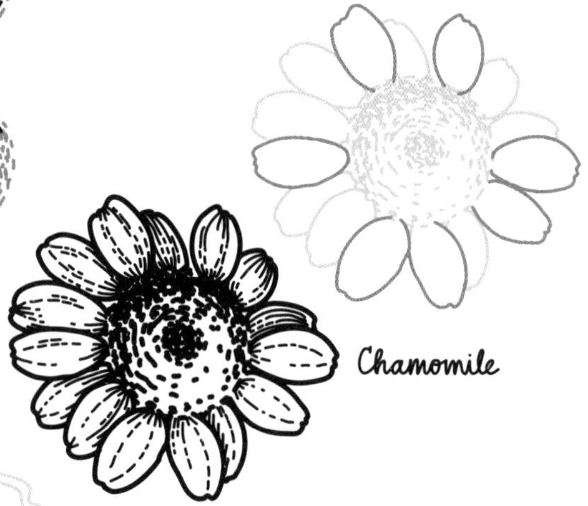

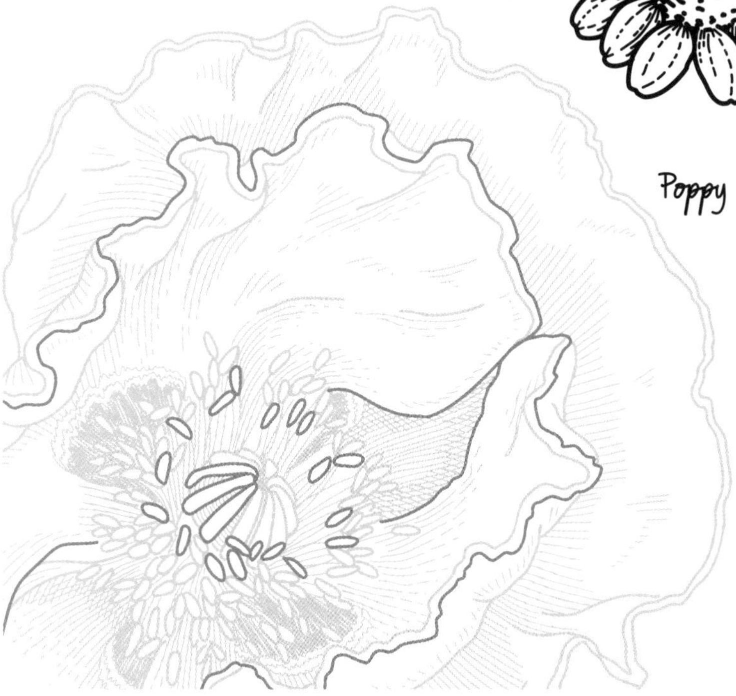

This poppy has lots of details. Start with the center, paying attention to the layers of the anthers. The black pattern on the inner petals makes this illustration pop. Draw the outline for the pattern first and then fill it in. The edges of the petals are heavily detailed too. This illustrates the natural folds of the flower.

Grab a thin pen, and start tracing the shading lines. I recommend choosing shorter sections to start. Add an extra layer of shading where needed.

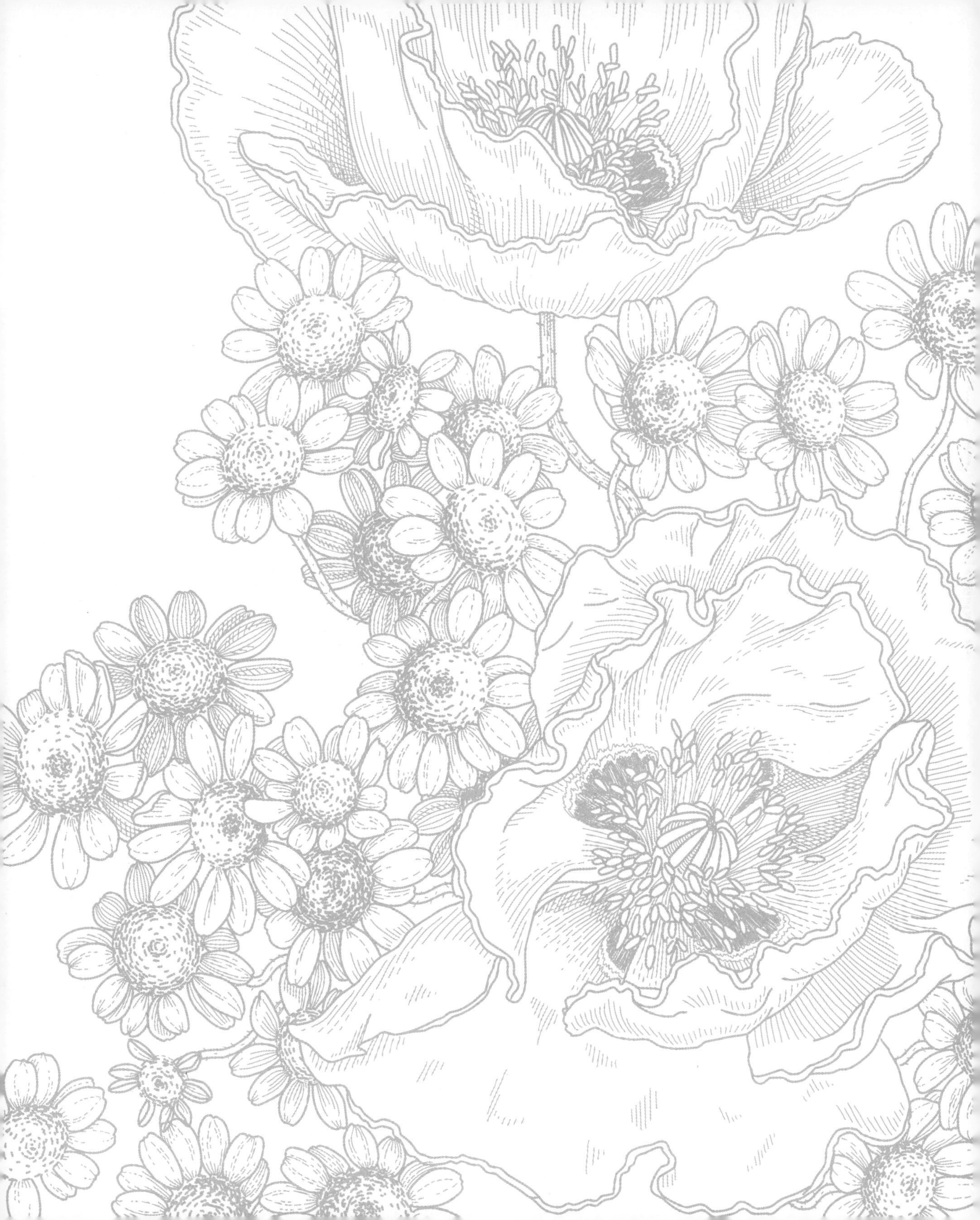

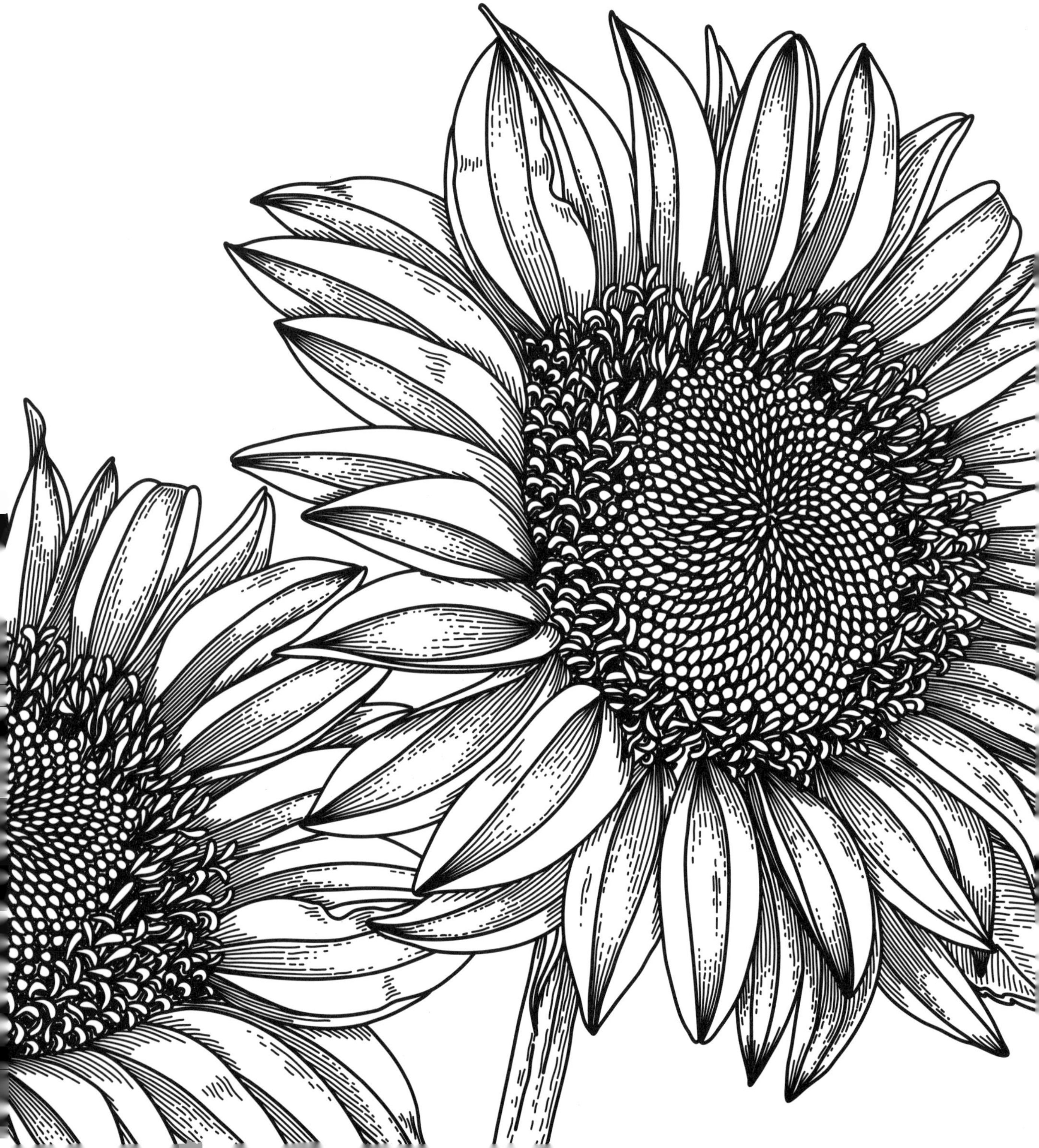

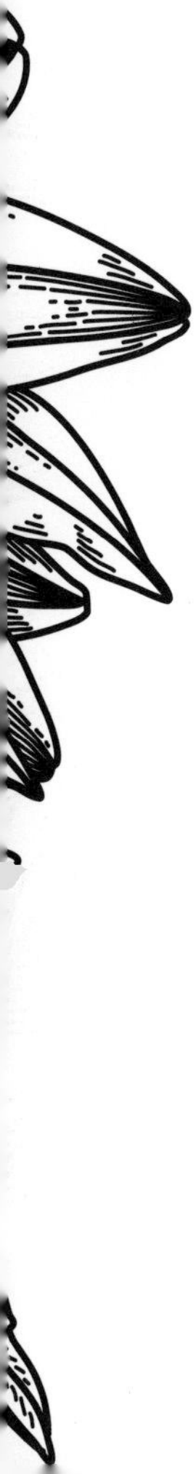

SHADING TEMPLATES

These templates are here for you to practice your shading. Create your own version of the shading, either based on the original illustration or your own imagination. Remember, you can always go back to the Basics chapter (page 14) for a refresher on the technique, and if you are still feeling unsure, grab a pencil and practice with that. Take advantage of having these outlines pre-drawn for you. You don't have to worry about proportions or composition. Just enjoy the best part of the process—the pen moving on the paper.

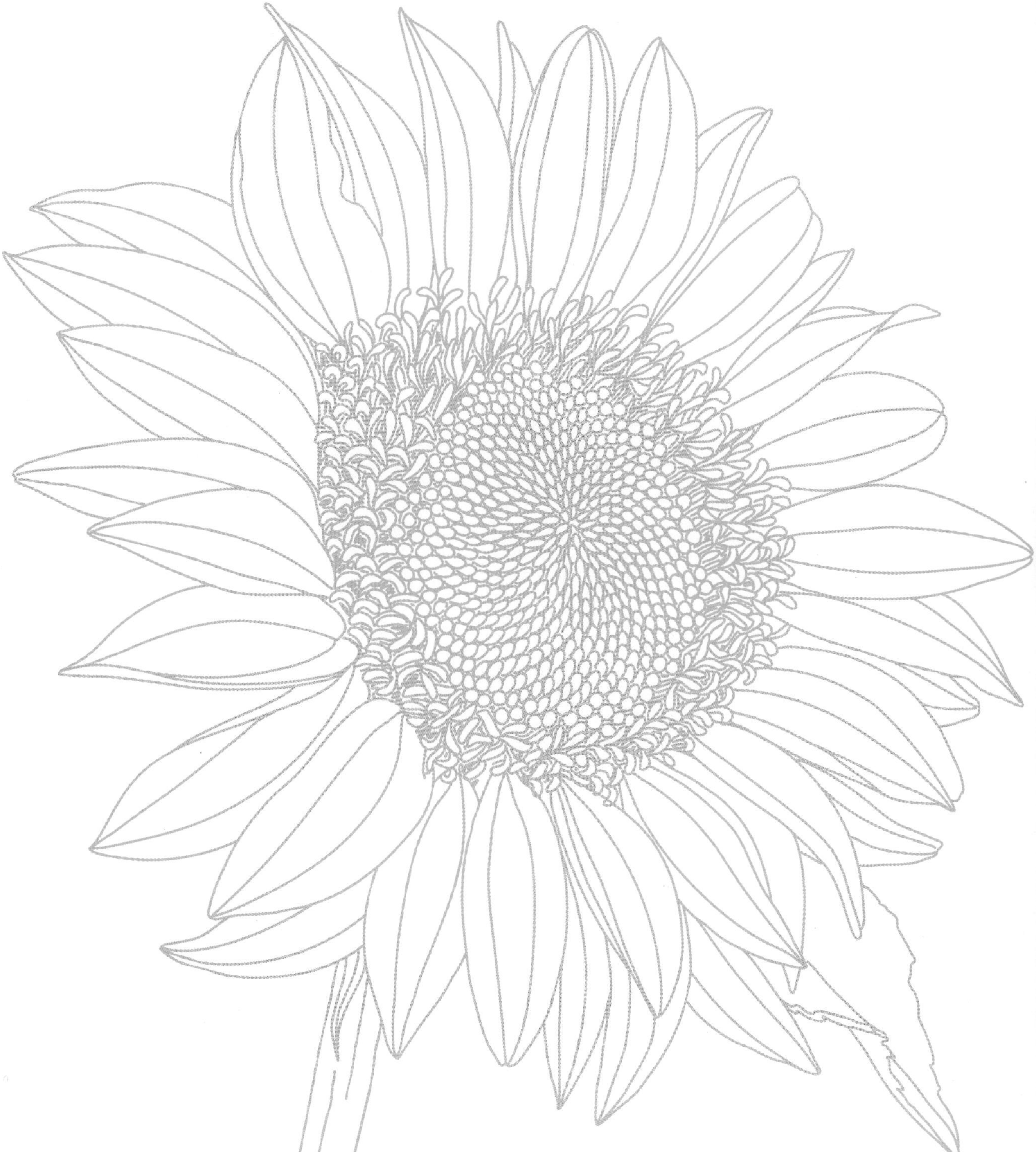

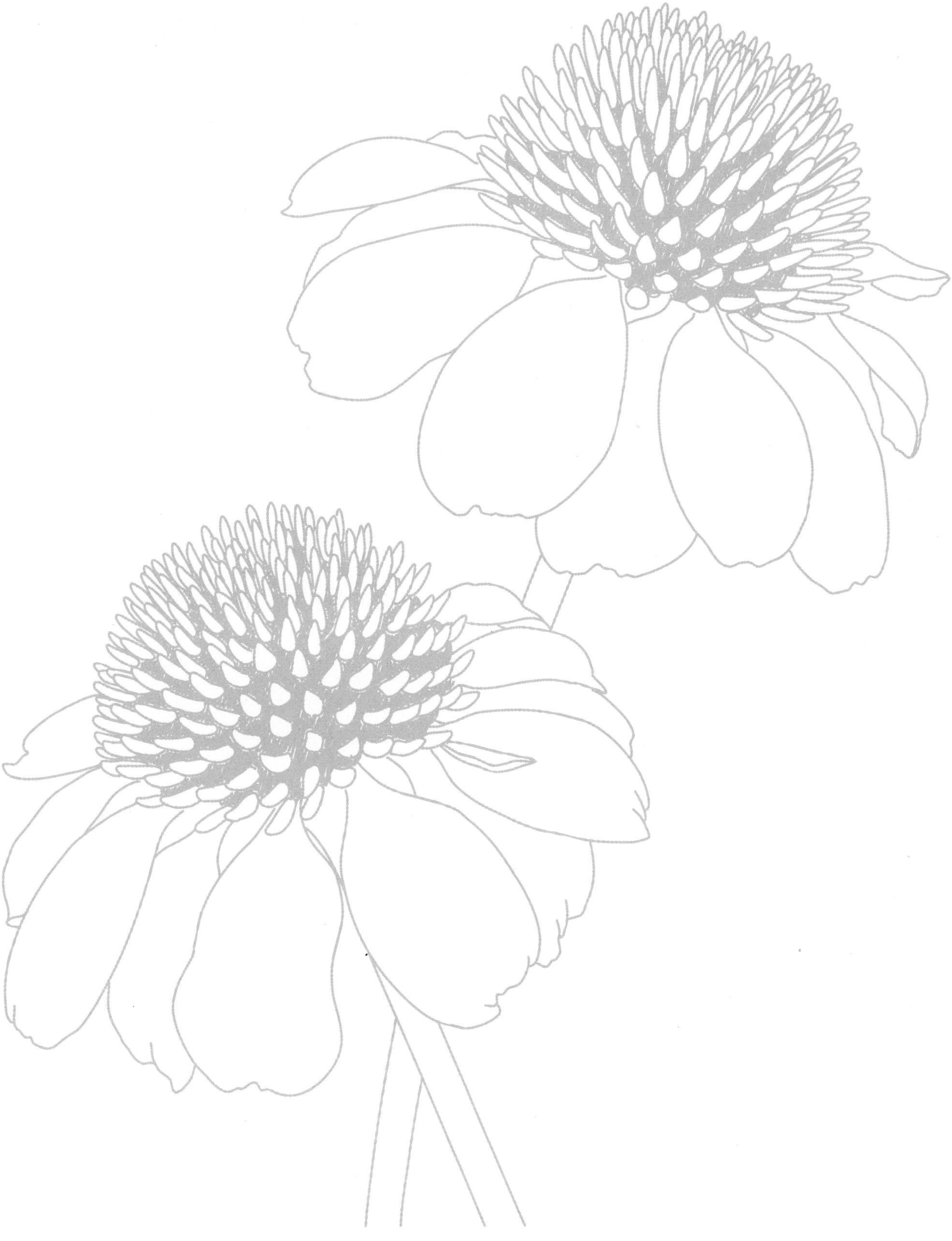

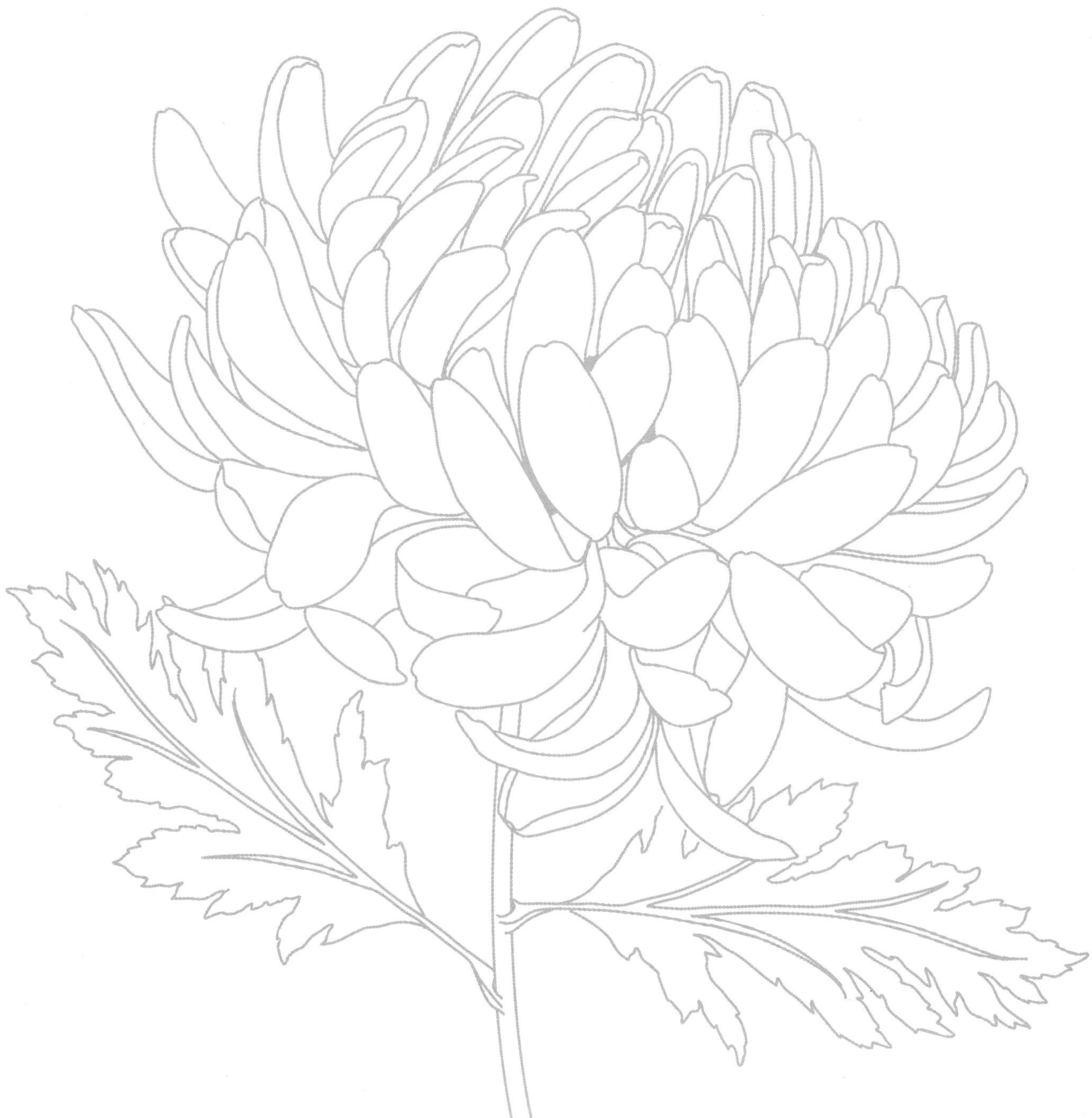

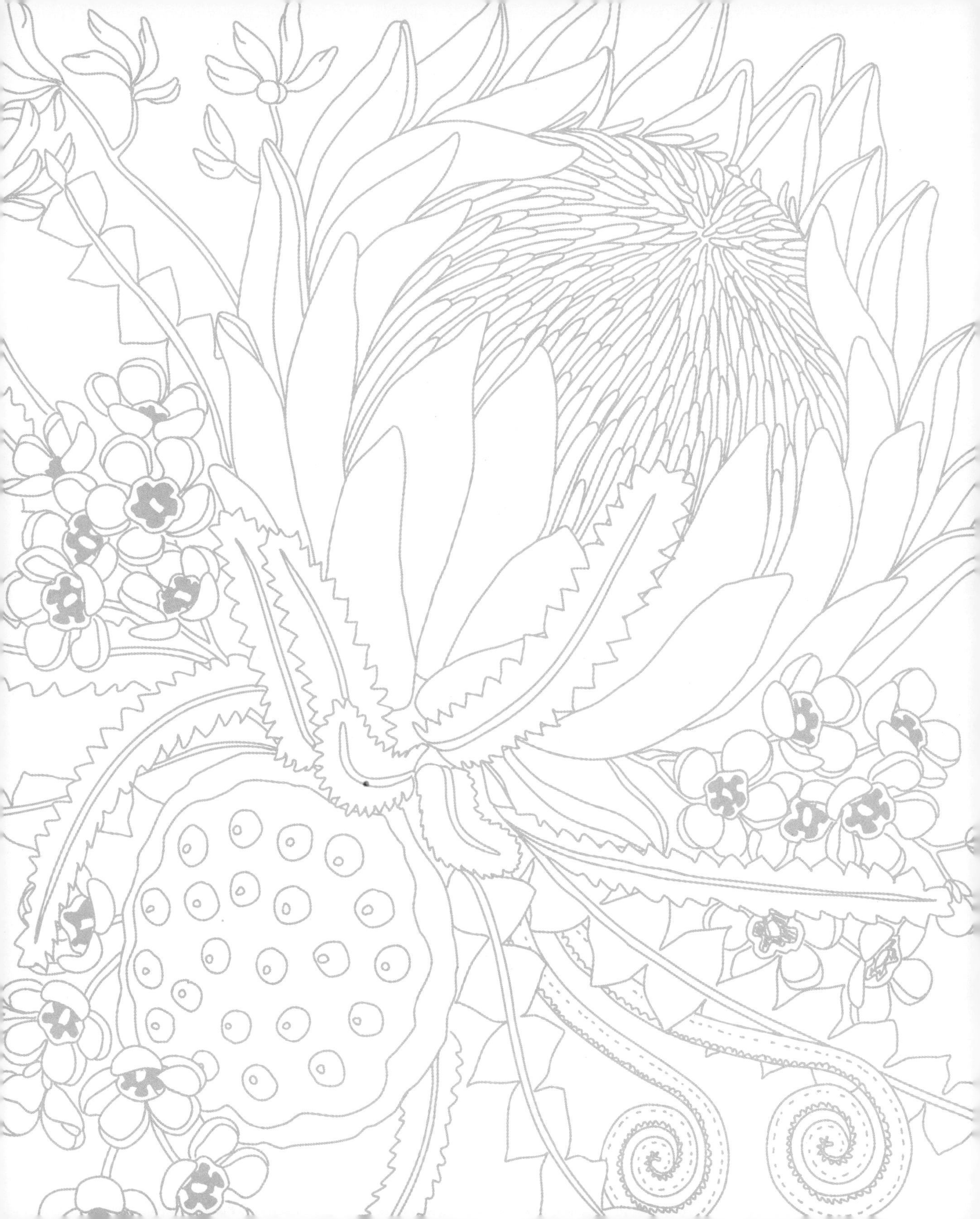

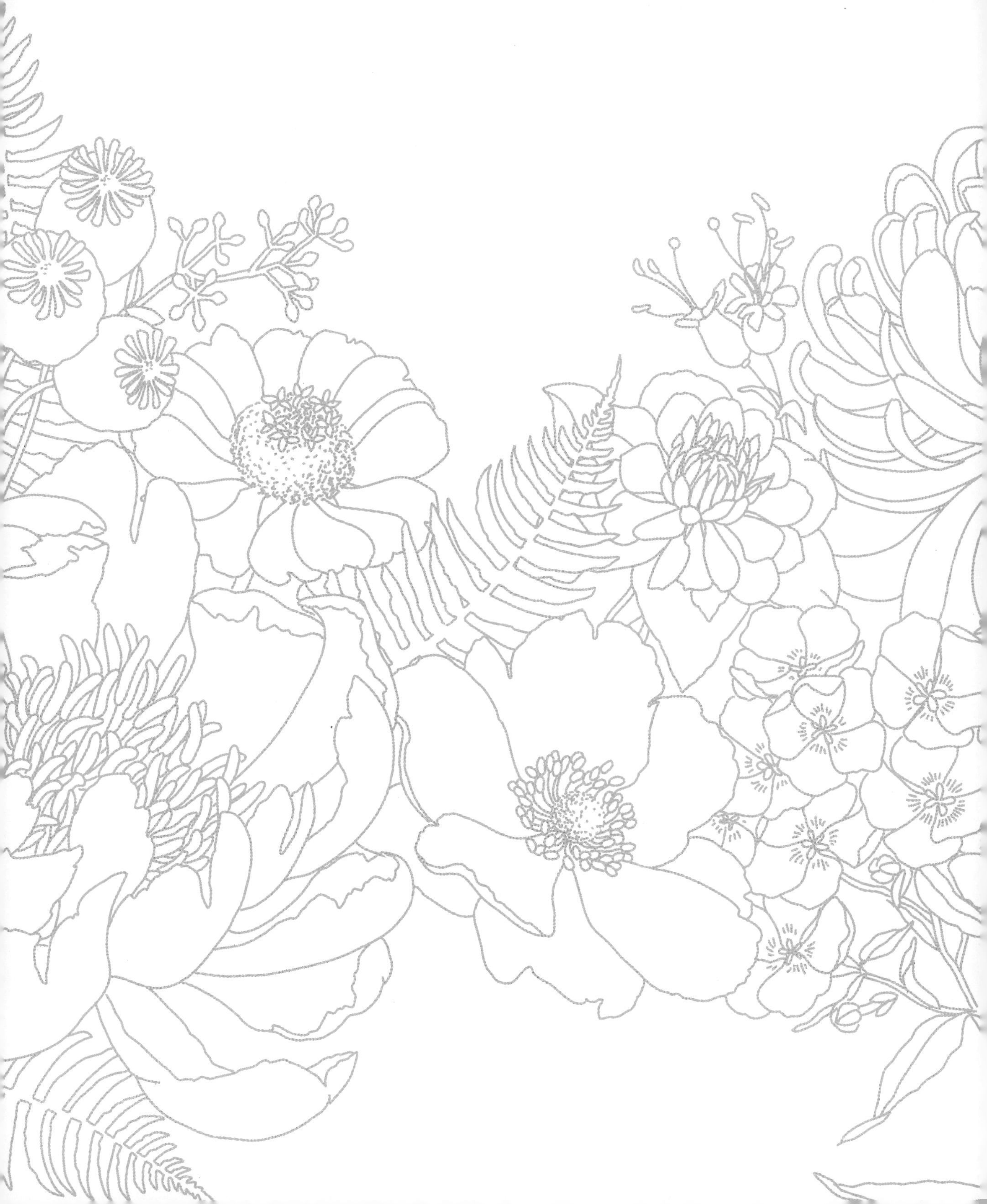

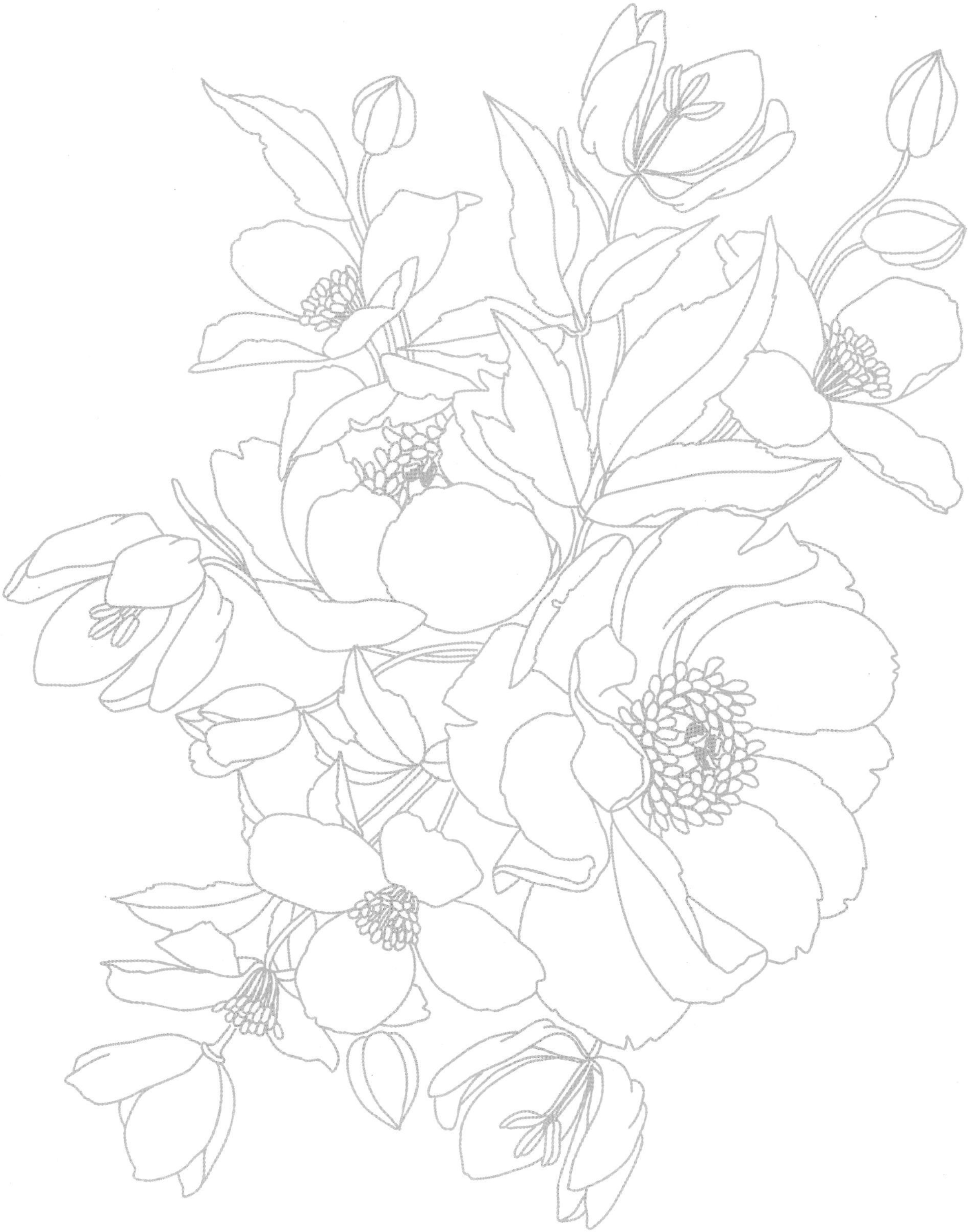

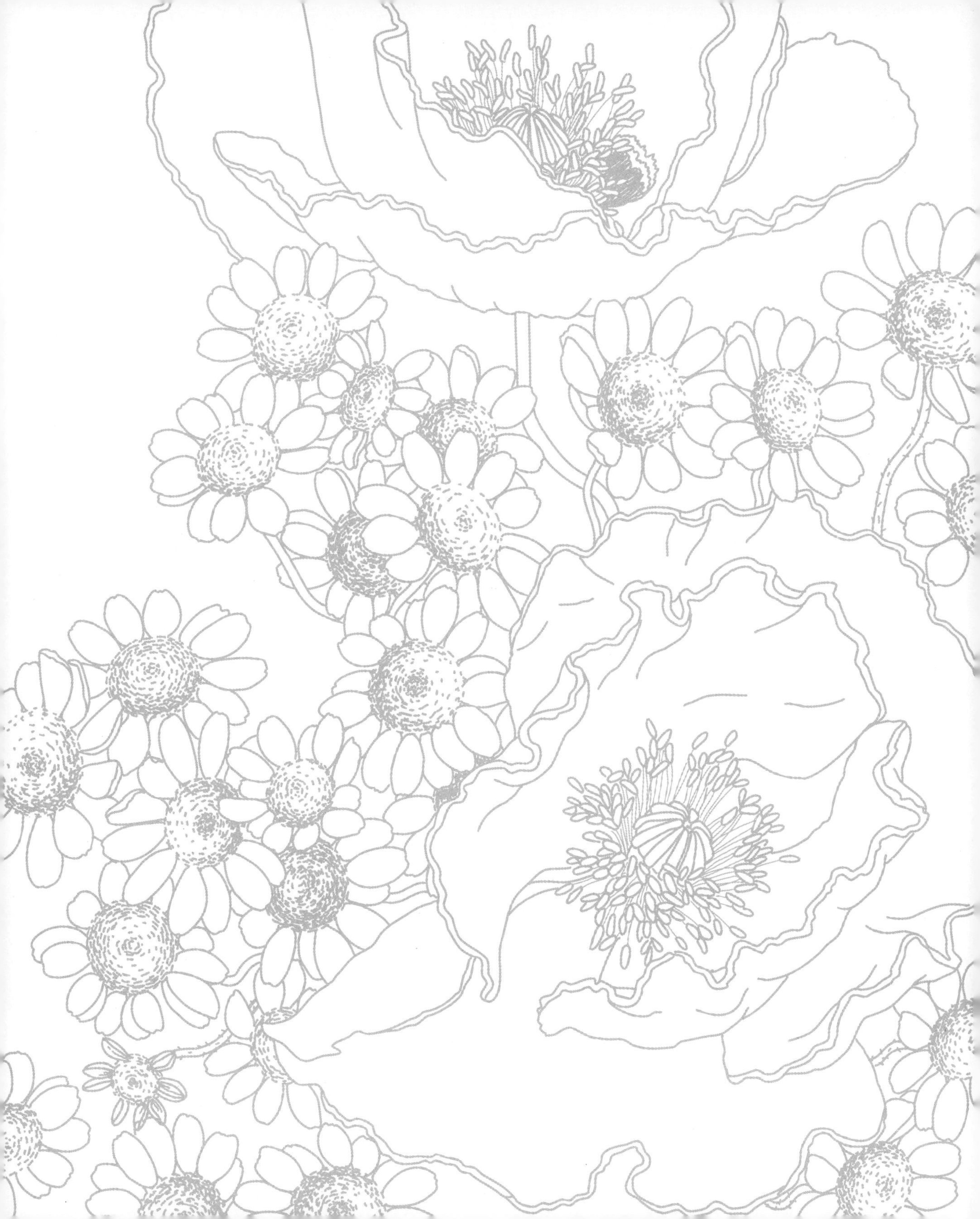

TEAR-OUTS

This chapter is a bonus gift for you atop of the 40 projects. These pages are perforated, so you can tear them out and work on them more freely, give them as a gift or hang on your wall. It is up to you!

I would consider preparing beautiful paints or markers, metallic gel pens and a cup of scented tea for your creative session.

And most importantly, have fun!

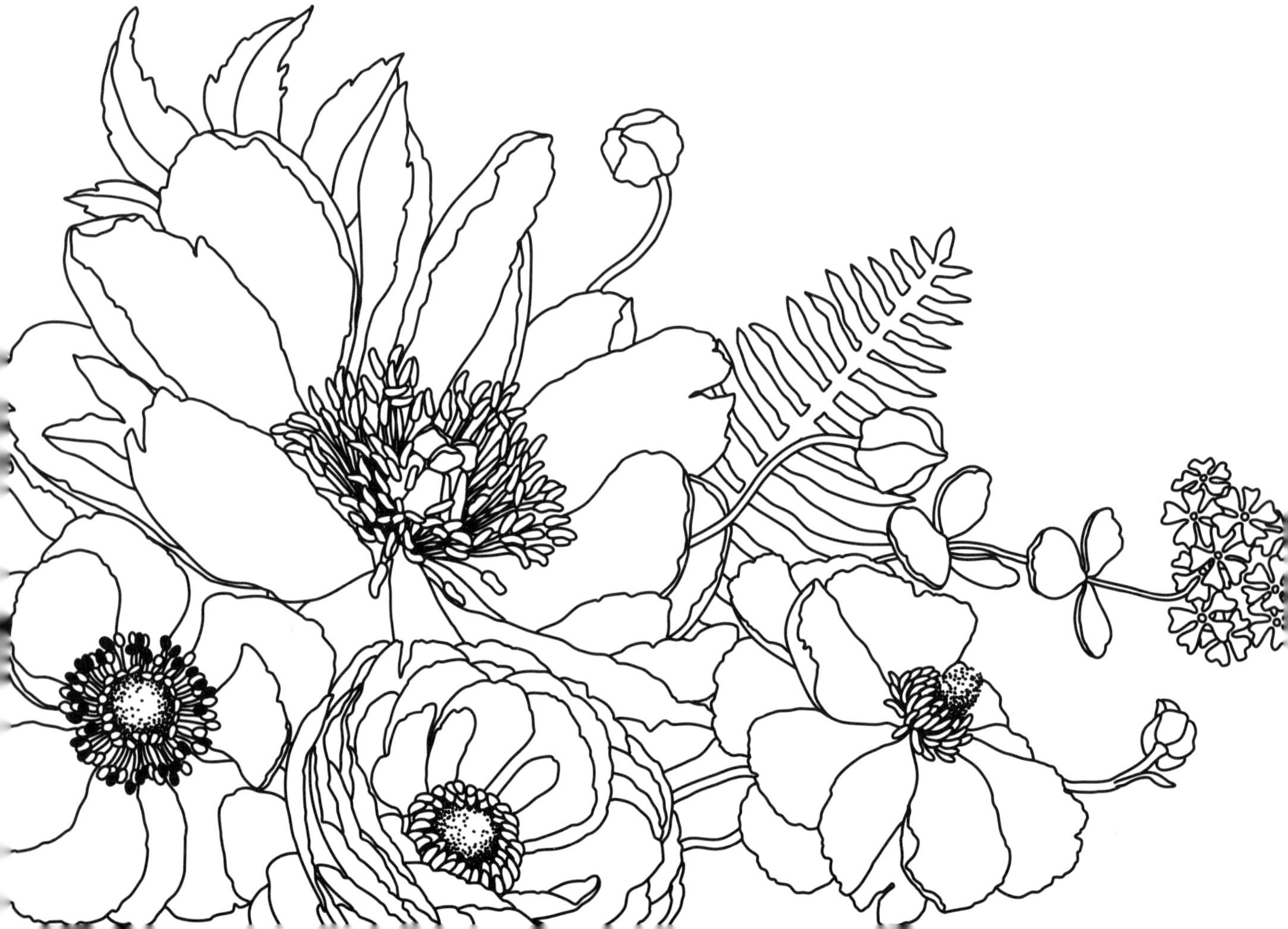

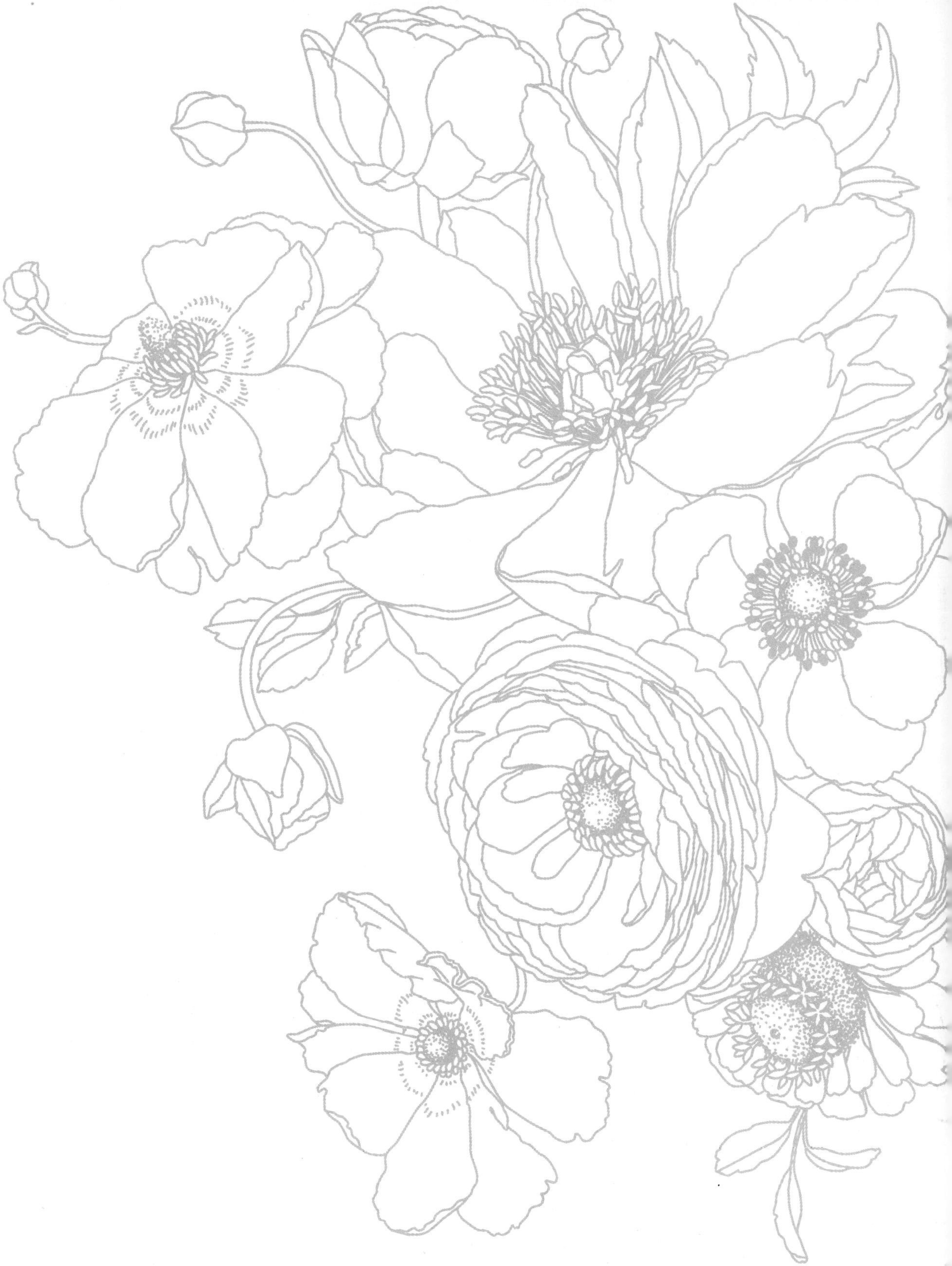

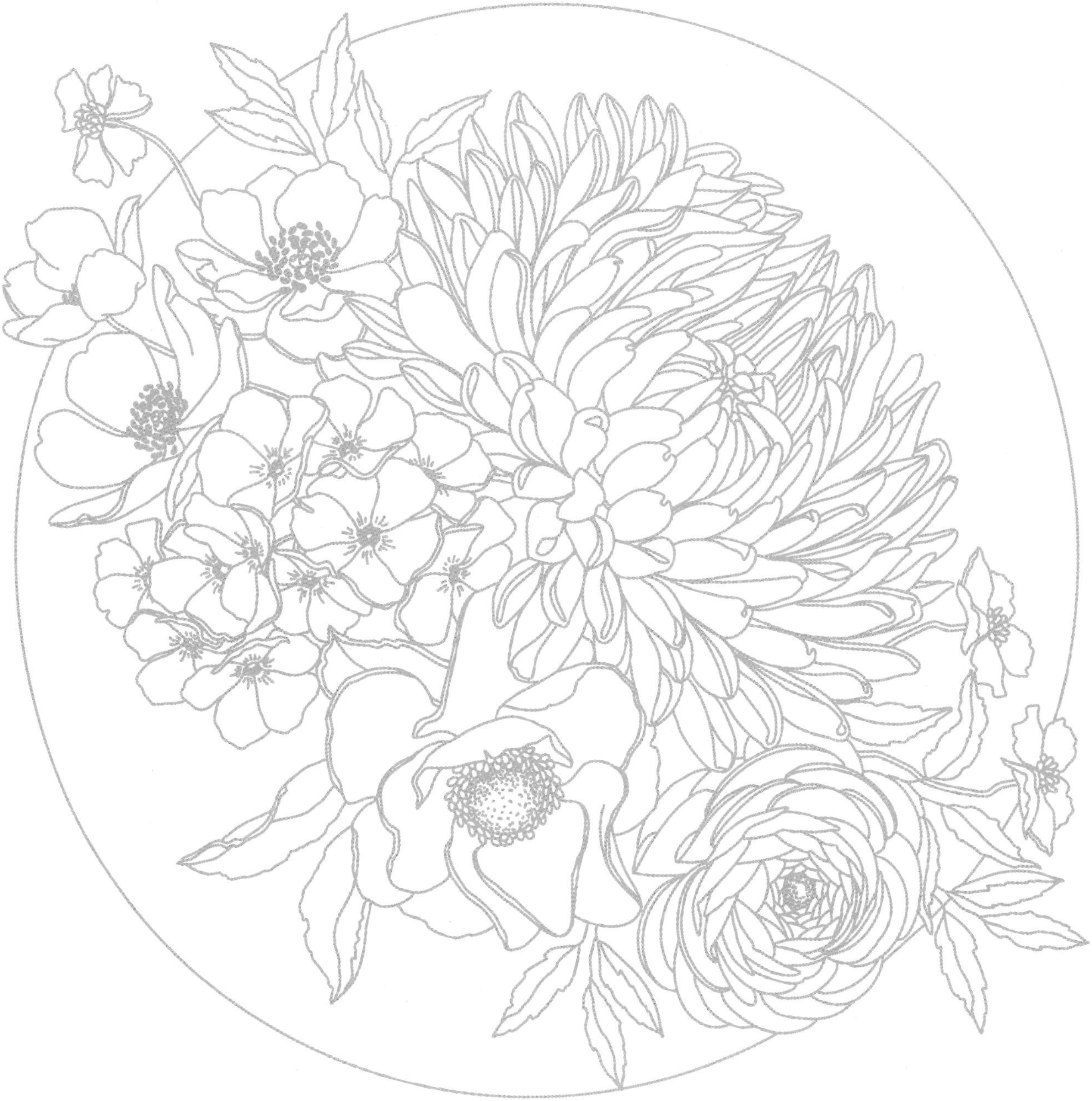

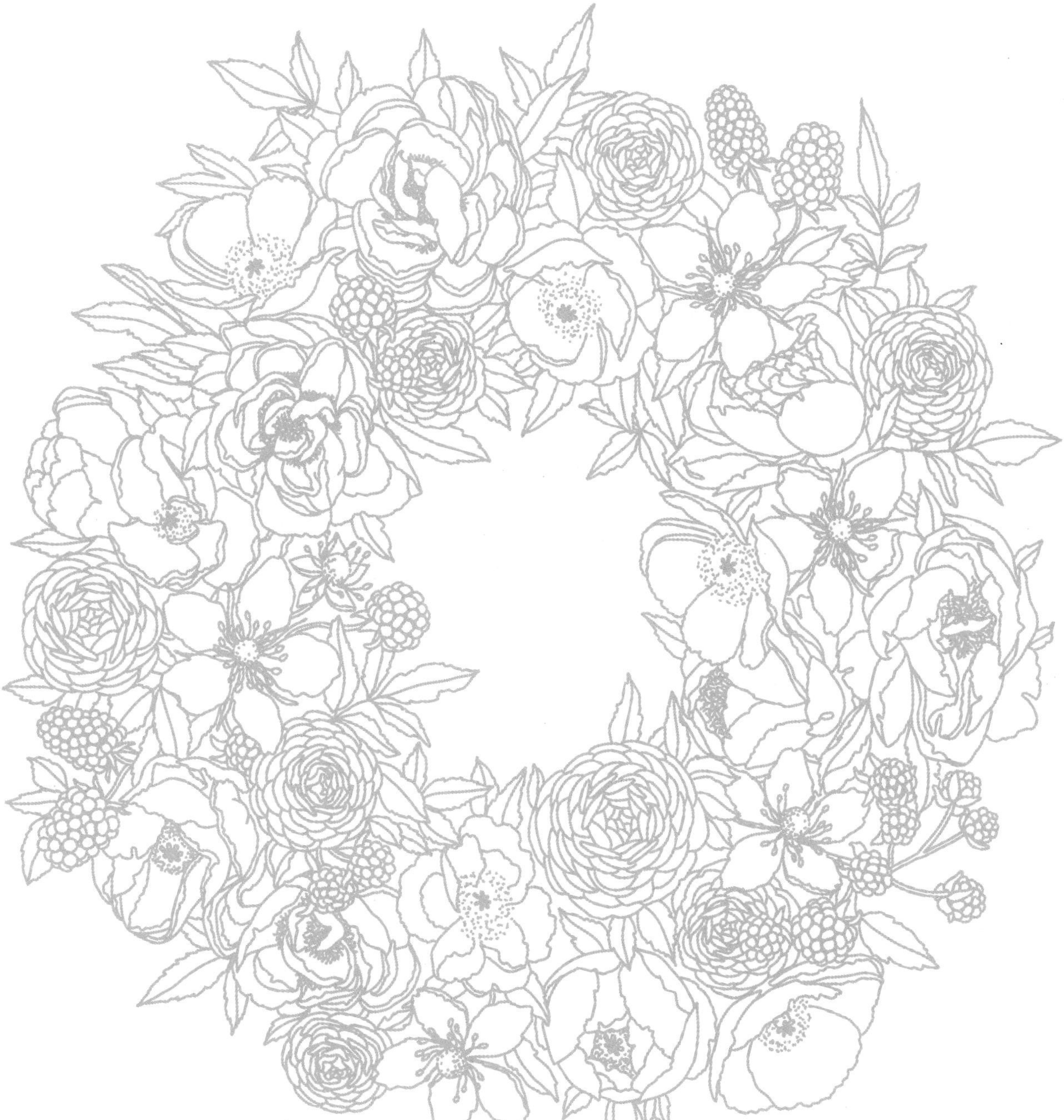

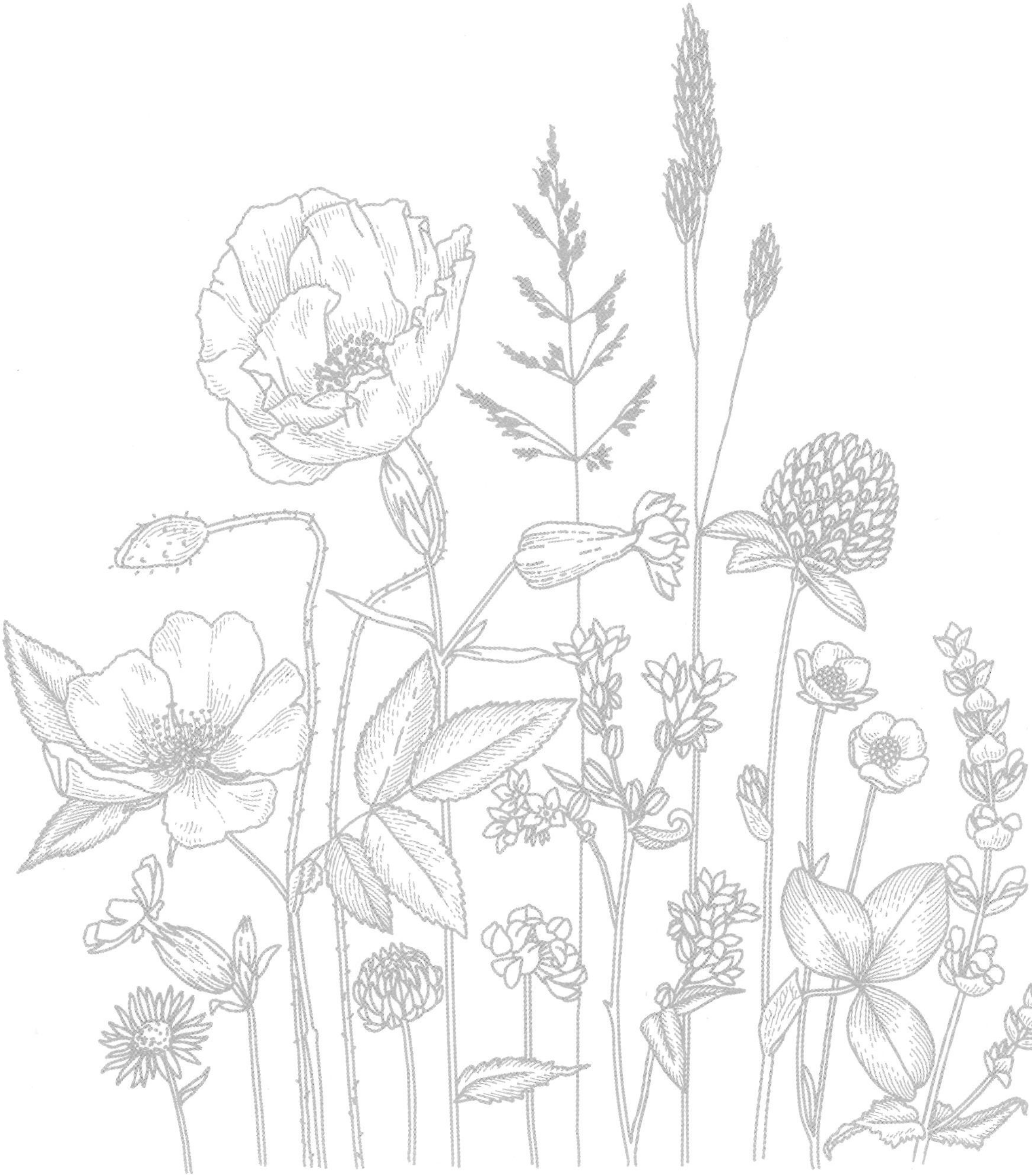

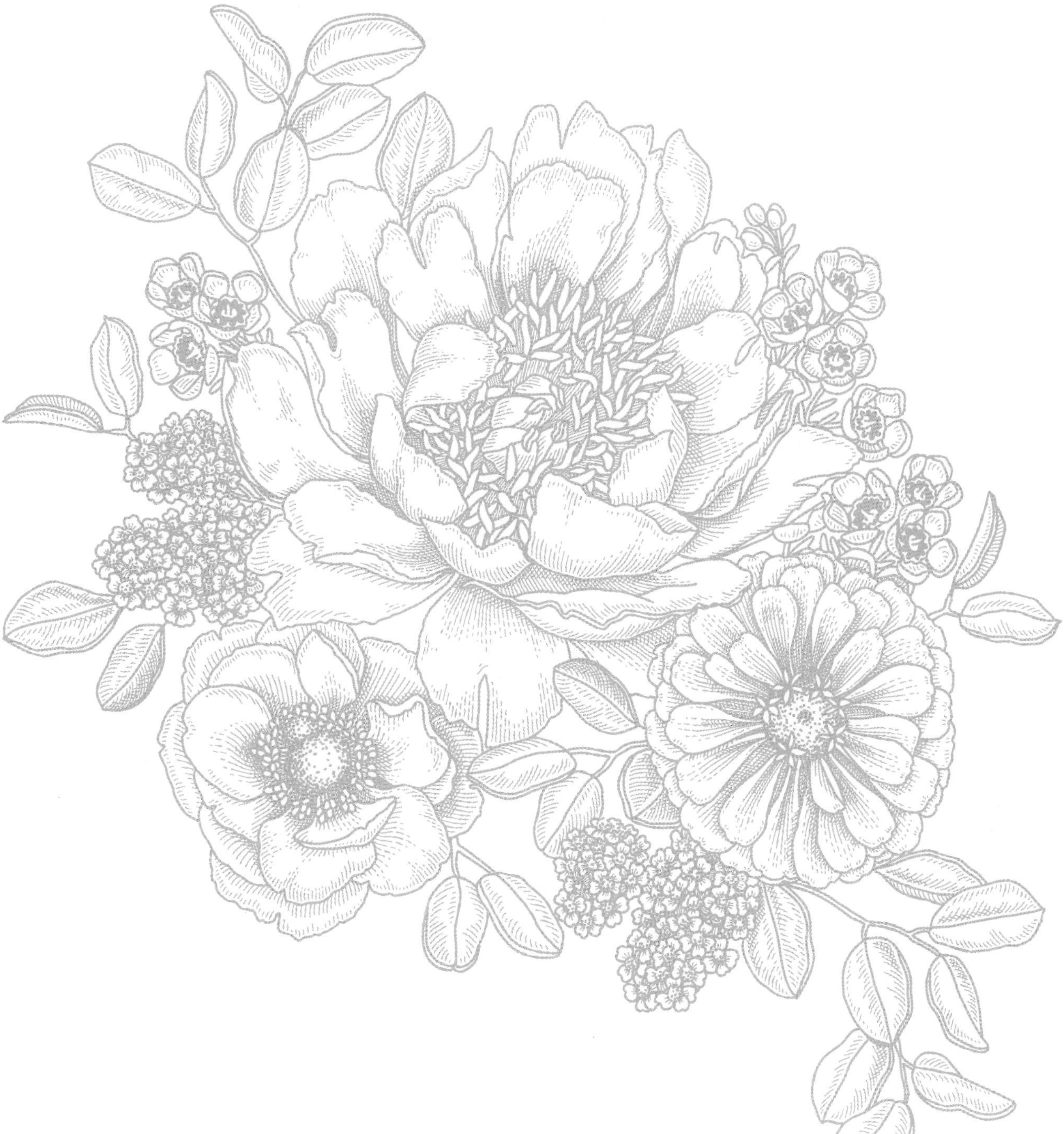

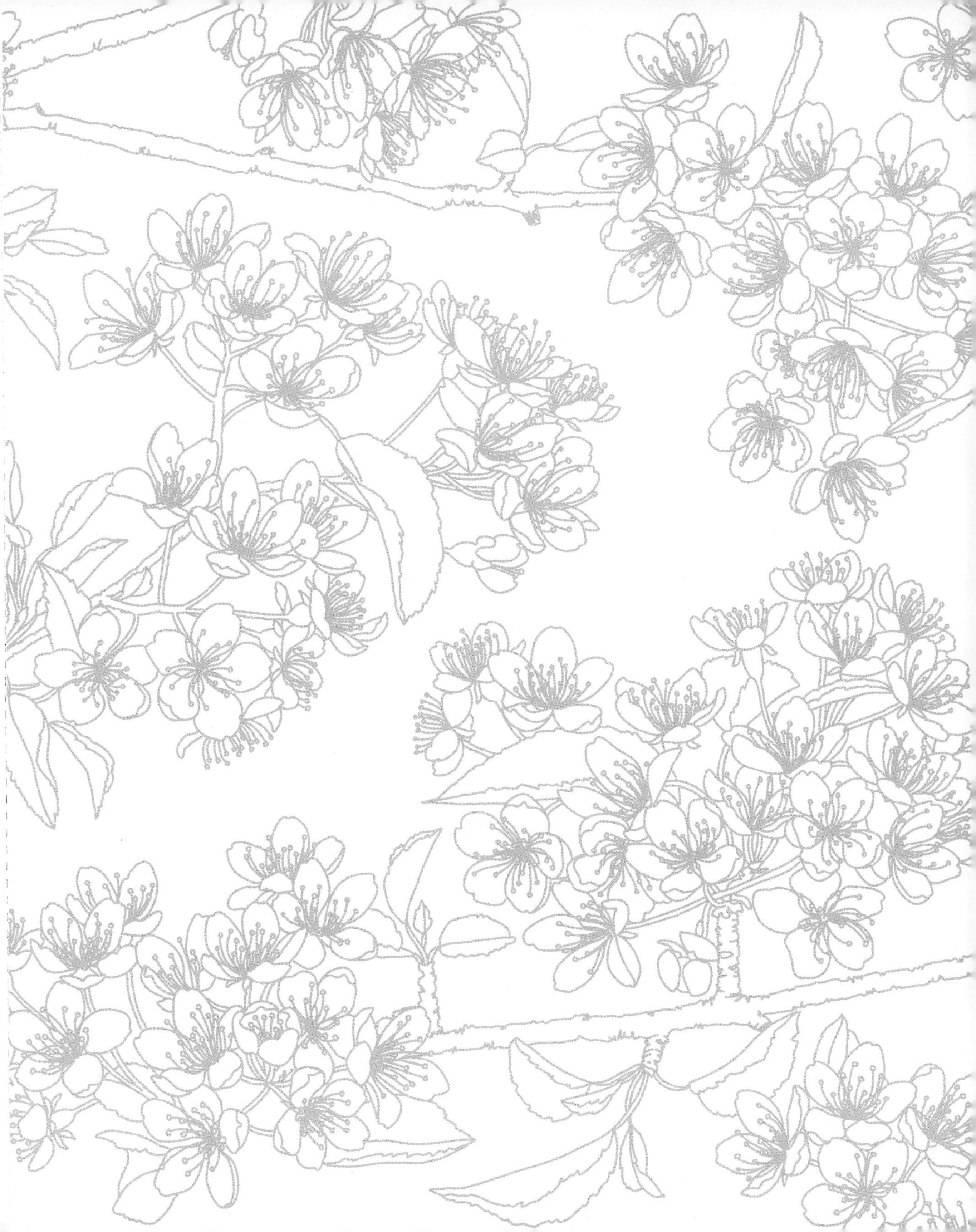

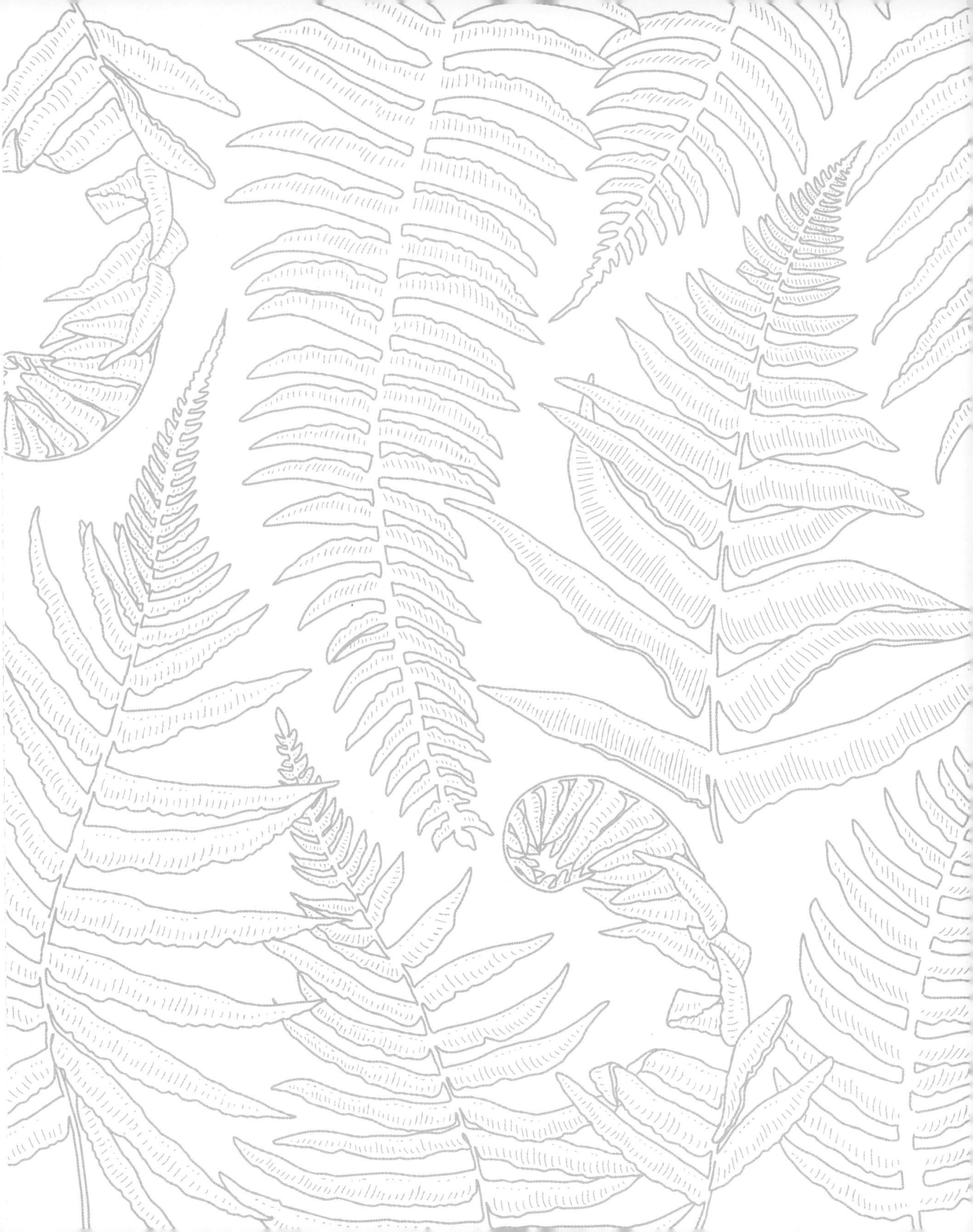

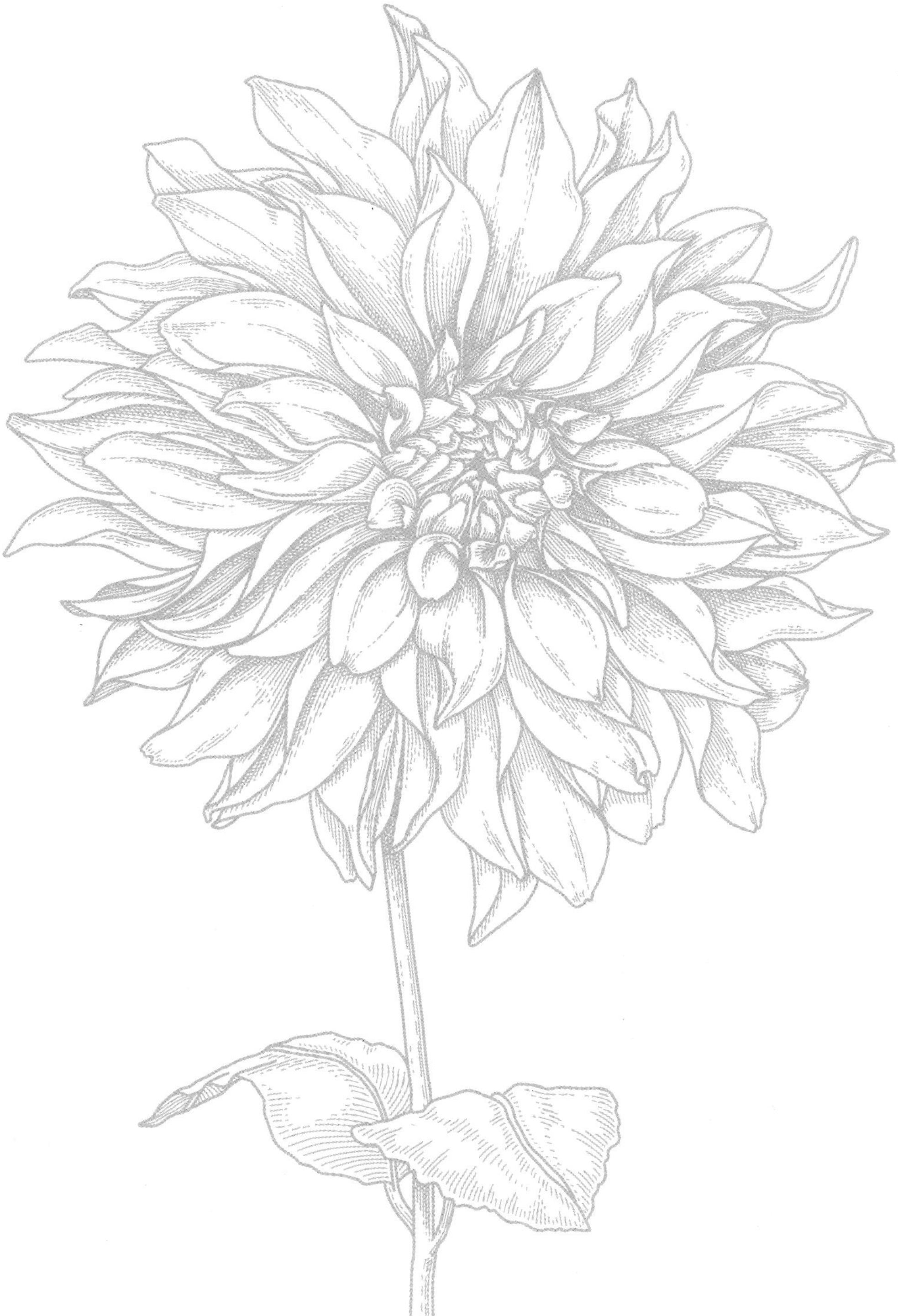

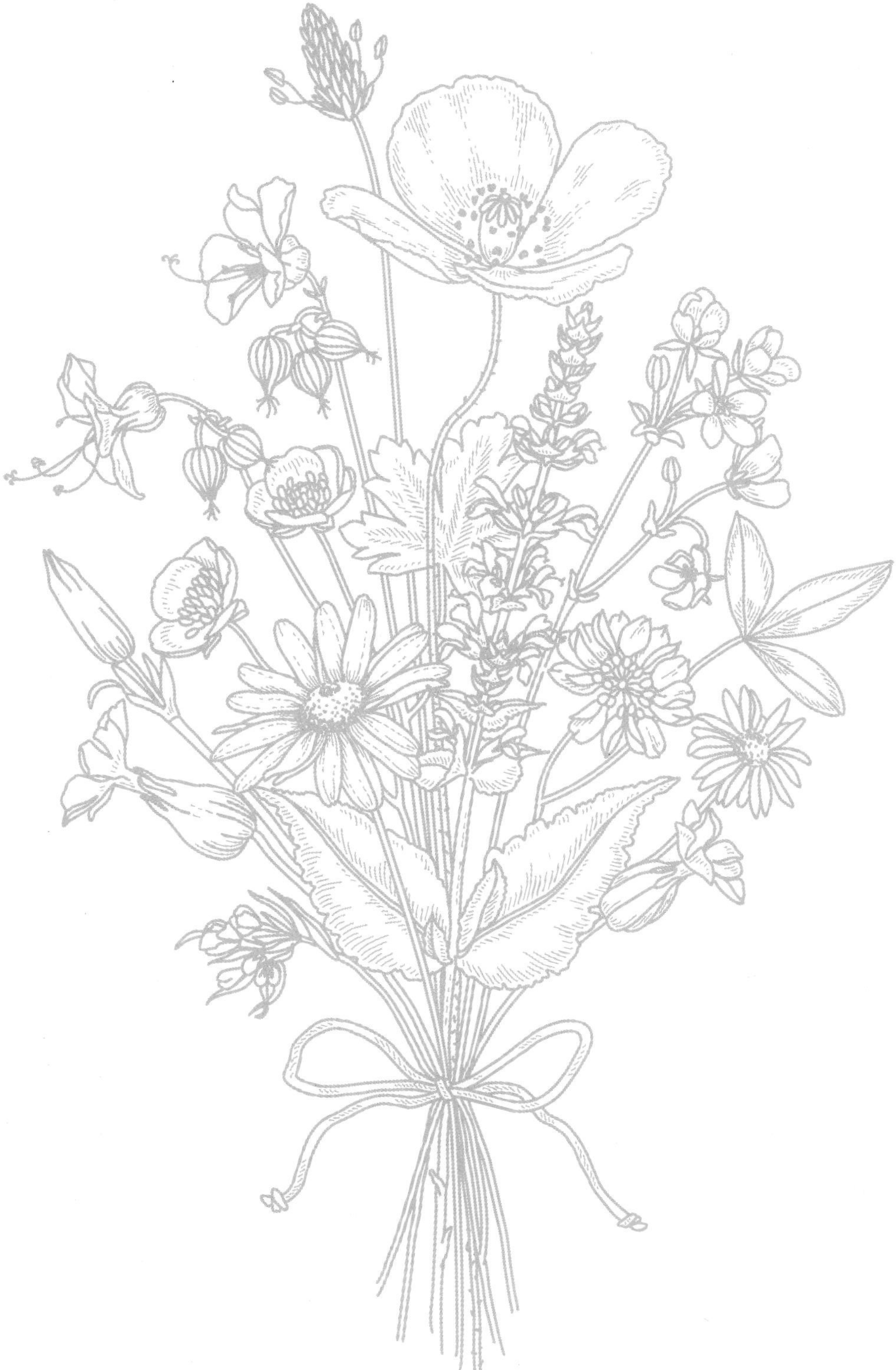

ACKNOWLEDGMENTS

When I was about to start my adult life, if someone had asked me what my plans were for the next ten years, I would not have even dreamed of writing a book, let alone writing a book about my passion! This is the most wonderful gift I have ever been given. I say gift, because beside the hard work I put into drawing flowers and building a career from it, there were a handful of people who made this book happen. I am truly thankful for them.

Ádám, my foundation, my best advisor, my safety net who catches me if I fall, my best friend, my love and the very special one who taught me to believe in myself. I could not be more thankful for you.

Áron, you are my sunshine. Thank you for accepting that Mommy has to work sometimes, thank you for your huge eyes when you look at my work and thank you for choosing our family. I am grateful for your presence and for opening my eyes to a new direction.

Franny, thank you for reaching out to me to write this book, for believing in me from the beginning, for being unbelievably supportive both emotionally and technically, for your great ideas and for your hard work. You are the kindest and most caring person I have ever worked with.

My parents, for spending a lot of time taking good care of Áron while I was working on this book, and for their constant, caring love.

The wonderful Floral Community on Instagram, who empowered my faith from the beginning of my art journey. The tremendous amount of positive feedback, caring words and all the heart-eyes are my constant motivation to create something beautiful for you. Thank you for your endless support.

My Patrons, whose support made it possible to quit my day job and step onto this artsy pathway surrounded with beautiful blooms. You are all awesome!

And I am truly thankful for the whole Page Street team, for all of your ideas and the hard work you put into creating this book.

ABOUT THE AUTHOR

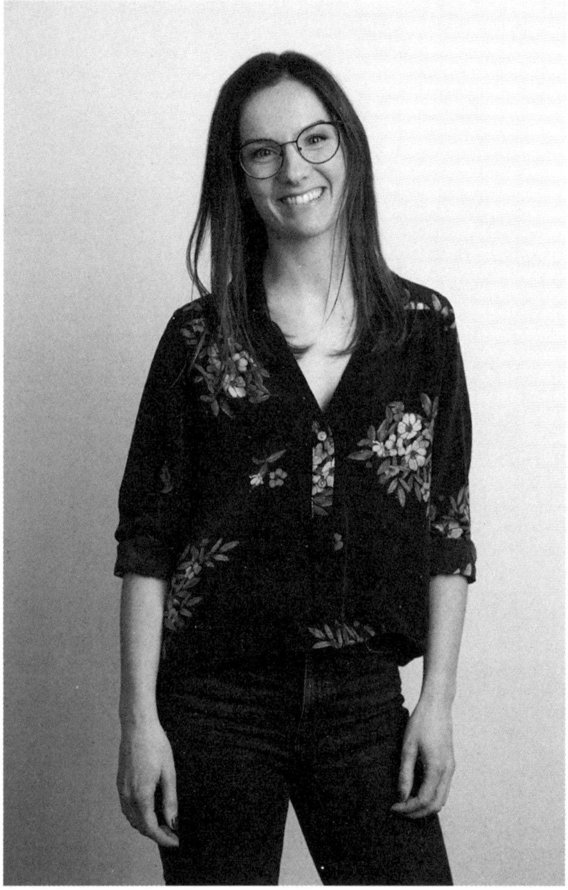

Anna Oszvald, a.k.a. @oszvaldann, is a botanical illustrator based in Budapest, Hungary. Her botanical journey started after her son was born, as a naptime escape. At that time she was working as an engineer in the automotive industry and needed a creative outlet. Drawing flowers started as a hobby with an Instagram account and taking part in a daily drawing challenge at @floralsyourway. Soon, Anna's passion had her staying up at night, drawing flowers every single stolen minute a mommy can afford. After creating her Instagram account and drawing her first ten flowers, Anna became inspired to teach others. She started to film how she drew her illustrations to show others how she created them. Showing her audience how to draw became her real passion. As this passion for teaching inspired her to create and show more and more, a wonderful audience started to build up and they wanted to learn from her. Creating a Patreon page was the next step. There she developed her method of teaching line drawing through different mediums. Her tracing technique quickly became the most popular method among her Patrons. As a natural next step, combining her own illustrations with teaching others gave her the idea for this book. Anna's work can be found on Amour Vert clothes, on stationary at Die Kartenmacherei, on stamps for Mama Elephant and notebooks for Denik.